THE EXPANSION OF EUROPE

4/22/83

A volume in
The Middle Ages Series
Edward Peters, General Editor

The Expansion of Europe:
The First Phase

Edited by
James Muldoon

University of Pennsylvania Press
1977

Library of Congress Cataloging in Publication Data
Main entry under title:

The Expansion of Europe.

(The Middle Ages)
  1. Middle Ages—History—Sources.   I. Muldoon,
James, 1935–   II. Series.
D113.E89   940.1   77-81455
ISBN 0-8122-7729-5

To the memory of my father
ROBERT J. MULDOON

Contents

THE EXPANSION OF EUROPE

Introduction

Until recently, textbooks have described the medieval world as being separated from the modern world by four major events; the Renaissance, the Reformation, the scientific revolution, and the expansion of European society overseas.[1] A generation of scholars has devoted a great deal of effort to demonstrating that, in reality, the roots of the Renaissance, the Reformation, and the scientific revolution lay in the Middle Ages, thus emphasizing the continuities in European experience rather than the discontinuities.[2] The medieval roots of European expansion overseas, however, have received less attention. As Professor Charles Verlinden has shown, many of the institutions and attitudes connected with expansion in the sixteenth and seventeenth centuries, and commonly accepted as being 'modern', were medieval in origin. To give but one example, the slave-operated plantation devoted to raising sugar cane, a phenomenon considered typical of the West Indies in the early modern era, is found fully developed in the Atlantic islands off the African coast by the late fifteenth century. It was this experience that encouraged the Spanish to develop similar plantations in the Americas.[3]

The voyages of Columbus, then, neither opened a new era nor marked the end of an old one. They marked the end of the period of internal European colonization and the beginning of a period devoted to spreading European values over the rest of the world. But Columbus' voyages were also a continuation of a process that had been going on since the tenth century, the process of expanding the borders of European culture.[4]

1. For a criticism of this approach to the study of modern history, see, Herbert Butterfield, *The Whig Interpretation of History* (London: G. Bell, 1931).
2. Two convenient introductions to the literature of this debate are, Karl H. Dannenfeldt, ed., *The Renaissance, Medieval or Modern?*, Problems in European Civilization (Boston: D. C. Heath, 1959) and Denys Hay, ed., *The Renaissance Debate*, European Problem Studies (New York: Holt, Rinehart and Winston, 1965). Concerning the relation of the Reformation to medieval religious movements, see, Lewis W. Spitz, ed., *The Reformation: Basic Interpretations*, Problems in European Civilization, 2nd ed. (Lexington, Mass.: D. C. Heath, 1972). A strong statement on the ties between medieval and modern science is A. C. Crombie, *Medieval and Early Modern Science*, 2 vols. (Garden City, N.Y.: Doubleday, 1959).
3. Charles Verlinden, *The Beginnings of Modern Colonization*, trans. Yvonne Freccero (Ithaca: Cornell Univ. Press, 1970), pp. 17–26.
4. The best introduction to Columbus, one that emphasizes Columbus as a man of both the medieval and the modern worlds, is Samuel Eliot Morison, *Admiral of the Ocean Sea* (Boston: Little, Brown, 1952), pp. 5–6.

3

The culture that can be termed uniquely European emerged during the eleventh century. This culture, as Christopher Dawson pointed out, consisted of three elements; the classical tradition of late Mediterranean antiquity, the barbarian or Germanic tradition, and the Christian tradition, which, in the changing institution of the Christian Church, blended these different traditions into a single culture. This culture first appeared "within the limits of the former Carolingian Empire, and found its centre in the old Frankish territories of Northern France and Western Germany . . . . this middle territory, reaching from the Loire to the Rhine . . . was the true homeland of mediaeval culture and the source of its creative and characteristic achievements."[5]

From the eleventh century on, European culture pushed outward from its homeland and gradually replaced or transformed the cultures on its borders. By 1095, the year in which Pope Urban II proclaimed the first crusade, European culture predominated in Italy, in Germany to a line along the Oder River, in France, with the exception of Celtic Brittany, in northern Spain, and in England, but not in Wales and Scotland.

The crusades are the best known movement of European expansion. Although the term crusade is usually employed only to describe attempts to defend Constantinople and to free the Holy Land from the Moslems, a series of crusades were fought along the borders of European culture from the eleventh to the fifteenth centuries. In 1095 the Moslems still controlled most of the Iberian peninsula and the southern and eastern Mediterranean littoral. The European Christian response was a series of wars in Spain and Portugal seeking not only to stop further Moslem expansion but also to regain lands previously lost. In northeastern Europe, adventurous German nobles warred against the non-Christian Prussians, Lithuanians, and other pagan tribes. In the far west, the kings of England fought a series of campaigns against the Celtic peoples of Wales, Ireland, and Scotland who, although Christians, were not always recognized as such.

All of these wars shared a common bond that marks them as crusades or holy wars.[6] They were all fought for explicitly religious reasons, to defend Christendom against the infidel, to convert the heathen to Christianity, or to reform the Church where it needed reforming. The religious inspiration that ostensibly moved men to go on crusade is seen clearly in the documents that mark the opening and closing of the medieval period of

---

5. Christopher Dawson, *The Making of Europe* (New York: Sheed and Ward, 1932; reprint ed., Cleveland: World, 1956), pp. 240–41.
6. The most recent studies of the crusades as holy wars are: James A. Brundage, *Medieval Canon Law and the Crusader* (Madison: Univ. of Wisconsin Press, 1969) and Frederick H. Russell, *The Just War in the Middle Ages*, Cambridge Studies in Mediaeval Life and Thought, no. 8 (Cambridge, Eng.: Cambridge Univ. Press, 1975).

expansion. From Urban II to Columbus, those who planted European flags outside of Europe claimed religious reasons. During the sixteenth century, however, the rhetoric and the concept of expansion changed gradually. Where earlier explorers bore commissions authorizing them to claim for their sovereigns any lands not occupied by Christians, by the beginning of the seventeenth century such commissions authorized the taking of any lands not held by Europeans.[7]

Religious motivation had never been the sole hallmark of medieval expansion. From the first, economic and social motives were inextricably associated in a religious culture. For example, Urban II saw in the crusades not only an opportunity to halt Moslem expansion, he also saw in them a means of giving employment to the restless younger sons of the European nobility who were engaging in fratricidal strife within Europe (docs. 1 and 2). The crusades, like the American frontier in the nineteenth century, were to be a safety valve, drawing off those who were too aggressive for peaceful life at home. Columbus may also have seen overseas expansion in the same terms. It is no coincidence that he set sail after the fall of Granada, the last Moslem stronghold in Spain (doc. 3). At the end of the fifteenth century, Spain was faced with the problem of numerous unemployed soldiers who were unable or unwilling to return to civilian life. The same was true in England after the end of the Irish wars in the late sixteenth century. Overseas expansion was a logical way to employ these men, both for royal profit abroad and royal peace at home.[8] As for economic motivation, writers from Urban II to Columbus emphasized the profits to be made in winning land and treasure from the infidel.

The documents selected for this collection reflect the various arguments advanced for expansion and the various ways in which Europeans sought to impose their culture on others. Every section contains documents ex-

7. Denys Hay, Europe: The Emergence of an Idea, rev. ed. (Edinburgh: Edinburgh Univ. Press, 1968).
8. The problem of the relationship between Europe's population and the movement overseas is a complicated one. While the population seems to have been rising during the sixteenth century, this pressure was not enough by itself to force men overseas; see H. G. Koenigsberger and G. L. Mosse, Europe in the Sixteenth Century, General History of Europe Series (New York: Holt, Rinehart and Winston, 1968), pp. 28–32. The notion that for the Spanish, at least, the New World served as a safety value for unemployed soldiers has recently been challenged by James Lockhart, The Men of Cajamarca (Austin: Univ. of Texas Press), pp. 17–22. The leading propagandist for English expansion overseas during the late sixteenth century, Richard Hakluyt, argued that colonization of the New World would "keep the mariner from idleness and from necessity," would provide a new start for "men of excellent wits . . . overthrown . . . by some folly of youth," and would serve as a place to unload for "the common profit and quiet of this realm" the unemployed and potential troublemakers; see Richard Hakluyt, "A Discourse Concerning Western Planting," in David C. Douglas, general editor, English Historical Documents, vol. 9, American Colonial Documents to 1776 (New York: Oxford Univ. Press, 1955), pp. 105–6.

plaining the expansion in religious terms, usually contained in a papal or episcopal letter. These papal or episcopal letters licensed Christian rulers to employ force against infidels or unreformed Christian societies, such as the Irish. Such licenses effectively divided the world into spheres of ecclesiastical jurisdiction with secular rulers acting as agents of the Church, or of Christendom.

In addition, the documents include selections from chronicles in which Europeans gave their less formal impressions of the people whom they encountered. From the beginning, contact with non-Europeans was embittered by the use of what would now be called racial and cultural stereotypes on both sides. The English considered the Irish treacherous while the Irish saw the English as hypocrites. At the same time, there were important instances of sympathetic understanding of the position of the non-Europeans. The Franciscans who went to visit the Mongols tried to understand the strange customs of these people. Medieval intellectuals even had qualms about the expansion of Europeans, at least as such expansion was linked with military conquest. Was it possible to spread the truth of the Christian faith when infidels identified the missionary with knightly warriors? Were the crusaders giving non-Europeans the wrong impression of Christian living?

One might raise the objection that European expansion between the eleventh and the fifteenth centuries consisted of a series of isolated incidents and did not form a coherent stage in the history of European expansion. Did the various figures in this period of expansion actually influence one another? The answer to this question must be given in parts.

In the first place, the crusades generated a continuous flow of materials, chronicles, papal letters, and calls for soldiers issued by various European rulers seeking new recruits for their own crusades. The crusade chroniclers routinely discussed earlier crusades and the lessons that might be learned from their failures. Papal and royal letters often alluded to previous letters on the topic, or even quoted whole sections of previous letters. Such letters often pointed to the long history of the wars and the need to carry on the work to its conclusion. Finally, the extensive travel literature that expansion had generated circulated widely in late medieval Europe. As a result, although the level of expansionist activity varied from generation to generation, with the period between the mid-thirteenth and the mid-fourteenth centuries marking its lowest point, the vision of lands beyond the frontiers of Europe remained. Even when the means of retracing the steps of earlier travellers were not available, the letters and chronicles reminded potential adventurers of what could be achieved when the circumstances were suitable. Columbus, for example, was inspired by reading Marco Polo's *Travels*, a copy of which he personally annotated.[9] Similar

---

9. Samuel Eliot Morison, ed., *Journals and Documents on the Life and Voyages of Christopher Columbus* (New York: Heritage Press, 1963), p. 384 n. 5.

stories can be told of others among his contemporaries. The medieval experience of expansion inspired succeeding generations of Europeans to look beyond the limited borders of Europe. When blended with the right mixture of naval and military technology, political support, and economic gain, the medieval experience led to the great expansion of European society in the centuries following Columbus's first voyage.

Bibliography

The best general introduction to the expansion of Europe in the late Middle Ages is Pierre Chaunu, *L'expansion européenne du XIIIe au XIVe siècle* (Paris: Presses universitaires de France, 1969). The most extensive introduction in English remains that by C. Raymond Beazley, *The Dawn of Modern Geography*, 3 vols. (Oxford, 1897–1906; reprint ed., New York: Peter Smith, 1949). A shorter introduction is provided by J. E. Wright, *Geographical Lore in the Time of the Crusades* (New York, 1925; reprint ed., New York: Dover, 1965). In recent years a number of works on the expansion of Europe in the sixteenth century have devoted one or two chapters to the period before Columbus. Among the better of these books are Boies Penrose, *Travel and Discovery in the Early Renaissance* (Cambridge, Mass.: Harvard Univ. Press; reprint ed., New York: Atheneum, 1962), and J. H. Parry, *The Age of Reconnaissance* (Cleveland: New American Library, 1963). Both of these volumes contain extensive bibliographies.

The life and career of Columbus have engendered a great deal of scholarly controversy. The best introduction is to be found in the works of Samuel Eliot Morison, which are mentioned in the notes. Morison, however, does not place much emphasis upon the pre-Columban voyages, a point on which he has been criticized; see David B. Quinn, *England and the Discovery of America, 1481–1620* (New York: Alfred A. Knopf, 1974), pp. 22–23. On medieval knowledge of the North Atlantic, see Vincent Cassidy, *The Sea Around Them* (Baton Rouge: Louisiana State Univ. Press, 1968).

A good historical atlas is very useful in seeing how the expansion took place. The best such atlas is the *Grosser Historisches Weltatlas*, vol. 2, *Mittlealter*, ed. Josef Engel (Munich: Bayerischer Schulbuch-Verlag, 1970). The standard historical atlas in English is William R. Shepherd, *Historical Atlas*, 9th ed. (New York: Barnes and Noble, 1967). A different kind of atlas, one that provides an overview of the movement of European history in the medieval period rather than detailing maps of particular regions, is Colin McEvedy, *The Penguin Atlas of Medieval History* (Harmondsworth: Penguin Books, 1961).

One of the by-products of medieval expansion was the improvement of maps and the gradual development of cartography as a science. Examples of the maps that were available to medieval and early modern seamen are provided in Nils A. E. Nordenskiöld, *Facsimile-Atlas to the Early History of Cartography*, trans. J. A. Ehelöf and C. R. Markham (Stockholm: 1889; reprint ed., New York: Dover, 1973).

Document 1*

Urban II's speech at Clermont (1095), in Fulcher of Chartres, *A History of the Expedition to Jerusalem, 1095–1127*, trans. Frances Rita Ryan, ed. Harold Fink (Knoxville: University of Tennessee Press, 1969; reprint ed., W. W. Norton: New York, 1973), pp. 65–67.

Fulcher of Chartres accompanied the First Crusade and lived in the Holy Land from 1100 to 1127. He was chaplain to Baldwin I, who ruled the crusader principality of Edessa from 1098 to 1100 and then ruled as king at Jerusalem from 1100 to 1118. It is not known whether Fulcher was present when Pope Urban II gave this address, which inspired a number of French nobles to undertake what has become known as the First Crusade. He is one of the most important sources of information about Urban's speech and its aftermath; so if he was not present, he must have obtained his information from fellow crusaders who had been present. This version of Urban's speech suggests that the pope was asking only that warriors go to the support of their Christian brethren who were threatened by the Moslems in the Near East. Toward the end, however, the pope indicates that Europe would have more peace internally if those who enjoyed fighting would go to the East to do so in this worthy cause. The second version of this speech, that of Robert the Monk (doc. 2) expands on this theme of the frontier wars as a safety valve for a warrior aristocracy.—*ed.*

Urban's Exhortation Concerning a Pilgrimage to Jerusalem

1. When these and many other matters were satisfactorily settled, all those present, clergy and people alike, spontaneously gave thanks to God for the words of the Lord Pope Urban and promised him faithfully that his decrees would be well kept. But the pope added at once that another tribulation not less but greater than that already mentioned, even of the worst nature, was besetting Christianity from another part of the world.

* From *A History of the Expedition to Jerusalem*, 1095–1127, by Fulcher of Chartres, translated by Frances Rita Ryan (Sisters of St. Joseph), edited by Harold S. Fink, by permission of the University of Tennessee Press. Copyright © 1969 by the University of Tennessee Press.

2. He said, "Since, oh sons of God, you have promised Him to keep peace among yourselves and to faithfully sustain the rights of Holy Church more sincerely than before, there still remains for you, newly aroused by Godly correction, an urgent task which belongs to both you and God, in which you can show the strength of your good will. For you must hasten to carry aid to your brethren dwelling in the East, who need your help for which they have often entreated.

3. "For the Turks, a Persian people, have attacked them, as many of you already know, and have advanced as far into Roman territory as that part of the Mediterranean which is called the Arm of St. George. They have seized more and more of the lands of the Christians, have already defeated them in seven times as many battles, killed or captured many people, have destroyed churches, and have devastated the kingdom of God. If you allow them to continue much longer they will conquer God's faithful people much more extensively.

4. "Wherefore with earnest prayer I, not I, but God exhorts you as heralds of Christ to repeatedly urge men of all ranks whatsoever, knights as well as foot-soldiers, rich and poor, to hasten to exterminate this vile race from our lands and to aid the Christian inhabitants in time.

5. "I address those present; I proclaim it to those absent; moreover Christ commands it. For all those going thither there will be remission of sins if they come to the end of this fettered life while either marching by land or crossing by sea, or in fighting the pagans. This I grant to all who go, through the power vested in me by God.

6. "Oh what a disgrace if a race so despicable, degenerate, and enslaved by demons should thus overcome a people endowed with faith in Almighty God and resplendent in the name of Christ! Oh what reproaches will be charged against you by the Lord Himself if you have not helped those who are counted like yourselves of the Christian faith!

7. "Let those," he said, "who are accustomed to wantonly wage private war against the faithful march upon the infidels in a war which should be begun now and be finished in victory. Let those who have long been robbers now be soldiers of Christ. Let those who once fought against brothers and relatives now rightfully fight against barbarians. Let those who have been hirelings for a few pieces of silver [Matt. 27:3] now attain an eternal reward. Let those who have been exhausting themselves to the detriment of body and soul now labor for a double glory. Yea on the one hand will be the sad and the poor, on the other the joyous and the wealthy; here the enemies of the Lord, there His friends.

8. "Let nothing delay those who are going to go. Let them settle their affairs, collect money, and when winter has ended and spring has come, zealously undertake the journey under the guidance of the Lord."

Document 2

Urban II's speech at Clermont, according to Robert the Monk in *The First Crusade*, ed. Edward Peters (Philadelphia: Univ. of Pennsylvania Press, 1971), pp. 2–4.

Like Fulcher of Chartres, Robert the Monk may have attended the Council of Clermont and heard Urban's speech. If he was not present, then he must have obtained this version of the speech from fellow crusaders. Robert's version places strong emphasis upon ousting the Moslems from the Holy Land and settling the crusaders on the conquered lands. The popes compared the Holy Land with Europe and suggested that aspiring landowners would be well advised to heed the call to go on crusade in order to acquire land that was superior to the land found in Europe.—ed.

Oh, race of Franks, race from across the mountains, race chosen and beloved by God—as shines forth in very many of your works—set apart from all nations by the situation of your country, as well as by your catholic faith and the honor of the holy church! To you our discourse is addressed and for you our exhortation is intended. We wish you to know what a grievous cause has led us to your country, what peril threatening you and all the faithful has brought us.

From the confines of Jerusalem and the city of Constantinople a horrible tale has gone forth and very frequently has been brought to our ears, namely, that a race from the kingdom of the Persians, an accursed race, a race utterly alienated from God, a generation forsooth which has not directed its heart and has not entrusted its spirit to God, has invaded the lands of those Christians and has depopulated them by the sword, pillage and fire; it has led away a part of the captives into its own country, and a part it has destroyed by cruel tortures; it has either entirely destroyed the churches of God or appropriated them for the rite of its own religion. . . .

The kingdom of the Greeks is now dismembered by them and deprived of territory so vast in extent that it can not be traversed in a march of two months. On whom therefore is the labor of avenging these wrongs and of recovering this territory incumbent, if not upon you? You, upon whom above other nations God has conferred remarkable glory in arms, great courage, bodily activity, and strength to humble the hairy scalp of those who resist you.

Let the deeds of your ancestors move you and incite your minds to manly achievements; the glory and greatness of king Charles the Great, and of his son Louis, and of your other kings, who have destroyed the kingdoms of the pagans, and have extended in these lands the territory of the holy church. Let the holy sepulchre of the Lord our Saviour, which is possessed by unclean nations, especially incite you, and the holy places which are now treated with ignominy and irreverently polluted with their filthiness. Oh, most valiant soldiers and descendants of invincible ancestors, be not degenerate, but recall the valor of your progenitors.

But if you are hindered by love of children, parents and wives, remember what the Lord says in the Gospel, "He that loveth father or mother more than me, is not worthy of me." "Every one that hath forsaken houses, or brethren, or sisters, or father, or mother, or wife, or children, or lands for my name's sake shall receive an hundred-fold and shall inherit everlasting life." Let none of your possessions detain you, no solicitude for your family affairs, since this land which you inhabit, shut in on all sides by the seas and surrounded by the mountain peaks, is too narrow for your large population; nor does it abound in wealth; and it furnishes scarcely food enough for its cultivators. Hence it is that you murder and devour one another, that you wage war, and that frequently you perish by mutual wounds. Let therefore hatred depart from among you, let your quarrels end, let wars cease, and let all dissensions and controversies slumber. Enter upon the road to the Holy Sepulchre; wrest that land from the wicked race, and subject it to yourselves. That land which as the Scripture says "floweth with milk and honey," was given by God into the possession of the children of Israel.

When Pope Urban had said these and very many similar things in his urbane discourse, he so influenced to one purpose the desires of all who were present, that they cried out, "It is the will of God! It is the will of God!"

Document 3

"The Journal of the first voyage of Columbus," *The Northmen, Columbus and Cabot*, Original Narratives of Early American History, eds., J. E. Olson and E. G. Bourne (New York: Scribners, 1906; reprint ed., Barnes & Noble, 1953), pp. 89–90, 110–11, 182.

Although the early life of Columbus is sufficiently obscure to encourage a good deal of scholarly debate about his origins and early career, his later life is fully documented. He kept journals of each voyage to the New World, wrote letters to important people about the voyages, and fought energetically with his pen to clear his name of various charges brought against him by his enemies. Also, his son, Ferdinand, wrote a biography of the great explorer. As a result, we have more information about the mind of the man than is usually available about men of the fifteenth and sixteenth centuries. Like many of his contemporaries, he was well aware of medieval contacts with China and saw his first voyage as picking up where the earlier contacts had left off. He saw the New World, too, as a place where a peaceful people could be put to work by Spaniards interested in acquiring land and status. At least in his writings, he never lost this initial optimism about the value of his discoveries. He died, however, before the Spanish realized the value of the discovery.—ed.

In the name of our Lord Jesus Christ

Because, O most Christian, and very high, very excellent, and puissant Princes, King and Queen of the Spains and of the islands of the Sea, our Lords, in this present year of 1492, after your Highnesses had given an end to the war with the Moors who reigned in Europe, and had finished it in the very great city of Granada, where in this present year, on the second day of the month of January, by force of arms, I saw the royal banners of your Highnesses placed on the towers of Alfambra, which is the fortress of that city, and I saw the Moorish King come forth from the gates of the city and kiss the royal hands of your Highnesses, and of the Prince my Lord, and presently in that same month, acting on the information that I had given to your Highnesses touching the lands of India, and respecting a Prince who is called Gran Can, which means in our language King of Kings, how he and his ancestors had sent to Rome many times to ask for learned men of our holy faith to teach him, and how the Holy Father had never complied, insomuch that many people believing in idolatries were lost by receiving doctrine of perdition: YOUR HIGHNESSES, as Catholic Christians and Princes who love the holy Christian faith, and the propagation of it, and who are enemies to the sect of Mahoma[1] and to all idolatries and heresies, resolved to send me, Cristóbal Colon, to the said parts of India to see the said princes, and the cities and lands, and their disposition, with a view that they might be converted to our holy faith; and ordered that I should not go by land to the eastward, as had been customary, but that I should go by way of the west, whither up to this day, we do not know for certain that any one has gone.

Thus, after having turned out all the Jews from all your kingdoms and lordships, in the same month of January, your Highnesses gave orders to me that with a sufficient fleet I should go to the said parts of India, and for this they made great concessions to me, and ennobled me, so that henceforward I should be called Don, and should be Chief Admiral of the Ocean Sea, perpetual Viceroy and Governor of all the islands and continents that I should discover and gain, and that I might hereafter discover and gain

---

1. Mohammed.

in the Ocean Sea, and that my eldest son should succeed, and so on from generation to generation for ever. . . .

[Friday, 12th of October]

. . . . Presently many inhabitants of the island assembled. What follows is in the actual words of the Admiral in his book of the first navigation and discovery of the Indies. "I," he says, "that we might form great friendship, for I knew that they were a people who could be more easily freed and converted to our holy faith by love than by force, gave to some of them red caps, and glass beads to put round their necks, and many other things of little value, which gave them great pleasure, and made them so much our friends that it was a marvel to see. They afterwards came to the ship's boats where we were, swimming and bringing us parrots, cotton threads in skeins, darts, and many other things; and we exchanged them for other things that we gave them, such as glass beads and small bells. In fine, they took all, and gave what they had with good will. It appeared to me to be a race of people very poor in everything. They go as naked as when their mothers bore them, and so do the women, although I did not see more than one young girl. All I saw were youths, none more than thirty years of age. They are very well made, with very handsome bodies, and very good countenances. Their hair is short and coarse, almost like the hairs of a horse's tail. They wear the hairs brought down to the eyebrows, except a few locks behind, which they wear long and never cut. They paint themselves black, and they are the color of the Canarians, neither black nor white. Some paint themselves white, others red, and others of what color they find. Some paint their faces, others the whole body, some only round the eyes, others only on the nose. They neither carry nor know anything of arms, for I showed them swords, and they took them by the blade and cut themselves through ignorance. They have no iron, their darts being wands without iron, some of them having a fish's tooth at the end, and others being pointed in various ways. They are all of fair stature and size, with good faces, and well made." . . .

Sunday, 16th of December

. . . . Your Highnesses may believe that these lands are so good and fertile, especially these of the island of Española,[2] that there is no one who would know how to describe them, and no one who could believe if he had not seen them. And your Highnesses may believe that this island, and all the others, are as much yours as Castile. Here there is only wanting a settlement and the order to the people to do what is required. For I, with

---

2. This is the island that is divided between Haiti and the Dominican Republic.

the force I have under me, which is not large, could march over all these islands without opposition. I have seen only three sailors land, without wishing to do harm, and a multitude of Indians fled before them. They have no arms, and are without warlike instincts; they all go naked, and are so timid that a thousand would not stand before three of our men. So that they are good to be ordered about, to work and sow, and do all that may be necessary, and to build towns, and they should be taught to go about clothed and to adopt our customs.

I

Exporting Feudalism

Introduction

If any single term summarizes for the modern mind the difference between the medieval and the modern eras it is the word *feudalism*—derived from the word *fief* (feudum), which referred to the basic economic-military-governmental unit of medieval Europe. Eighteenth- and nineteenth-century writers, however, gave the word a pejorative connotation that remains current; editorial writers still use the term "feudal" to describe regimes of which they disapprove. In this sense, "feudalism" is a synonym for primitive, arbitrary, or reactionary. Feudalism, using the term in its proper sense, did not die out completely in Europe until the late eighteenth century. One of the earliest actions of the French Revolutionaries was the publication of a "Decree Abolishing Feudalism" in August 1789. Feudalism, like so many other aspects of the medieval world, lingered well into the modern era and only gradually gave way to political and economic institutions that we would call "modern."

As a basis for organizing a society, feudalism reached its fullest development in France during the Middle Ages and survived there until the Revolution of 1789. From the late fifteenth century until the mid-eighteenth century, France was either the dominant power in Europe or shared the dominant role with one other power. The result was that, although the style of feudal government developed and was modified in the course of the centuries, feudalism was logically associated with the strength and success of the French monarchy. When the French undertook to colonize the New World, it was logical for them to apply contemporary feudalism to the North American continent, creating what Francis Parkman called "Canadian feudalism." This was not identical with the feudalism of the early Middle Ages, but it was clearly "an offshoot of the feudalism of France, modified by the lapse of centuries, and further modified by the royal will."[1] These modifications of which Parkman spoke centered on restricting the military power of the nobility that had battled for domination of the French kingdom during the medieval and early modern period. The French did not export to North America the medieval feudal lord whose castle and vassals could stand in the way of royal centralization of the kingdom. What was exported was the

---

1. Francis Parkman, *The Old Régime in Canada*, 8th ed. (Boston: Little, Brown, 1893), p. 243.

seigneur, who took up land in Canada under royal patent, did homage for it, and then subdivided it among peasant farmers who paid him annually in cash and in kind. The seigneur had administrative and judicial powers over those who settled on his manor, although here again the powers granted to Canadian landlords were generally more restricted than those granted in France. The Canadian landlord was rarely authorized to erect his own gibbet, the symbol of high justice, the power to execute criminals.[2]

The imposition of "feudal" government in Canada is often seen as one of the features of French colonization that caused its downfall. As Parkman argued, "An ignorant population, sprung from a brave and active race, but trained to subjection and dependence through centuries of feudal and monarchical despotism, was planted in the wilderness by the hand of authority, and told to grow and flourish."[3] In other words, the French colonists in the New World were the prisoners of an outmoded system of government, one not suitable for export to North America. The English, in Parkman's opinion, were capable of more successful adaption to the conditions of the Americas because they were not the prisoners of a system. They were the heirs of an historical experience that trained them "in habits of reflection, forecast, industry, and self-reliance,—a training which enabled them to adopt and maintain an invigorating system of self-rule, totally inapplicable to their rivals."[4]

Parkman was clearly correct in seeing historical experience in the shaping of the French and English responses to the challenge of the New World. What he failed to consider was why the French assumed that a modified feudal structure would serve the needs of their new colony. The obvious answer was that from the French perspective "feudalism" was a perfectly suitable means for administering a colonial society. Having learned the dangers inherent in the existence of an armed feudal nobility, the French monarchs of the seventeenth and eighteenth centuries, and their ministers, strove to draw the fangs of the nobles in France by transforming them into army officers or courtiers. In the overseas possessions, however, the local nobleman who retained the administrative and judicial, if not the military, powers of the old nobility, provided local government at almost no cost to the monarch.

The experience of the French in creating colonies in the course of the Crusades indicated that feudalism could be successfully adapted for export. William the Conqueror, for example, brought French feudalism in his baggage train, as did the Normans who conquered Sicily and southern

2. Ibid., p. 252.
3. Ibid., p. 394.
4. Ibid., p. 396.

Italy and those others who crossed the Pyrenees to join in the reconquest of Spain. The fullest development of French feudal practice came in the eastern Mediterranean. French noblemen took quite seriously Urban II's injunction to settle overseas. The population growth in northern France, especially among noble families, meant an increasing number of younger sons who had no possibility of acquiring fiefs of their own, and these men joined the crusade at the first call. What these men intended to do was not only to oust the infidel from the Holy Land, they also intended to re-create the style of life that was expected of men of their class in France.

The selections in this section focus on the establishment of feudal societies in the lands conquered by the crusaders. One of the most important aspects of medieval feudalism, and one that is often overlooked, was its emphasis on the need of rulers to possess a wide range of skills, not only military but administrative as well. Fulcher of Chartres and Robert of Clari both describe the process of selection by which leaders were chosen not simply because of their birth but because of their abilities (docs. 4 and 5). The oath of homage that vassals were expected to give to their lords was similar to the one that vassals routinely swore in Europe (doc. 6).

The response of the crusaders to the Byzantines whom they were expected to assist and to the Moslems whom they fought against reflected the interests of the crusaders as a social and economic class. The desire for land of their own led the crusaders to reject any policy that would require them to hold lands they took from the Moslems as fiefs of the Byzantine emperor. Furthermore, the crusaders came to mistrust the Byzantines and to characterize them as untrustworthy and not even good Christians. As for the Moslems, the crusaders tended to describe them as bloodthirsty villains quite capable of killing wounded prisoners, as Joinville points out (doc. 7). On the other hand, Joinville seems able to understand a Moslem nobleman and to respect him. Furthermore, the longer crusaders remained in the East, the more they acculturated and took wives from among the Moslem population. Fulcher of Chartres even describes a society in which the Europeans and the native population learn to live together in harmony, surely an exaggerated view of the situation but perhaps an indication of the hopes that the crusaders had for the future of the conquest.

The gradual collapse of the crusader states during the thirteenth century as the Moslems returned to the offensive meant the end of feudalism in the East. It did not mean, however, that feudalism was judged unsuitable for overseas colonies. In the fifteenth century a French nobleman, the Lord of Bethencourt, attempted to settle the Canary Islands along feudal lines (doc. 8). As a result, when the French began to settle Canada in the seventeenth century, they could look to a long tradition of organizing colonies along feudal lines. One problem continuously recurred in these attempts, a problem that plagued the Canadian settlement. Frenchmen were not anxious to emigrate if they could avoid it. There generally seem to have been sufficient opportunities for Frenchmen at home.

Bibliography

When completed, the most extensive history of the crusades in English will be Kenneth M. Setton, general editor, A History of the Crusades. Three of the five proposed volumes have appeared: vol. 1, The First Hundred Years, ed. Marshal W. Baldwin (Philadelphia: Univ. of Pennsylvania Press, 1955; reprint ed., Madison: Univ. of Wisconsin Press, 1969); vol. 2, The Later Crusades, eds. Robert L. Wolfe and Harry W. Hazard (Philadelphia: Univ. of Pennsylvania Press, 1962; reprint ed., Madison: Univ. of Wisconsin Press, 1969); vol. 3, The Fourteenth and Fifteenth Centuries, ed. Harry W. Hazard (Madison: Univ. of Wisconsin Press, 1975). In addition, see Steven Runciman, A History of the Crusades, 3 vols. (Cambridge, Eng.: Cambridge Univ. Press, 1951–54). A good brief treatment is contained in Hans Eberhard Mayer, The Crusades (Oxford: Oxford Univ. Press, 1972). The pioneering work in the survival of the crusading spirit in the fourteenth and fifteenth centuries is Aziz S. Atiya, The Crusades in the Later Middle Ages (London: Methuen, 1938). The crusades as a kind of colonial expansion are discussed in Joshua Prawer, The Crusaders' Kingdom: European Colonialism in the Middle Ages (New York: Praeger, 1972).

Two basic introductions to feudalism are: Carl Stephenson, Medieval Feudalism (Ithaca: Cornell Univ. Press, 1942) and François L. Ganshof, Feudalism, trans. Philip Grierson (London: Longmans, Green, 1952). The most complete picture of feudalism as it actually functioned is in Marc Bloch, Feudal Society, trans. L. A. Manyon (Chicago: Univ. of Chicago Press, 1961). There has been a good deal of debate about the use of the term feudalism and about its applicability to societies other than that found in medieval Europe. These topics are dealt with in Rushton Coulborn, ed., Feudalism in History (Princeton: Princeton Univ. Press, 1956). Some of the reasons why the French retained the feudal style so long into the modern period are explored in P. S. Lewis, *Later Medieval France* (New York: St. Martin's, 1968).

The long series of wars with the Moslems gave rise to a number of myths about them, which are discussed in Norman A. Daniel, *Islam and the West: The Making of an Image* (Edinburgh: Edinburgh Univ. Press, 1960) and R. W. Southern, *Western Views of Islam in the Middle Ages* (Cambridge, Mass.: Harvard Univ. Press, 1962). One result of the growing interest in the conversion of the Moslems by prayer and example, coupled with the failure of the crusades by the end of the thirteenth century, was the appearance of a number of critics who opposed the crusades; see Palmer A. Throop, *Criticism of the Crusades* (Amsterdam: Swets and Zeitlinger, 1940).

Document 4*

Fulcher of Chartres, *A History of the Expedition to Jerusalem, 1095–1127*, trans. Frances Rita Ryan, ed. Harold Fink (Knoxville: Univ. of Tennessee Press, 1969; reprint ed., W. W. Norton: New York, 1973), pp. 124, 148–51, 192–93, 225, 231, 266–72.

Because Fulcher of Chartres moved within the ruling circles of the crusaders, he was able to observe at first hand the leaders of the crusade. The excerpts presented here illustrate the way the French nobles chose leaders for their new principalities. While the description no doubt idealizes the situation, nevertheless it reveals the way feudal governments functioned. Fulcher also points out that the crusade was a success, so that men who had come as poor men remained to become rich men. His optimistic opinion about the future of the crusading movement was, of course, shattered by the resurgence of the Moslems after their initial defeats. This optimism was typical of the first period of expansion.—ed.

All the people of the Lord's army in the Holy City chose Godfrey prince of the realm because of the nobility of his character, military skill, patient conduct, no less than for his elegance of manners, to protect and govern it. Then too, they placed canons in the Church of the Lord's Sepulcher and in His Temple to serve Him. Moreover they decided at that time that a patriarch should not be created as yet until they had inquired from the Roman pope whom he wished to place in authority. . . .

The Accession of King Baldwin and the Smallness of His Kingdom

In the year 1101 after the Incarnation of our Lord, and on the anniversary of His Nativity, Baldwin was ceremoniously appointed and crowned king by the above-mentioned patriarch in the presence of the other bishops, the priests, and the people in the Basilica of the Blessed Mary at Bethlehem. This had not been done for his brother and predecessor because Godfrey had not wished it, and there were others who did not approve of it. Still, upon wiser consideration they decided that it should be done.

* From *A History of the Expedition to Jerusalem, 1095–1127*, by Fulcher of Chartres, translated by Frances Rita Ryan (Sisters of St. Joseph), edited by Harold S. Fink, by permission of the University of Tennessee Press. Copyright © 1969 by the University of Tennessee Press.

"Why should it be objected," they said, "since Christ our Lord was dishonored by abuse as a criminal and crowned with thorns in Jerusalem, and since He willingly gave Himself unto death for us? Besides, this crown was not, in the minds of the Jews, an emblem of honor and kingly dignity, but rather of ignominy and disgrace. But what those murderers did as an insult to Him was by the grace of God turned to our salvation and glory.

"Moreover a king is not made king against the mandate of God, for when he is chosen rightly and according to God's will he is sanctified and consecrated with a lawful blessing. Anyone who receives that kingly power together with a golden crown takes upon himself at the same time the honorable duty of rendering justice. To him certainly as to the bishop in regard to the episcopate can this be fitly applied: 'He desires to do good work who desires to rule, but if he does not rule justly, he is not a true king.' "

In the beginning of his reign Baldwin as yet possessed few cities and people. Through that same winter he stoutly protected his kingdom from enemies on all sides. And because they found out that he was a very skillful fighter, although he had few men, they did not dare to attack him. If he had had a greater force he would have met the enemy gladly. . . .

The Substitution of Tancred at Antioch

Then it happened, in the month of March, that Tancred turned over to King Baldwin Haifa, a city which he possessed, and Tiberias, and with his men marched to Antioch. The people of Antioch had sent representatives to him saying, "Do not delay, but come to us and rule us, and possess the city of Antioch and the land subject to it until the Lord Bohemond, our master and yours, shall come forth from captivity. For you are his kin, a prudent and excellent soldier, and more powerful than we are. You are better able to hold this our land than we. If sometime Lord Bohemond shall return then what is right shall be done." This was requested, and it was so done. . . .

Bohemond, Having Collected an Army, Devastated the Territory of the Emperor

In that same year Bohemond, after he had returned from Gaul, collected as many men as possible and prepared a fleet in the port of Brindisi, which is in Apulia. After waiting for a favorable time for crossing, the men embarked on the seventh day before the Ides of October and sailed to Bulgaria, landing at the port of Avlona.

Capturing Avlona very quickly, they proceeded to the city of Durazzo and laid siege to it on the third day before the Ides of October. But because that city was well supplied with men and provisions, it wore down the besiegers for a long time. Lord Bohemond had five thousand knights and sixty thousand footmen. Then too he allowed no women to cross with him lest they be an impediment and a burden to the army.

The Emperor of Constantinople, Alexius by name, was at that time strongly opposed to our people. By trickery or open violence he thwarted or tyrannized over the pilgrims going to Jerusalem by land or sea. It was for this reason that Bohemond invaded Alexius' territory, trying to take his cities and fortresses.

The Peace Between the Emperor and Bohemond, Which Was Solemnized by Oaths

In the year 1108 after the Incarnation of Our Lord, after Bohemond had already besieged Durazzo for one year, he had accomplished nothing whatever. He had prepared stratagems against the emperor, and the emperor had done the same against him. Finally after a treaty had been discussed through intermediaries and after the emperor with his army had approached Bohemond, they became friends with each other after several conferences.

The emperor, swearing upon the most precious relics, promised Bohemond that the pilgrims, of whom mention often has been made, would from that day forward be safe and unharmed by land and sea as far as the emperor's power extended, and that no one of them should be seized or maltreated. Bohemond on his part swore to observe peace and loyalty to the emperor in all things.

Afterwards Bohemond, when occasion offered, returned to Apulia leading back the smaller portion of his army. The greater part proceeded by sea to Jerusalem where it had vowed to go. . . . As a result of the death of King Baldwin the people of Jerusalem called a council at once lest lacking a king they be considered the weaker. They chose as their king Baldwin, Count of Edessa, a kinsman of the deceased king. It happened that he had crossed the Euphrates River and had come to Jerusalem to consult with his predecessor. On Easter Day he was chosen unanimously and was consecrated. . . .

The King Obtained the Principality of Antioch

However, the king remained in Antioch because necessity demanded it until he granted out the lands of the deceased nobles in legal form to the living, until he had united widows, of whom he found many, to husbands in pious affection, and until he had reorganized much else in need of restitution. For as much as up to this time he had been simply king of the people of Jerusalem, now by the death of Prince Roger of Antioch, Baldwin was made king of the people of Antioch in that other realm as well.

I, therefore, admonish the king and beseech that he love God with his whole heart and all his understanding and all his strength and that as a faithful servant he dedicate himself completely and with thanksgiving to God and that he who has found the Lord to be his faithful friend confess himself His humble servant. For which of Baldwin's predecessors has the Lord elevated as much as he? The Lord has made others the possessor of one kingdom but Baldwin of two. Without fraud, without the shedding of blood, without the trouble of litigation, but peacefully by divine will he acquired them.

God gave to him the land far and wide from Egypt to Mesopotamia. The Lord has shown a bountiful hand toward him; let him then take care not to have a grudging hand toward God, who gives abundantly and does not cavil. If Baldwin desires to be a king let him endeavor to rule justly. . . .

The Surrender of the City of Tyre

1. When the king of Damascus saw that his Turks and the Saracens, shut up in the city, could in no way escape from our hands he preferred to redeem them alive with some humiliation rather than mourn after them dead. Therefore he inquired through sagacious intermediaries how he might get out his people with all of their property and then turn over the empty city to us.

After both sides had haggled over this matter for a long time, they mutually exchanged hostages, the Muslims came forth from the city, and the Christians entered peacefully. However, those of the Saracens who chose to remain within the city did so in peace according to the terms of the agreement. . . .

Therefore we ought not to cease nor indeed to hesitate to seek out the Lord as our kind and beneficent Helper in our tribulations, and to entreat Him with prayers to lend a favorable ear to our entreaties. This indeed we did in Jerusalem by repeatedly visiting the churches, shedding tears, distributing alms, and mortifying the body with fasts. God, seeing this from on high, as I believe, did not leave without bestowing His benediction behind Him [Joel 2:14], and He will hear our prayer.

While we were waiting with ears open to learn any bit of news, behold! three messengers arrived in great haste bearing letters from our patriarch announcing the capture of Tyre.

When this was heard a most joyful clamor arose. The "Te Deum laudamus" was forthwith sung with exultant voices. Bells were rung, a procession marched to the Temple of God, and flags were raised on the walls and towers. Through all the streets many-colored ornaments were displayed, thankful gestures made, the messengers suitably rewarded according to their deserts, the humble and the great mutually congratulated themselves, and the girls were delightful as they sang in chorus.

Justly Jerusalem like a mother rejoices over her daughter Tyre at whose right hand she sits crowned as befits her rank. And Babylon mourns the loss of her prestige, which sustained her until recently, and the loss of her hostile fleet, which she used to send out against us each year.

Indeed although Tyre is lessened in worldly pomp she is augmented in divine grace. For whereas among the heathen the city had a high priest or arch-priest in authority, according to the institutions of the fathers she shall have a primate or patriarch in Christian law. For where there were high priests Christian archbishops shall be instituted to rule over provinces.

Where there was a metropolis, which is interpreted "mother city," there were metropolitans who presided over three or four cities within the province of the mother or greater city.

For when smaller cities had priests or counts there bishops were instituted. Moreover the priests and the rest of the clergy in minor orders were known, not foolishly, as tribunes of the people.

Every secular-power corresponds in dignity to its rank, that first there is the Augustus or emperor, then the Caesars, then kings, dukes, and counts. So said Popes Clement, Anaclete, Anicet, and many others. . . .

From time to time Pope Paschal confirmed these privileges and transmitted them to the Church of Jerusalem, which privileges, by the authority of the Roman Church, she should enjoy in perpetual right. These privileges are contained in this document. . . .

The Distribution of the Lands Around Tyre

The affairs of Tyre were settled as was proper. A tripartite division was made in which two equal parts were turned over to the authority of the city. The third part, lying within the city as well as around the harbor, was as a result of reciprocal concessions made one by one turned over to the Venetians to hold by hereditary right. Then all returned home.

The patriarch of Jerusalem returned to Jerusalem with the soldiers of the city, and the clergy and people received the Holy Cross of the Lord with due veneration.

The Sign That Appeared at That Time

At that time the sun appeared to us in dazzling color for almost one hour. It was changed by a new and hyacinthine beauty and transformed into the shape of the moon as in a two-pronged eclipse. This happened on the third day before the Ides of August when the ninth hour of the day was waning.

Therefore do not marvel when you see signs in the heavens because God works miracles there as he does on earth. For just as in the heavens so also on earth He transforms and arranges all things as He wills. For if those things which He made are wonderful, more wonderful is He who made them. Consider, I pray, and reflect how in our time God has transformed the Occident into the Orient.

For we who were Occidentals have now become Orientals. He who was a Roman or a Frank has in this land been made into a Galilean or a Palestinean. He who was of Rheims or Chartres has now become a citizen of Tyre or Antioch. We have already forgotten the places of our birth; already these are unknown to many of us or not mentioned any more.

Some already possess homes or households by inheritance. Some have taken wives not only of their own people but Syrians or Armenians or even Saracens who have obtained the grace of baptism. One has his father-in-law as well as his daughter-in-law living with him, or his own child if not his step-son or step-father. Out here there are grandchildren and great-grandchildren. Some tend vineyards, others till fields.

People use the eloquence and idioms of diverse languages in conversing back and forth. Words of different languages have become common property known to each nationality, and mutual faith unites those who are ignorant of their descent. Indeed it is written, "The lion and the ox shall eat straw together" [Isa. 62:25]. He who was born a stranger is now as one born here; he who was born an alien has become as a native.

Our relatives and parents join us from time to time, sacrificing, even though reluctantly, all that they formerly possessed. Those who were poor in the Occident, God makes rich in this land. Those who had little money there have countless bezants here, and those who did not have a villa possess here by the gift of God a city.

Therefore why should one return to the Occident who has found the Orient like this? God does not wish those to suffer want who with their crosses dedicated themselves to follow Him, nay even to the end.

You see therefore that this is a great miracle and one which the whole world ought to admire. Who has heard anything like it? God wishes to enrich us all and to draw us to Himself as His dearest friends. And because He wishes it we also freely desire it, and what is pleasing to Him we do with a loving and submissive heart in order that we may reign with him throughout eternity.

Document 5

Robert of Clari, *The Conquest of Constantinople*, trans. Edgar H. McNeal, Records of Civilization, Sources and Studies, no. 23 (New York: Columbia Univ. Press, 1936), pp. 113–15, 118–19.

Robert of Clari, a minor French nobleman, wrote this chronicle sometime after he returned from the Fourth Crusade in 1216. This crusade was marked by the capture of Constantinople by the western crusaders who had ostensibly come to protect the Eastern Empire from the Moslems. Instead, the crusaders turned on the East Romans whom they came to despise as schismatics in matters of religion and untrustworthy in matters of politics and war. Having taken Constantinople in 1204, the crusaders then selected a new emperor. It is in observing the selection process of the emperor at Constantinople that we learn a good deal about how Western European feudalism operated. On the frontier, the leaders of the crusade formed a feudal society in miniature. The ruler was selected in negotiations that involved the crusaders who led the group, the Venetians who underwrote some of the cost of transporting the crusaders, and leading Churchmen. Also typical of the feudal world was the fact that disputes over the possession of land caused internal divisions among the crusaders. In large measure the crusaders tried to impose western feudal social and political institutions on an urbanized, merchantile society. They failed, of course, because they were unable to adapt to the social, economic, and political realities of a world very unlike their own.—ed.

Afterwards it came about that all the counts and all the high men came together one day at the palace of Boukoleon, which belonged to the marquis, and they said to one another that they ought to decide on an emperor and ought to choose their ten electors, and they told the doge of Venice to choose his ten. When the marquis heard this, he wanted to put in his own men and those who he thought would choose him as emperor, and he wanted to be emperor forthwith. And the barons were not at all agreed that he should put in his own men, but they were quite willing that he should have some of his men among the ten. When the doge of Venice, who was a right worthy man and wise, saw this, he spoke in the hearing of all and said: "Lords, now hear me," said the doge. "I propose that before an emperor is elected the palaces be placed under the common guard of the host. For if they should elect me emperor, I would go straightway without any gainsaying and take possession of the palaces, and likewise if they elected the count of Flanders, he should have the palaces without any gainsaying, or if they elected the marquis or Count Louis or the count of St. Pol, or even if they should elect a poor knight, whoever is to be emperor should have the palaces without any gainsaying, whether from the marquis or from the count of Flanders or from any one else." When the marquis heard this, he could not gainsay it; instead he vacated the palace which he was holding. Then they went and put guards in the palaces from the commonalty of the host, to hold the palaces. When the doge of Venice had spoken thus, then he told the barons to choose their ten and he would soon have his ten chosen. And when the barons heard this, then each one wanted to put in his own men. The count of Flanders wanted to put in his men, and so did Count Louis and the count of St. Pol and the other rich men, and in this way they could never agree as to whom they should put in or whom they should choose. So they took another day to choose these ten and when it came to that day, again they could not agree as to whom they should choose. The marquis always wanted to put in those who he thought would elect him emperor, and he wanted to be emperor whether or no. This discord lasted a good fortnight without their ever being able to agree. And there was no day on which they did not assemble for this affair, until at length they agreed that the clergy of the host, the bishops and abbots who were there, should be the electors. Then when they had come to an agreement, the doge of Venice went and chose his ten in such a way as I shall tell you. He called four of those whom he thought the worthiest in his land, and he made them swear on relics that they would choose to the best of their knowledge ten of the worthiest of his land who were in the host, and they did so. And when they called one of them, he had to come forward, and he dared not afterwards talk or take counsel with anyone. Instead they placed him straightway in a church, and one after another likewise, until the doge had his ten. And when they were all in that church, the ten Venetians and the bishops, a mass of the Holy Spirit was chanted, that the Holy Spirit might guide them and give them to choose such a man as would be meet and good for the office.

When the mass was chanted, the electors assembled and took counsel together, and they talked of one and of another, until the Venetians and the bishops and abbots, all twenty electors, agreed all together that it should be the count of Flanders, nor was there one of them who was against it. When they were agreed together and their council was about to break up, they gave the bishop of Soissons the charge of saying the word. When they had separated, all those of the host assembled to hear and to learn whom they would name emperor. When they were thus assembled, they were all very quiet, and most of them were afraid and fearful that they would name the marquis, but those who held to the marquis were greatly afraid that they would name someone other than the marquis. And as they were waiting there all quiet, the bishop of Soissons rose to his feet and said to them: "Lords," said the bishop, "by the common consent of all of you we have been delegated to make this election. We have chosen one whom we ourselves knew to be a good man for it, one in whom rule is well placed and who is right well able to maintain the law, a man of gentle birth and a high man. We will name him to you. He is Baldwin, count of Flanders." When the word was heard, all the French were right glad of it, but there were some others, like those who held for the marquis, who were greatly displeased. . . .

It was not long afterwards that the emperor sent for all the high barons and the doge of Venice and Count Louis and the count of St. Pol and all the high men, and said he wanted to go and conquer some of the land, and they decided who should go with the emperor and who should stay to guard the city. And it was decided that the doge of Venice should stay and Count Louis and some of their people with them. And the marquis stayed and he married the wife of Isaac, the former emperor, who was sister to the king of Hungary. When the marquis saw that the emperor was about to go and conquer the land, he came and asked him to give him the kingdom of Salonika, a land which was fully fifteen days' journey from Constantinople. And the emperor answered him that it was not his to give, for the barons of the host and the Venetians had the larger part of it. As far as it rested with him he would give it him very gladly and with great good will, but the part belonging to the barons of the host and to the Venetians he could not give him. When the marquis saw that he could not have it, he was in a great rage. Then the emperor went away where he had planned to go, with all his people. And as he came to the castles and the cities, they were yielded to him without resistance, and the keys were brought out to him, and the priests and the clerks came in their vestments in procession to meet and welcome him, and all the Greeks worshipped him as the sacred emperor. And the emperor placed his guards in the castles and the cities everywhere as he came to them. And so he conquered much of the land up to fifteen days' journey from Constantinople, until he came within a day's journey of Salonika. In the meantime, while the emperor was thus conquering the land, the marquis had set out with his wife and all his people to follow after the emperor and he came up with the host of the emperor before the emperor came to Salonika. And when he was come up with the host, he went and encamped a good league on this side, and when he had made camp, he took messengers and sent them to the emperor, and sent word to him not to go into his land of Salonika, that had been given to him. For he should know well that if he went there he would not go with him any longer and would not hold to him longer, but rather he would go back to Constantinople and do the best he could for himself.

Document 6

"Livre de Jean d'Ibelin," Assises de Jérusalem, Recueil des historiens des croisades, Lois, 2 vols. (Paris: 1841, 1843), 1: 313–14. Translated by James Muldoon.
Jean d'Ibelin (d. 1266) played an important role in the first crusade of St. Louis, but he is most remembered for compiling a volume of the laws of the feudal kingdom of Jerusalem. In many ways, this volume provides one of the best guides to the legal and institutional structure of feudalism to be found anywhere. The reason is that in the East, the imposition of a feudal structure was a conscious move, not, as in Western Europe, a structure that had evolved piecemeal to meet changing circumstances. Lands taken from the Moslems were to be held as fiefs and the holders of such fiefs were required to take oaths of fealty to their lords, just as they had been expected to do for fiefs that they had held in the lands from whence they had come.—ed.

When a man or a woman does homage to the chief lord of the kingdom, he should be on his knees before him and place his joined hands between his and say to him, "Sire, I become your liege-man for this fief," and say what fief it is for which he is doing homage, "and I promise to guard and protect you against everything that can live and die." And the lord answers him saying, "And I acknowledge this by the faith of God and my own, saving my rights." And he should kiss him in good faith on the mouth. But if he who did homage, if as is said above, to the chief lord, had previously become the liege man or done homage to a man or woman who was not a man of the chief lord, or to a man who was a man of the chief lord, he ought to save it when doing homage; for one who is a man of another cannot do homage afterwards to yet another, if he does not save [the rights] of his first lord, or if the lord does not give his consent. . . . And he who does homage for something which is in a kingdom other than that of the chief lord ought to make it in the manner set down above, so that he does not do liege homage for it; because no one ought to make more than one liege homage. . . .

Document 7

Jean, Sire de Joinville, "Chronicle of the Crusade of St. Lewis," in Memoirs of the Crusades, trans. Frank Marzials (London: J. M. Dent, 1908; reprint ed., New York: E. P. Dutton, 1958), pp. 148, 170–71, 197–98, 205–6, 216–17.
Joinville (1224–1317) was an associate of St. Louis, though not a

member of that king's inner circle of advisors. His chronicle or, more accurately, his life of St. Louis was written at the request of St. Louis's great-grandson, Louis X, who wished a record of his illustrious ancestor's life as a model for future kings of France. Joinville accompanied Louis on his first crusading expedition but not on the second. His opinions, written down almost fifty years after the events described, are those of a soldier and gentleman. In this selection he gives some current opinions about non-Christians. He quotes with approval St. Louis's story about a disputation between a Christian and a Jew that ended with the Jew being struck by a knight, almost a parody of the debates between Christians and nonbelievers described elsewhere in this volume. His descriptions of the Moslems are those of a soldier interested in his opponents. Joinville even seems to have found it easy to understand and to deal with his captor who was, after all, a knight and gentleman like himself.—ed.

He told me that there was once a great disputation between clergy and Jews at the monastery of Cluny. And there was at Cluny a poor knight to whom the abbot gave bread at that place for the love of God; and this knight asked the abbot to suffer him to speak the first words, and they suffered him, not without doubt. So he rose, and leant upon his crutch, and asked that they should bring to him the greatest clerk and most learned master among the Jews; and they did so. Then he asked the Jew a question, which was this: "Master," said the knight, "I ask you if you believe that the Virgin Mary, who bore God in her body and in her arms, was a virgin mother, and is the mother of God?"

And the Jew replied that of all this he believed nothing. Then the knight answered that the Jew had acted like a fool when—neither believing in her, nor loving her—he had yet entered into her monastery and house. "And verily," said the knight, "you shall pay for it!" Whereupon he lifted his crutch and smote the Jew near the ear, and beat him to the earth. Then the Jews turned to flight, and bore away their master, sore wounded. And so ended the disputation.

The abbot came to the knight and told him he had committed a deed of very great folly. But the knight replied that the abbot had committed a deed of greater folly in gathering people together for such a disputation; for there were a great many good Christians there who, before the disputation came to an end, would have gone away misbelievers through not fully understanding the Jews. "And I tell you," said the king, "that no one, unless he be a very learned clerk, should dispute with them; but a layman, when he hears the Christian law mis-said, should not defend the Christian law, unless it be with his sword, and with that he should pierce the mis-sayer in the midriff, so far as the sword will enter." . . .

At the time when we came to Cyprus, the Soldan[1] of Iconium[2] was the richest king in all paynimry. And he had done a marvellous thing, for he had melted a great part of his gold in earthen jars, such as are used oversea to hold wine, and may contain three or four measures, and he had caused the jars to be broken, so that the ingots of gold remained uncovered in one of his castles, and every one who entered the castle could see and handle them; and of these ingots there were at least six or seven.

His great wealth might well be seen from a pavilion which the King of Armenia sent to the King of France, and which was worth some five hundred livres; and the King of Armenia told the King of France that a ferrais of the Soldan of Iconium had given it him. Now a ferrais is he who has care of the soldan's pavilions and keeps his houses clean. . . .

As it pertains to my subject, I will here tell you what kind of people the Bedouins are. The Bedouins do not believe in Mahomet, but they believe in the law of Ali, who was uncle to Mahomet; and so also believes the Old Man of the Mountain, who entertains the Assassins. And they believe that when a man dies for his lord, or in any good cause, his soul goes into another body, better and more comfortable; and for this reason the Assassins are not greatly concerned if they are killed when carrying out the commands of the Old Man of the Mountain. But of the Old Man of the Mountain we will say no more at this present, but speak only about the Bedouins.

The Bedouins live neither in villages, nor cities, nor castles, but lie always out in the fields; and they establish their households, their wives and their children, at night, and by day when the weather is bad, in a sort of lodging that they make with the hoops of barrels tied to poles, like ladies' chariots; and over these hoops they throw sheepskins, called skins of Damascus, cured with alum. The Bedouins themselves wear great pelisses that cover the whole of their body, their legs, and their feet.

When it rains in the evening, or the weather is foul by night, they wrap themselves round in their cloaks, and take the bits out of their horses' mouths, and leave their horses to browse near. When the morrow comes, they spread out their cloaks to the sun, and rub and cure them; nor does it afterwards appear as if the cloaks had been wetted. Their belief is that no one can die save on the day appointed, and for this reason they will not wear armour; and when they wish to curse their children they say to them: "Be thou accursed like a Frank, who puts on armour for fear of death!" In battle they carry nothing but sword and spear.

Nearly all are clothed in a surplice, like priests. Their heads are all bound round with cloths, that go beneath their chins, wherefore they are an

1. Sultan.
2. Kingdom of the Seljuk Turks in Asia Minor.

ugly people, and hideous to behold, and the hairs of their heads and of their beards are all black. They live on the milk of their beasts, and purchase, in the plains belonging to wealthy men, the pasturage on which their beasts subsist. Their number no man can tell; for they are to be found in the kingdom of Egypt, in the kingdom of Jerusalem, and in all the other lands of the Saracens, and of the misbelievers—to whom they pay, every year, a great tribute. . . .

THE "HALCA" OR GUARD OF THE SOLDAN

It is convenient, in pursuing our story, to disturb its course somewhat, at this point, for the purpose of showing how the soldans kept their forces ordered and conditioned. And it is sooth that they had formed the main part of their chivalry of foreigners, whom merchants had brought for sale out of strange lands, and whom they bought right willingly and at a high price. And these people that the merchants brought into Egypt were obtained in the East, because when one Eastern king defeated another, he took the poor people whom he had conquered, and sold them to the merchants, and the merchants came and sold them in Egypt.

As to the children, the soldan brought them up in his own house till their beards began to grow; and he would see that they had bows proportioned to their strength; and so soon as they waxed stronger, the weaker bows were cast into the soldan's arsenal, and the master artilleryman provided them with bows as strong as they could bend.

The arms of the soldan were or, and such arms as the soldan wore were worn by these young people also; and they were called *bahariz*. So soon as their beards began to grow the soldan made them knights. And they wore the soldan's arms, save for one difference, viz., that they added on to the arms or, crimson devices, roses, or crimson bends, or birds or other devices, according to their pleasure.

And these people, of whom I am speaking to you, were called of the *Halca*, because the *bahariz* slept in the tent of the soldan. When the soldan was in camp, those of the *Halca* were lodged about his quarters, and set to guard his person. At the entrance to his quarters were lodged, in a little tent, the porters of the soldan, and his minstrels, who had horns, and drums, and cymbals. And with these they made such a noise at the point of day and at nightfall, that those who were near could not hear one another speak; and clearly were they heard throughout the camp.

Nor would the minstrels have been rash enough to sound their instruments during the day, save by order of the master of the *Halca*; whence it happened that if the soldan wished to give an order, he sent for the master of the *Halca*, and gave the order through him; and then the master caused the soldan's instruments to be sounded, and all the host assembled to hear the order of the soldan: the master of the *Halca* spoke it, and all the host carried it out.

When the soldan went to war, the knights of the *Halca*, if so be that they approved themselves well in battle, were made emirs by the soldan, and he placed them in command of two hundred knights, or three hundred; and the better they approved themselves the more knights did he set them over.

The reward reserved for their deeds of chivalry is this: when they become famous and rich beyond question, and the soldan is afraid lest they should kill or disinherit him, then he causes them to be taken and put to death in his prison, and their wives deprived of all they possess. This is how the soldan dealt with those who captured the Count of Montfort, and the Count of Bar; and so did Bondocdar deal with those who had discomfited the King of Armenia. For these latter, thinking to have some reward, dismounted and went to salute Bondocdar while he was hunting wild beasts; and he replied: "I salute you not," because they had disturbed his hunting; and he caused them to be beheaded. . . .

The chief emir of the galleys sent for me and asked me if I were cousin to the king; and I said "No," and told him how and why the mariner had said I was the king's cousin. And he said I had acted wisely, for otherwise we should all have been put to death. And he asked me if I was in any manner of the lineage of the Emperor Frederic of Germany, who was then living. I replied that I thought my lady mother was the emperor's cousin-german. And he said that he loved me the more for it.

While we were at meat, he caused a citizen of Paris to be brought before us. When the citizen came in, he said to me: "Lord, what are you doing?" "Why, what am I doing?" said I. "In God's name," said he, "you are eating flesh on a Friday!" When I heard that, I put my bowl behind me. And the emir asked my Saracen why I had done so, and he told him. And the emir replied that God would not take what I had done amiss, seeing I did it unwittingly. And you must know that this same reply was given to me by the Legate after we were out of prison; and yet, notwithstanding, I did not afterwards forbear to fast on bread and water, every Friday in Lent; wherefore the legate was very wroth with me, seeing that I was the only man of substance that had remained with the king.

On the Sunday after, the emir caused me, and all the other prisoners taken on the water, to be landed on the bank of the river. While they were taking my Lord John, my good priest, out of the hold of the galley, he fainted, and they killed him and threw him into the river. His clerk fainted also, by reason of the sickness of the host that was upon him, and they threw a mortar on his head, so that he died, and they threw him into the river.

While the other sick people were being disembarked from the galleys in which they had been kept prisoners, there were Saracens standing by, with naked swords, who killed those that fell, and cast them all into the river. I caused them to be told, through my Saracen, that it seemed to me this was not well done; for it was against the teachings of Saladin, who said you ought never to kill a man after he had partaken of your bread and of your salt. And the emir answered that the men in question were of no account, seeing they were helpless because of the sickness they had upon them.

He caused my mariners to be brought before me, and told me they had all denied their faith; and I told him never to place confidence in them, for lightly as they had left us so lightly, if time and opportunity occurred, would they leave their new masters. And the emir made answer that he agreed with me; for that Saladin was wont to say that never did one see a bad Christian become a good Saracen, or a bad Saracen become a good Christian.

After these things he caused me to be mounted on a palfrey, and to ride by his side. And we passed over a bridge of boats and went to Mansourah, where the king and his people were prisoners; and we came to the entrance of a great pavilion, where the soldan's scribes were; and there they wrote down my name. Then my Saracen said to me: "Lord, I shall not follow you further, for I cannot; but I pray you, lord, always to keep hold of the hand of the child that you have with you, lest the Saracens should take him from you." And this child was called Bartholomew, and he was the bastard son of the Lord of Montfaucon. When my name had been written down, the emir led me into the pavilion where the barons were, and more than ten thousand persons with them. When I entered, the barons made such joy that we could not hear one another speak, and they gave thanks to our Saviour, and said they thought they had lost me.

Document 8

Jean de Bethencourt, The Canarian, trans. R. H. Major, Hakluyt Society Publications, no. 46 (London: The Society, 1872), pp. 3–5, 42–45, 162–64, 167–69, 185–87, 203–5.

The attempt by Jean de Bethencourt (d. 1425) to establish a colony in the Canary Islands is an interesting example of the way in which the desire for land moved fifteenth-century nobles. The Canaries had long been known to exist, and during the fourteenth century European seamen occasionally landed there. The fierceness of the native population prevented any permanent settlements at first. The tone of this volume is that of the epic poem describing heroic adventures of a chivalrous knight. Bethencourt is Roland off to the wars. He was not, however.

able to get much support from either his own lord, the king of France, or from the king of Castile whom he tried to interest in the venture. The argument that possession of these islands would aid in the wars against the Moslems fell on deaf ears, and the islands did not at that point seem to possess any economic significance. The Castilians did eventually employ the islands as a base where ships sailing westward could refit for the trip across the Atlantic.—ed.

It was the custom in old times to record in writing the deeds of chivalry and marvellous feats of the valiant conquerors of former days, as is seen in our ancient histories. We here propose to speak of the enterprise undertaken by the Sieur de Bethencourt, chevalier and baron, born in the kingdom of France in Normandy, who set out from his house of Grainville la Teinturière en Caux, and came to Rochelle, and there fell in with Gadifer de la Sale, a good and worthy knight, who was then starting on his adventures. . . .

Accordingly, on the first of May 1402, Monseigneur de Bethencourt, with Messer Gadifer and all his retinue, set sail from La Rochelle for the lands of Canary, to see and explore all the country, with the view of conquering the islands and bringing the people to the Christian faith. They had a very good ship, well provided with men, victual, and everything requisite for their voyage. They had intended to make for Belle Isle, but at the Isle de Ré they met with a foul wind, and consequently steered a course for Spain, and arrived at the port of Vivières (Vivero in Gallicia), where Monseigneur de Bethencourt and his company stayed eight days. . . .

Before Monsieur de Bethencourt took his departure from the island of Lancerote and the Canaries, he had put everything in order to the best of his power, and had left Messire Gadifer the entire command, promising to return as soon as he could with reinforcements both of men and provisions, and never contemplating such disorder as afterwards ensued. Still, as one may readily understand, it is not easy to obtain an early audience of so great a prince as the King of Castile upon such a matter as this. When he had made his reverence to the King, who received him very graciously, and inquired what he wanted, Bethencourt said, "I come, Sire, to pray you to be pleased to grant me permission to conquer and bring to the Christian faith certain islands called the Islands of Canary, in which I have been and have so far made a commencement, that I have left some of my people there, who are daily looking for my return. I have also left a good knight named Master Gadifer de la Salle, who was pleased to join me in the expedition. And, inasmuch, Sire, as you are king and lord of all the country adjacent to these islands, and the nearest Christian sovereign, I am come to ask that you will be graciously pleased to permit me to do you homage for them." On hearing this, the king was very pleased, gave him welcome, and commended him highly for having conceived so good and honourable a project as to come from such a distance as the kingdom of France with the view of making conquests and winning honour. The king further said, "It shows a very good intention on his part to come to do me homage for a country, which, as I understand, is at two hundred leagues distance, and of which I never heard before." The king then spoke encouragingly to De Bethencourt, and told him that he was pleased with his proposition and accepted his homage, and in so far as it was possible, gave him the lordship of those Canary islands. He also granted him the fifth of the merchandise, which should come from those islands to Spain; which fifth Monsieur de Bethencourt received for a long time. The king further made him an immediate grant of twenty thousand maravedies, to be received in Seville, for the purchase of provisions for Gadifer and those who were left with him. This money was made payable by order of Monsieur de Bethencourt to Enguerrant de la Boissière, who seems not to have done his duty with respect to it, for it is said that he went off to France with all, or at any rate a part of it. However, Monsieur de Bethencourt soon supplied the loss by sending stores of provisions, and himself returned to the islands as soon as he could, as will be seen presently. The king also gave him leave to coin money in the Canaries, which he did, when he came into peaceful possession of those islands. . . .

The king who came first to M. de Bethencourt was the one who ruled that part of the island towards Lancerote; and he was baptized, and all the people he brought with him, on the eighteenth day of January, one thousand four hundred and five. He received the name of Lewis; and three days afterwards came twenty-two persons, and they were baptized on the day of their arrival. On the twenty-fifth day of January, the king of that part of the island which lies towards the Great Canary presented himself to M. de Bethencourt with forty-seven of his people, but they were not baptized until the third day from their arrival. The king received the name of Alphonse. From that time forward all the people came to be baptized; some now, some then, according as their dwellings might happen to be scattered about the country; so that by this time, thank God, they are all Christians, and bring their little children, as soon as they are born, to the court of Baltarhayz, where they are baptized in a chapel that M. de Bethencourt has had built; and they mingle with his people and share all their comforts. The said Lord de Bethencourt has commanded that they should be treated with the utmost gentleness; and he issued an order, in the presence of the two kings, that John le Courtois should continue to be his lieutenant as he had hitherto been, for he himself wished to visit his own country of France, where he proposed to stay as short a time as possible. He kept his word; for he had such favourable weather, that he only spent four months and a half from the time of his departure till his return. He desired Messire John le Verrier and Messire Pierre Bontier to remain, in order to explain and teach without intermission the Catholic faith. He took as few people as possible with him; but among them were three Canarian men and one Canarian woman, as he wished them to see for themselves the manners and customs of the kingdom of France, and to give an account of them when he brought them back to the Canaries. So he left the island of Erbanie on the last day of January with tears of joy; and all those whom he left behind wept on account of his departure, and the Canarians even more than the others, for the said lord had always treated them with great kindness. . . .

M. de Bethencourt did not find his wife at Grainville, for she was at Bethencourt; he sent for her, and when she arrived we need not say how joyous was their meeting. . . .

After a stay of about a week at Grainville, Messire Ystace d'Erneville and others proposed to take leave of M. de Bethencourt. He then informed them that he meant to return to the Canaries as soon as possible, and to take as many people as he could from Normandy; and that it was his intention to conquer the Great Canary if possible, or at least to have a touch at it. Messire Ystace, who was present, said that, with his leave, he would go with him. "My nephew," answered de Bethencourt, "I will not give you this trouble; I will take less important persons than you." Upon this several noblemen then present volunteered their services; for example, one named Richard de Grainville, a relative of de Bethencourt's, one named Jean de Boville, another named Jean de Plessis, as well as Maciot de Bethencourt and some of his brothers: indeed, the greater part of the company, consisting of people of various stations in life, were willing to go. M. de Bethencourt then said, "I wish to take with me people of all the different trades that can be mentioned or thought of; and when they arrive there they need have no doubt of finding a profitable country and one easy to live in without hard labour; and to those who come I will give sufficient land to till, if they will only undertake the trouble. There are many mechanics in this country who have not a foot of ground of their own, and who live very hardly; now if they will come with me yonder, I promise them that I will do the best for them that I can, better than for any others that may come in future, and much better even than for the natives who have embraced Christianity." . . .

After that M. de Bethencourt had conquered the islands of Palma and of Ferro, he returned to Fuerteventura with his two vessels, and took up his quarters in the tower of Baltarhayz, which Messire Gadifer had commenced building while he was in Spain; and he arranged many things in this country which it would take a long time to describe. He established, as I have stated, a hundred and twenty households in the island of Ferro, and placed the remainder in Fuerteventura and Lancerote. To each he allotted portions of land, manors, and houses, and dwellings, to every one as it seemed good to him, and managed so well that every one was satisfied, and he decreed that none of the people whom he had brought from his own country should pay anything whatever for nine years, but at the end of nine years they were to pay like the others, that is to say, a fifth— the fifth head of cattle, the fifth bushel of corn; in fact, a fifth of everything. . . .

As for the two priests of Erbanie and Lancerote, it is quite clear that they have a right to their tithes; but inasmuch as there are many people and little ecclesiastical help, they will only receive a thirtieth when a prelate is appointed; "and please God, when I leave this," said Monsieur, "I will go to Rome and obtain for this country a bishop, who shall uphold the discipline and the dignity of the Catholic faith." M. de Bethencourt then appointed his nephew to be lieutenant and governor of all the islands which he had conquered, and commanded him to look to the due observance of God's laws and to give all possible honour to Him; and he desired that the people of the country should be treated with gentleness and affection. . . .

Monsieur de Bethencourt arrived at Rome and remained there three weeks; he presented himself before the Pope, and gave him the letters sent by the King of Spain; and when His Holiness had caused them to be read twice over, and had comprehended the substance thoroughly, he summoned M. de Bethencourt, who kissed the Pope's feet, and was thus addressed by him, "You are one of our children, and as such I hold you. You have achieved a goodly deed, and have made a goodly beginning, which will be the forerunner, by God's grace, of a still greater conclusion. The King of Spain writes me word that you have conquered certain islands, whose inhabitants have now embraced the faith of Jesus Christ, and that you have caused them all to be baptized; for which cause I wish to hold you as my son and as a son of the Church, because you are the originator of conquests which other sons [of our Holy Church] shall hereafter achieve, for, from what I gather, the main-land of Guinea and Barbary is not far distant from the islands, indeed only twelve leagues from them. Furthermore, the King of Spain informs me that you penetrated ten leagues into the land of Guinea, and that you killed and brought away Saracens from that country. You are indeed a man worthy of honour, and it is my wish that you may not be forgotten, but that you may have now a place amongst other kings and be mentioned in their list. With respect to your desire for the appointment of a prelate and bishop over the country, your reason and your wish are both praiseworthy, and I consent to appoint whomsoever you may name, provided he be suitable for the office." . . .

After he had been about fifteen days at Rome, he desired to take leave of the Pope. The Bulls were drawn up in due form, and Albert de las Casas was appointed Bishop of all the Canary Islands. Monsieur de Bethencourt then took his leave of the Pope, who gave him his blessing, and desired that he should not hesitate to ask of him whatever might give him pleasure, and that it should be willingly conceded.

II

Portugal Leads
the Way West

Introduction

The creation of the Portuguese overseas empire has an epic quality about it. The vast size of the empire in comparison to the small size of Portugal itself causes the modern observer to wonder how such a small country could have achieved so much. Furthermore, the Portuguese retained a significant part of their empire until the middle decades of the twentieth century.[1]

Like the great empire that the Spanish created in the sixteenth and seventeenth centuries, the Portuguese empire was rooted in the reconquest of the Iberian peninsula from the Moslems in the Middle Ages. Portugal traces its origin to the award of the county of Portugal to Henry of Burgundy upon his marriage to an illegitimate daughter of the king of Castile in 1093. Henry of Burgundy, the French knights who accompanied him, and the warriors who joined them from other parts of Europe paved the way for Afonso Henriques who asserted the independence of Portugal from Castile in the 1140s. In 1179 Pope Alexander III recognized the independence of Portugal and accepted the kingdom as a papal fief, thus giving international recognition to Portuguese independence.[2]

The motives that impelled the founders of the Portuguese empire were the same mixed motives impelling crusaders elsewhere. Some obviously were anxious to roll back the Moslem threat from southern Europe, while others saw in the reconquest an opportunity to acquire land and the status that accompanied its possession—a situation that is quite clearly given in the chronicle that describes the recapture of Lisbon (doc. 9). While a bishop points out the religious reasons for their work, the leaders of the crusaders and King Afonso draw up an agreement rewarding the warriors in more tangible fashion.

By the fifteenth century, the Moslems had been pushed out of Portugal, and the impetus of the crusading movement made it possible to take the war to Africa, where they could be attacked on their home ground. In 1415 the Portuguese captured Ceuta, a city in North Africa opposite

---

1. On the general history of Portugal in the Middle Ages, see A. H. de Oliveira Marques, *History of Portugal*, vol. 1: *From Lusitania to Empire* (New York: Columbia Univ. Press, 1972), and H. V. Livermore, *A New History of Portugal* (Cambridge, Eng.: Cambridge Univ. Press, 1967).
2. Oliveira Marques, pp. 36–43; Livermore, pp. 44–65.

Gibraltar. From here the Christians began to work down the west coast of Africa. Gradually, the west coast of Africa and the islands that lay off it, the Canaries, the Azores, the Cape Verde, and Madeira groups, appeared on maps. The discoveries even entered into European wars. The general state of war between Portugal and Castile during the fifteenth century spilled over into the Atlantic, as the Castilians sought to gain control of the Atlantic by attacking Portuguese bases on the islands. These conflicts were the forerunners of the great wars for control of the colonial empires that broke out in the seventeenth and eighteenth centuries.[3]

The success of the Portuguese in gaining and holding their great empire may be linked to a significant change that took place in the Portuguese approach to expansion during the fifteenth century. Initially, the Portuguese expansion movement was marked by crusading zeal and a desire for land. These qualities appear as late as the early fifteenth century in letters such as that of King Duarte I of Portugal to Pope Eugenius IV, a letter in which the pope is asked to authorize Portuguese conquest of islands in the Canaries (doc. 10). At the same time, this letter contained some new ideas. The king wanted not only to conquer the islands and baptize the natives, but he also wanted to civilize them, that is to bring them up to what he considered the higher cultural standards of Europeans. One can see in his argument a faint hint of the "White Man's Burden" argument that the Victorians later employed.

During the last half of the fifteenth century, however, the Portuguese appear to have rejected the policy of establishing colonies, and converting the native population to Christianity, in favor of a policy emphasizing trade with the peoples whom they encountered. What emerged was a trading empire, one in which the Portuguese monopolized the carrying trade. As the documents dealing with trade along the Guinea coast make clear, the Portuguese developed an extensive administrative network to insure that the monarchy received its proper share of the trade's proceeds (docs. 16, 17). Settlement and missionary efforts became proportionately less attractive to the monarchy as the value of the trade came to be realized. The Portuguese empire began to collapse in the sixteenth century as the Portuguese lost their monopolistic position to larger kingdoms that were more capable of supporting the fleets necessary to insure the security of the monopoly. The entry of the Dutch and then the English into the spice trade spelled the end for the Portuguese monopoly.

Involvement on a large scale in the trade with West Africa had two important consequences for Portugal and, eventually, for the rest of Europe. The Portuguese began the trade in African slaves.[4] Furthermore, the desire

3. The most convenient introduction to Portuguese expansion is C. R. Boxer, *The Portuguese Seaborne Empire 1415-1825* (New York: Alfred A. Knopf, 1969).
4. Oliveira Marques, pp. 260-61.

for trading rights caused the Portuguese to become increasingly involved in the internal politics of African societies in order to insure the continuation of their monopoly. The Portuguese monopoly required sympathetic native rulers. The description of Portuguese involvement in dynastic politics in Senegal indicates the nature of outside involvement (doc. 13). Eventually, the Portuguese promised military aid to a ruler who had been ousted in return for his baptism and his agreement that the Portuguese would be allowed to construct a fort to be used as a base for their trading activities. The Portuguese created armies, led by European officers, consisting of native troops, sepoys, which were used to defend Portuguese trading enclaves and to implement policies involving native politics. To a large extent, the Portuguese developed many of the institutions and techniques of imperial control later followed by larger nations.

One of the most interesting aspects of Portuguese expansion overseas was the attitude of the Portuguese to the peoples they encountered. It is often argued, especially by Portuguese and Brazilian historians, that the Portuguese, of any European people, showed the least antipathy to non-European peoples and the greatest willingness to marry non-Europeans. In recent years, this view has been developed extensively in the work of the Brazilian historian Gilberto Freyre, who has argued that Brazil is the most integrated society in the world because of its Portuguese heritage.[5] Although the selections included here do not demonstrate that degree of toleration, they do indicate a significant degree of toleration. As Gomes Eannes de Azurara remarked about the people encountered in Guinea, the Portuguese "made no difference between them and their free servants, born in our own country" (doc. 11). The Portuguese appear anxious to encourage the adoption of European religion and culture by their slaves with the aim of encouraging them to blend into Portuguese society. Unlike the Spanish, the Portuguese do not appear to have allowed their crusading zeal to narrow and harden their attitudes toward non-Europeans. Perhaps the decline of crusading ardor among the Portuguese and the emergence of a mercantile ethos encouraged the development of a kind of toleration of non-Europeans not generally found elsewhere at this time.

5. Gilberto Freyre, *The Masters and the Slaves*, 2nd ed. (New York: Alfred A. Knopf, 1956), p. 3. The views of Freyre and of the Portuguese defenders of the racial situation in the Portuguese empire have been strongly criticized by C. R. Boxer, *Race Relations in the Portuguese Empire 1415–1825* (Oxford: Clarendon Press, 1963).

Bibliography

A basic introduction to medieval Portuguese exploration is provided in Edgar Prestage, *The Portuguese Pioneers*, The Pioneer Histories (London: A. and C. Black; reprint ed., New York: Barnes and Noble, 1967). There is no recent scholarly study of Henry the Navigator, who was responsible for so much of the Portuguese interest in overseas expansion. There are two older books that are still useful, C. Raymond Beazley, *Prince Henry the Navigator* (New York and London: G. P. Putnam, 1895), and J. P. Oliveira Martins, *The Golden Age of Henry the Navigator*, trans. J. J. Abraham and W. E. Reynolds (London: Chapman and Hall, 1914). On the relationship between Africa and Brazil, Portugal's only colony in the New World, see, José Honório Rodrigues, *Brazil and Africa* (Berkeley: Univ. of California Press, 1965).

Document 9

Charles W. David, ed., *De expugnatione Lyxbonensi: The Conquest of Lisbon*, Records of Civilization, Sources and Studies, no. 24 (New York: Columbia Univ. Press, 1936), pp. 53–57, 111–13, 115–17.

The conquest of Lisbon in 1147 was a major step in the creation of the kingdom of Portugal. Soldiers from all over Europe came to participate and to profit from the Christian victory. The anonymous chronicler who recorded the campaign may have come with the party of northern Europeans he describes in the opening selection. The writer may also have had some acquaintance with classical Roman and Greek historians because he followed the practice of placing speeches in the mouths of the participants, just as the ancient historians had done. The speech he attributes to a bishop was a justification of the war as a war of defence. The arguments that the bishop employed are similar to those used by ecclesiastical theorists anxious to justify the crusades (see Part 7).—*ed.*

To begin, then, men of divers nations, customs, and speech assembled in the port of Dartmouth in about one hundred and sixty-four vessels. The whole expedition was divided into three parts. Under Count Arnold of Aerschot, nephew of Duke Godfrey, were the forces from the territories of the Roman Empire; under Christian of Ghistelles, the Flemings and the men of Boulogne. All the others were under four constables: the ships of Norfolk and Suffolk under Hervey de Glanvill, those of Kent under Simon of Dover, those of London under Andrew, and all the rest under Saher of Archelle.

Among these people of so many different tongues the firmest guarantees of peace and friendship were taken; and, furthermore, they sanctioned very strict laws, as, for example, a life for a life and a tooth for a tooth . . . Furthermore, they constituted for every thousand of the forces two elected members who were to be called judges or *coniurati*, through whom the cases of the constables were to be settled in accordance with the proclamation and by whom the distribution of moneys was to be carried out. . . .

[The archbishop who had accompanied the crusaders then addressed them:]

"Now, as worthy sons of the mother church, repel force and injury; for in law it happens that whatever anyone does in self-defense he is held to have done lawfully. Brothers, you have laid aside the arms [of violence] by which the property of others is laid waste—concerning which it is said,

51

'He that strikes with the sword shall perish with the sword,' that is, he who, without the command or consent of any higher or legitimate power, takes up arms against the life of his brothers—but now by God's inspiration you are bearing the arms [of righteousness] by means of which murderers and robbers are condemned, thefts are prevented, acts of adultery are punished, the impious perish from the earth, and parricides are not permitted to live nor sons to act unfilially. Therefore, brothers, take courage with these arms, courage, that is to say, either to defend the fatherland in war against barbarians or to ward off enemies at home, or to defend comrades from robbers; for such courage is full of righteousness. Indeed, such works of vengeance are duties which righteous men perform with a good conscience. Brothers, be not afraid. For in acts of this sort you will not be censured for murder or taxed with any crime; on the contrary you will be adjudged answerable if you should abandon your enterprise. 'Indeed, there is no cruelty where piety towards God is concerned.' Engage in a just war with the zeal of righteousness, not with the bile of wrath. 'For a war is just,' says our Isidore,[1] 'which is waged after a declaration, to recover property or to repulse enemies'; and, since it is just to punish murderers and sacrilegious men and poisoners, the shedding of their blood is not murder. Likewise he is not cruel who slays the cruel. And he who puts wicked men to death is a servant of the Lord, for the reason that they are wicked and there is ground for killing them. Certainly the children of Israel waged a just war against the Amorites when they were refused a peaceful passage [through their borders]. And you, therefore, being people of Israel, sons of Christ, and servants of the cross, shall it be permitted to the adversaries of the cross to insult you with impunity?

Representatives were chosen from among our leaders and from the leaders of the men of Cologne and the Flemings, through whom the terms of the engagements and agreements between ourselves and the king should be defined. And afterwards they, in association with the king, the archbishop, his fellow bishops, and the clergy and laity, caused the charter of confirmation of the agreements to be made known before all in the following words:

> Let the covenant of agreement between me and the Franks be known to all the sons of the church, both present and to come. To wit, that I Affonso,[2] king of the Portuguese, with the assent of all my men, in order that it may be forever held in memory by future generations, grant by this charter of confirmation that the Franks who are about to remain with me at the siege of the city of Lisbon may take into their own power

1. Isidore of Seville (560–636), a bishop and scholar wrote the *Etymologiae*, an encyclopedia that brought together much of the learning of the ancient world. During the Middle Ages this work was the standard reference work for ancient thought and learning.
2. Afonso Henriques (1139–85).

and possession, and may keep, all the possessions of the enemy, myself and all my men having absolutely no share in them. If any shall wish to have enemy captives redeemed alive, they shall freely have the ransom money, and they shall turn the said captives over to me. If perchance they should take the city, they shall have it and hold it until it has been searched and despoiled, both through putting everyone to ransom and otherwise. And so, at last, after it has been ransacked to their full satisfaction, they shall hand it over to me. And afterwards the city and subjugated lands shall, with me presiding, be divided among them in accordance with their respective ranks, as each may be best known to me, to be held according to the most honorable customs and liberties of the Franks, I myself retaining in them only the overlordship of an "advocate." Moreover, I release, absolutely and in good faith, the ships and the goods of those who were with me at the siege of Lisbon, and of their heirs, from all the merchant toll which is commonly called *pedatica*, from now henceforth in perpetuity throughout all my lands. . . .

When these matters had been thus confirmed, it was decided by the common counsel of all that commissioners should be sent to parley with the enemy, so that we might not appear to be attacking them except unwillingly. Accordingly, the archbishop of Braga and the bishop of Oporto and a few of our men were sent to the city. After signals had been exchanged, as the alcayde stood in person on the wall with the bishop and chief men of the city, a truce was mutually ratified in order that on each side they might say what they wished. Then the archbishop made the following speech:

May the God of peace and love remove the veil of error from your hearts and convert you to himself. And therefore have we come to you to speak of peace. For in concord small things grow great, in discord the greatest go to ruin. But, in order that discord may not forever reign between us, we have come hither to you with a message of conciliation. For Nature so begat us from one and the same principle that, by reason of the common bond of humanity and the chain of harmony derived from the mother of all, one ought not to be unacceptable to another. And, if you will, we have come hither to this city which you possess not to subdue you and drive you out and despoil you. For the inborn kindliness of Christians ever holds to this principle, that, while it seeks its own, it seizes not the property of others.

We demand that the see of this city shall be under our law; and surely, if a natural sense of justice had made any progress among you, you would go back unbidden to the land of the Moors from whence you came, with your baggage, money, and goods, and your women and children, leaving to us our own. However, we already know full well that you would only do such a thing unwillingly and as a result of force. But consider a voluntary departure; for, if you yield willingly to our demands, you have already escaped the bitterest part of them. For how otherwise there could be peace between us I know not, since the lot assigned to each from the beginning lacks its rightful possessor. You Moors and Moabites fraudulently seized the realm of Lusitania from your king and ours. From then until now there has been desolation of cities, villages, and churches without number, and it still goes on. On the one side in this struggle your fealty, on the other human society itself, has been violated.

Document 10

Letter from King Duarte I of Portugal to Pope Eugenius IV, Vatican Archives, Reg. Lat. 336, Folios 189–189^v. Translated by James Muldoon.

In 1436, King Duarte I of Portugal (1433–38) requested that Pope Eugenius IV (1431–37) lift the papally imposed ban on further European colonization of the Canary Islands. The ban resulted from attacks that European invaders had made upon some natives of the islands who had already been converted to Christianity. The king requested that the Portuguese be allowed to continue their advance into the islands because the papal ban would not really protect the natives from unscrupulous invaders. Such men would not be deterred by a papal threat of excommunication. Only by allowing Christian rulers to occupy the islands would the armed force necessary to protect the natives be available. Furthermore, the king asserted that the Portuguese would help the natives to advance to a civilized way of life as the Portuguese defined civilized. This letter also pointed out a major difficulty that the papacy faced in dealing with the problem of the European conquest of the world overseas. Condemnation of expansion without adequate military support would have little effect. Should, therefore, the papacy accept the argument, that conquest by responsible European powers would benefit the conquered in the hope that the papacy could then influence the conquerors in the direction of humane treatment of the conquered? Or, should the papacy ignore what was happening? These questions, reflecting both moral concern and political reality, plagued the papacy throughout the period of expansion.—ed.

O most blessed Father, among the countless islands which the sea encompasses, there are included seven islands close to one another in the ocean south of Portugal which are popularly called the Canary Islands. The nearly wild men who inhabit the forests are not united by a common religion, nor are they bound by the chains of law, they are lacking normal social intercourse, living in the country like animals. They have no contact with each other by sea, no writing, no kind of metal or money. They have no houses and no clothing except for coverlets of palm leaves or goat skins which are worn as an outer garment by the most honored men. They run barefoot quickly through the rough, rocky and steep mountainous regions, hiding . . . in caves hidden in the ground.

The illustrious and magnificent prince, Henry, the Infante,[1] brother of the most serene King Duarte of Portugal, considered that it is better that the talent given him grow in order to provide a profit for the Lord rather than be buried in the ground. And thus, according to the vocation to which he had been called, the spread of the Christian name more extensively, he conducted himself according to the model and example of that most victorious and unconquered prince of illustrious memory, John, from whom the task was left to him as an inheritance. Having prepared a fleet of ships and armed galleys with the consent and at the command of the most serene king and lord, Duarte, his brother, he went to the aforementioned Canary Islands, first in order that he might convert those pagans to the Christian faith. So that he might make them loyal subjects of the Portuguese crown, he gave them civil laws and an organized form of society. When the aforementioned fleet came to one of these islands and a large number of armed men stepped ashore, about 400 of the pagans there, reborn in the font of holy baptism, obtained the Christian faith, in which many of them remain up to the present. What a significant achievement! Where the name of Christ had never been known, Christ is now worshipped, and where from the beginning God was unknown, now He is known and adored. But because many of the pagans, monstrous with ferocity, terrified by the courage of the armed men, fled through the wide spaces of the desert with wonderous speed, while others remained hidden in caves, and others sat upon the highest, almost inaccessible mountain peaks, and because the army could not find enough food anywhere on that island, a council was held in Portugal to prepare for the wars so that when a supply of food had been acquired again, he might return at a convenient time to the work which had been begun. And because, as so often happens, of a contrary wind that was blowing, the fleet was delayed longer than anticipated, so that some of the men descended on two small islands of the Canaries that were occupied by Christians, and scarcely even the wild goats were safe from their desires. When this happened, the bishop who ruled those islands, having asked, received from Your Holiness an edict of prohibition so that no one under pain of excommunication might wage war or take anything not only in those islands, but anywhere else in the islands as well. Certainly, Blessed Father, this is most prejudicial to the most serene prince, the lord king of Portugal, who through that famous young man, his brother Henry, has begun the war for the remaining islands as we have previously mentioned. Because he was the first to begin the conquest of the islands, more indeed for the salvation of the souls of the pagans of the islands than for his own personal gain, for there was nothing for him to gain, Your Holi-

1. Henry the Navigator (1394–1460).

ness ought not be the last obstacle in such a noble cause for one worthy of the help and assistance of Your Holiness. Also, since these islands are next to Africa, how near Africa can be seen by looking at a map and at the sailing directions, it is more true to say indeed that they are part of Africa, the conquest of which the most serene King Duarte has pursued on his own authority for a long time, a conquest begun by his father, that ever victorious and unconquered prince, King John, and left as an inheritance to his heirs.

The aforementioned most serene prince, your most devoted son, Duarte, King of Portugal and the Algarve and Lord of Ceuta, entreats and begs your holiness that you deign to restrict that edict of prohibition and that threat of excommunication with regard to those islands in which only a few Christians dwell so that the aforementioned remaining islands that the prince has begun to conquer and to add to the church of God, the fear of excommunication having been removed, he might take up these islands in his mailed fist with the help of God and of Your Holiness. The same most serene prince begs Your Holiness that those islands that he has taken from the hands of the infidels, Your Holiness will grant and give to him out of generosity to that king. If this is done, he will be greatly encouraged to prosecute this renowned work, which is already under way, and led to an increased devotion toward Your Holiness. Although many will strive on their own authority to wage war and to occupy the lands of the infidels, nevertheless, because the earth and its fullness are the Lord's who left to Your Holiness the fullness of this power over the entire world, whatever is possessed by the authority and permission of Your Holiness is understood to be held in a special way and with the permission of almighty God.

Document 11

Gomes Eannes de Azurara, *The Chronicle of the Discovery of Guinea*, eds. C. R. Beazley and E. Prestage, Hakluyt Society Publications, nos. 95, 100 (London: The Society, 1896, 1899), 1: 8–9, 27–30, 83–85; 2: 230–32.

Gomes Eannes de Azurara (d. after 1472) was a member of the Order of Christ, a Portuguese crusading religious community, that spearheaded the Portuguese advance against the Moslems. His history dealt with Portuguese expansion in the first half of the fifteenth century. Although he placed heavy emphasis upon the conversion of the non-Christians as a motive for expansion, he also pointed to the economic benefits that the kingdom of Portugal was reaping from its overseas territories. He was also interested in describing the life-styles of those people whom the Portuguese encountered and the relations of the Portuguese with them. It is interesting to note his claim that many of the slaves captured in the advance eventually became Christians and married Portuguese. Defenders of Portuguese colonial policy often point to what they see as the lack of race or color consciousness in the Portuguese world, something reflected in the number of marriages that took place between the conquerors and the conquered throughout the Portuguese empire.—ed.

For here in Portugal I meet with great lords, prelates, nobles, widowed ladies, Knights of the Orders of Chivalry, Masters and Doctors of the holy faith, with many graduates of every science, young scholars, companies of esquires, and men of noble breeding, with mechanics and an untold multitude of the people. And some of these shew me towns and castles; others villages and fields; others rich benefices; others great and wealthy farms; others country houses and estates and liberties; others charters for pensions and for marriages; others gold and silver, money and cloth; others health in their bodies and deliverance from perils which they have gained by means of thee; others countless servants both male and female; while others there are that tell me of monasteries and churches that thou didst repair and rebuild, and of the great and rich ornaments that thou didst offer in many holy places. Others, again, pointed out to me the marks of the chains they bore in the captivity from which thou didst rescue them. What shall I say of the needy beggars that I see before me laden with alms? And of the great multitude of friars of every order that shew me the garments with which thou didst clothe their bodies, and the abundance of food with which thou didst satisfy their necessities? I had already made an end of this chapter, had I not descried the approach of a multitude of ships with tall sails laden from the islands thou didst people in the great Ocean Sea, which called on me to wait for them, as they longed to prove that they ought not to be omitted from this register. And they displayed before me their great cattle-stalls, the valleys full of sugar cane from which they carried store to distribute throughout the world: they brought also as witnesses to their great prosperity all the dwellers in the kingdom of the Algarve. Ask, said they, whether these people ever knew what it was to have abundance of bread until our Prince peopled the uninhabited isles, where no dwelling existed save that of wild beasts. Next they shewed me great rows of beehives full of swarms of bees, from which great cargoes of wax and honey are carried to our realm; and besides these, lofty houses towering to the sky, which have been and are being built with wood from those parts. . . .

In which five reasons appear why the Lord Infant was moved to
command the search for the lands of Guinea.

WE imagine that we know a matter when we are acquainted with the doer
of it and the end for which he did it. And since in former chapters we
have set forth the Lord Infant as the chief actor in these things, giving as
clear an understanding of him as we could, it is meet that in this present
chapter we should know his purpose in doing them. And you should note
well that the noble spirit of this Prince, by a sort of natural constraint,
was ever urging him both to begin and to carry out very great deeds. For
which reason, after the taking of Ceuta he always kept ships well armed
against the Infidel, both for war, and because he had also a wish to know
the land that lay beyond the isles of Canary and that Cape called Bojador,
for that up to his time, neither by writings, nor by the memory of man,
was known with any certainty the nature of the land beyond that Cape.
Some said indeed that Saint Brandan had passed that way; and there was
another tale of two galleys rounding the Cape, which never returned. But
this doth not appear at all likely to be true, for it is not to be presumed
that if the said galleys went there, some other ships would not have en-
deavoured to learn what voyage they had made. And because the said
Lord Infant wished to know the truth of this—since it seemed to him that
if he or some other lord did not endeavour to gain that knowledge, no
mariners or merchants would ever dare to attempt it—(for it is clear that
none of them ever trouble themselves to sail to a place where there is
not a sure and certain hope of profit)—and seeing also that no other prince
took any pains in this matter, he sent out his own ships against those
parts, to have manifest certainty of them all. And to this he was stirred up
by his zeal for the service of God and of the King Edward his Lord and
brother, who then reigned. And this was the first reason of his action.

The second reason was that if there chanced to be in those lands some
population of Christians, or some havens, into which it would be possible
to sail without peril, many kinds of merchandise might be brought to this
realm, which would find a ready market, and reasonably so, because no
other people of these parts traded with them, nor yet people of any other
that were known; and also the products of this realm might be taken there,
which traffic would bring great profit to our countrymen.

The third reason was that, as it was said that the power of the Moors
in that land of Africa was very much greater than was commonly supposed,
and that there were no Christians among them, nor any other race of
men; and because every wise man is obliged by natural prudence to wish
for a knowledge of the power of his enemy; therefore the said Lord Infant
exerted himself to cause this to be fully discovered, and to make it known
determinately how far the power of those infidels extended.

The fourth reason was because during the one and thirty years that he had warred against the Moors, he had never found a Christian king, nor a lord outside this land, who for the love of our Lord Jesus Christ would aid him in the said war. Therefore he sought to know if there were in those parts any Christian princes, in whom the charity and the love of Christ was so ingrained that they would aid him against those enemies of the faith.

The fifth reason was his great desire to make increase in the faith of our Lord Jesus Christ and to bring to him all the souls that should be saved—understanding that all the mystery of the Incarnation, Death, and Passion of our Lord Jesus Christ was for this sole end—namely the salvation of lost souls—whom the said Lord Infant by his travail and spending would fain bring into the true path. For he perceived that no better offering could be made unto the Lord than this; for if God promised to return one hundred goods for one, we may justly believe that for such great benefits, that is to say for so many souls as were saved by the efforts of this Lord, he will have so many hundreds of guerdons in the kingdom of God, by which his spirit may be glorified after this life in the celestial realm. For I that wrote this history saw so many men and women of those parts turned to the holy faith, that even if the Infant had been a heathen, their prayers would have been enough to have obtained his salvation. And not only did I see the first captives, but their children and grandchildren as true Christians as if the Divine grace breathed in them and imparted to them a clear knowledge of itself.

But over and above these five reasons I have a sixth that would seem to be the root from which all the others proceeded: and this is the inclination of the heavenly wheels. For, as I wrote not many days ago in a letter I sent to the Lord King, that although it be written that the wise man shall be Lord of the stars, and that the courses of the planets (according to the true estimate of the holy doctors) cannot cause the good man to stumble; yet it is manifest that they are bodies ordained in the secret counsels of our Lord God and run by a fixed measure, appointed to different ends, which are revealed to men by his grace, through whose influence bodies of the lower order are inclined to certain passions. And if it be a fact, speaking as a Catholic, that the contrary predestinations of the wheels of heaven can be avoided by natural judgment with the aid of a certain divine grace, much more does it stand to reason that those who are predestined to good fortune, by the help of this same grace, will not only follow their course but even add a far greater increase to themselves. But here I wish to tell you how by the constraint of the influence of nature this glorious Prince was inclined to those actions of his. And that was because his ascendent was Aries, which is the house of Mars and exaltation of the sun, and his lord in the XIth house, in company of the sun. And because the said Mars was in Aquarius, which is the house of Saturn, and in the mansion of hope, it signified that this Lord should toil at high and mighty conquests, especially in seeking out things that were hidden from other men and secret, according to the nature of Saturn, in whose house he is. And the fact of his being accompanied by the sun, as I said, and the sun being in the house of Jupiter, signified that all his traffick and his conquests would be loyally carried out, according to the good pleasure of his king and lord. . . .

Although the sorrow of those captives was for the present very great, especially after the partition was finished and each one took his own share aside (while some sold their captives, the which they took to other districts); and although it chanced that among the prisoners the father often remained in Lagos, while the mother was taken to Lisbon, and the children to another part (in which partition their sorrow doubled the first grief)—yet this sorrow was less felt among those who happened to remain in company. For as saith the text, the wretched find a consolation in having comrades in misfortune. But from this time forth they began to acquire some knowledge of our country; in which they found great abundance, and our men began to treat them with great favour. For as our people did not find them hardened in the belief of the other Moors; and saw how they came in unto the law of Christ with a good will; they made no difference between them and their free servants, born in our own country; but those whom they took while still young, they caused to be instructed in mechanical arts, and those whom they saw fitted for managing property; they set free and married to women who were natives of the land; making with them a division of their property, as if they had been bestowed on those who married them by the will of their own fathers, and for the merits of their service they were bound to act in a like manner. Yea, and some widows of good family who bought some of these female slaves, either adopted them or left them a portion of their estate by will; so that in the future they married right well; treating them as entirely free. Suffice it that I never saw one of these slaves put in irons like other captives, and scarcely any one who did not turn Christian and was not very gently treated.

And I have been asked by their lords to the baptisms and marriages of such; at which they, whose slaves they were before, made no less solemnity than if they had been their children or relations.

And so their lot was now quite the contrary of what it had been; since before they had lived in perdition of soul and body; of their souls, in that they were yet pagans, without the clearness and the light of the holy faith; and of their bodies, in that they lived like beasts, without any custom of reasonable beings—for they had no knowledge of bread or wine, and they were without the covering of clothes, or the lodgment of houses; and worse than all, through the great ignorance that was in them, in that they had no understanding of good, but only knew how to live in a bestial sloth.

But as soon as they began to come to this land, and men gave them prepared food and coverings for their bodies, their bellies began to swell, and for a time they were ill; until they were accustomed to the nature of the country; but some of them were so made that they were not able to endure it and died, but as Christians. . . .

In the land of the Negroes there is no walled place save that which they call Oadem, nor are there any settlements except some by the water's edge, of straw houses, the which were emptied of their dwellers by those that went there in the ships of this land. True it is that the whole land is generally peopled, but their mode of living is only in tents and carts, such as we use here when our princes do happen to go upon a warlike march; and those who were captured there gave testimony of this, and also John Fernandez, of whom we have already spoken, related much concerning the same. All their principal study and toil is in guarding their flocks, to wit, cows and sheep and goats and camels, and they change their camp almost every day, for the longest they can rest in one spot will be eight days. And some of their chief men possess tame mares, of which they breed horses, though very few.

Their food consisteth for the great part of milk, and sometimes a little meat and the seeds of wild herbs that they gather in those mountains, and some who have been there have said that these herbs (but of them there are few) seem to be the millet of that land. Also they eat wheat when they can obtain it, in the same way that we in this land eat confetti. And for many months of the year they and their horses and dogs maintain themselves by no other thing except the drinking of milk. And those that live by the sea shore eat nothing save fish, and all for the most part without either bread or anything else, except the water that they drink, and they generally eat their fish raw and dried. Their clothing consisteth of a skin vest and breeches of the same, but some of the more honourable wear bournouses; and some pre-eminent men, who are almost above all the others, have good garments, like the other Moors, and good horses and good saddles, and good stirrups, but these are very few.

The women wear bournouses which are like mantles, with the which they only cover their faces, and by that they think they have covered all their shame, for they leave their bodies quite naked. "For sure," saith he who compiled this history, "this is one of the things by the which one may discern their great bestiality, for if they had some particle of reason they would follow nature, and cover those parts only which by its shewing ought to be covered, for we see how naturally in each one of these shameful parts it placeth a circle of hair in proof that it wished to hide them; and also some naturalists hold that if those hairs be let alone, they will grow so much as to hide all the parts of your shame." And the wives of the most honourable men wear rings of gold in their nostrils and ears, as well as other jewels.

Document 12

"The Asia of João de Barros," in *The Voyages of Cadamosto and other Documents on Western Africa in the Second Half of the Fifteenth Century,* ed. G. R. Crone, Hakluyt Society Publications, series 2, no. 80 (London: The Society, 1937), pp. 114–15, 142–43.

João de Barros (1496–1570) wrote to praise the great days of Portuguese expansion during the reign of King Afonso V (1438–81). His knowledge of the Portuguese efforts in West Africa was first-hand because he had served as an official at El Mina, the great trading center in that region. He emphasized the role that the African empire was playing in the Portuguese economy and, at the same time, the difficulty of obtaining permanent settlers from among the Portuguese population.—*ed.*

As the King, D. João,[1] already had in the time of his father, D. Afonso,[2] the trade of Guiné as part of the revenue of his household, and had drawn from it gold, ivory, slaves, and other things which enriched his Kingdom, and as each year new lands and peoples were discovered, his hope of the discovery of India by these seas became ever the stronger. Being a very Christian prince and lord of great prudence, he ordered the building of a fortress, to be the first stone of the Oriental Church, which he wished to build in praise and glory of God for the possession he took of that which he had discovered and which remained to be discovered, through the Pope's grant, as we said before. And knowing that in the land through which ran the traffic of gold the negroes liked silk, woollen, and linen clothes, and other domestic goods, that they displayed a clearer understanding than others of that coast, and that in the trade with our men they showed they would be easily converted, he commanded that this fortress should be erected in the place, where our men usually made the traffic of gold. Thus, with the bait offered by the worldly goods which would always be obtainable there, they might receive those of the Faith through our doctrine, which was his principal aim. And though opinions in his Council about the building of this fortress were divergent because of the distance, and the ill-effects of the climate,

1. John II (1481–95).
2. Afonso V (1438–81).

the food of the country, and the labour of navigation upon those who went thither, the King considered that the possibility of getting even one soul to the Faith by baptism through the fortress, outweighed all the inconveniences. For he said that God would take care of them, since the work was to his praise, that his subjects would win profit, and that the patrimony of this Kingdom would be increased. Once the building of this fortress was decided upon, he ordered the equipping of a Fleet of ten caravels and two urcas,—to carry hewed stones, tiles and wood, as well as munitions and provisions for six hundred men, one hundred of whom were craftsmen and five hundred soldiers. . . .

Although the death of Prince D. João Bemoy, as related above, changed all the purposes which the King had set before himself from Bemoy's return and from the building of the fortress, he did not abandon the trade with the rivers Çanagá[3] and Gambea, which was carried on as usual each year. From the ships coming thence he learned that the fleet which he had sent to Çanagá had not been as unsuccessful as he thought. For, though it had not served to restore Bemoy, it had benefited the trade, and caused the interior to become better known than it had been before. The princes of those parts had been accustomed to see one or two ships only in their ports, on which were poor and ill-clothed sailors, so that they had not formed a very high opinion of the power of the King, despite all the interpreters had told them of the Kingdom. But when they saw so many ships, so many gallant people, and such warlike equipment, as went on that fleet, they were so amazed that from one to the other its fame spread through the whole of Guiné. Thus the friendship of the King came to be much more highly appreciated, and as most of them were quarrelling or fighting with one another, when they saw that the King had sent a large fleet merely to restore Bemoy, whose sole merit had been to deal expeditiously with the King's trading ships, they all began to do their best to dispatch the ships, each in his own fashion, and to send presents and promises, in their own interests and in the hope of obtaining similar help from him should they need it, or from fear of angering him. This resulted in so much intercourse with these peoples, that the King began with more confidence to send his agents with messages to their greatest princes, and to intervene in their affairs and wars, as a known and valued friend. During this time he sent Pero de Evora, and Gonçalo Eanes to the King of Tucuról,[4] and also to the King of Timbuktu,[5] and at other times he sent, by the river Cantor, to Mandi Mansa, one of the most powerful

3. Senegal River.
4. This was the region between the Senegal River and Darfur.
5. A major trading center in West Africa, located near the Niger River along the edge of the Sahara.

of that part of the Province of Mandinga.[6] On this mission went one Rodrigo Rabelo, a squire of his household, Pero Reinel, gentleman of the spurs, and João Colaço, crossbow man of the chamber, with other auxiliaries, making a total of eight persons. They took him as a present horses, beasts of burden, and mules with their harnesses and several other gifts much appreciated in that land, for they had been sent before. Of them all Pero Reinel alone escaped, being more accustomed to these parts; the others died of disease.

Document 13

John W. Blake, ed., *Europeans in West Africa, 1450–1560*, 2 vols., Hakluyt Society Publications, series 2, nos. 86, 87 (London: The Society, 1942), 1: 64–67, 80–81, 83–86.

The success of Portuguese trading efforts, like those of the later empires, depended initially at least on good relations with the existing traders. The Europeans entered into existing trade networks and depended upon the flow of trade continuing to flow through their outposts into Europe. Therefore, the creation of a secure trading post required careful negotiations with the existing population. The story of the conversion of Bemoym, a ruler whose territory embraced the mouth of the Senegal River, shows how both the Europeans and the native population tried to take advantage of each other's needs for their own ends. The Portuguese wanted a trading post. Bemoym wanted to be returned to his throne. Each side wished to dominate the relationship. The result was mistrust on both sides culminating in the failure of this attempt to secure the mouth of the Senegal River for the Europeans.—ed.

Grant of Rights of Trade in Guinea to the Santiagians. 12 June 1466

Dom Affonso V[1] [etc.]. To all to whom this letter shall come, we make known that prince dom Fernando, my most dear and beloved brother, has sent to inform us that some four years ago he began to populate his island of Santiago, which is opposite Cabo Verde,[2] and that, because it is so remote from our kingdoms, people are unwilling to go to live there, unless they are given very wide privileges and franchises and go at his expense. He, knowing the great profit it would yield us and him, if the island were thus populated, as he wished, in which cause he was ready to go to much

6. Mali.
1. Afonso V (1438–81).
2. Cape Verde.

personal expense so as to carry it to perfection, and being hopeful of success with God's help, prayed us to be pleased to grant him some privileges for them. We, having seen his petition and having considered it carefully, believe that we may thereby be very well served. And so that we may graciously reward my said brother, we are pleased to command him to be given the following privileges, namely: first, we give and grant him civil and criminal authority over all Moors, black and white, free and captive, and over all their descendants, who are in the said island, although they be Christians, and this while our favour continues. This civil and criminal authority, which we thus grant him in the manner stated, is additional to the authority which already before this we gave him in the said island, as is contained in the patent of the said grant which he has from us.

Furthermore, we are pleased to authorise him that henceforward and always the inhabitants of the said island may have and hold licence, whenever they wish, to be able to go with ships to trade and to buy in all our trades of the parts of Guiné (save our trade of Arguim,[3] where we do not wish anyone to trade or do anything either in the said trade or in its limits, except him to whom we are pleased to grant licence and permission) all the goods, which the said inhabitants of the said island have and desire to carry, except arms and iron tools, ships and their equipment, because our pleasure is that none of these things should be bartered in any manner in the said trades, and we have strictly forbidden this before, under the penalty for such a thing already imposed.

They may do this, without further approaching us or sending to us, or to our officers and others, to ask or apply for the said licence, or for clerks so that they may have them with them in their ships in the said parts, according to our ordinance with reference to those who go there from our kingdoms; but we will that they ask and apply for the said licences and clerks from the customs officer or receiver, whom we command to be appointed there to be our deputy in order to collect and gather our dues, which are to be the fourth of all things, which the inhabitants of the said island thus barter in the said parts of Guiné.

These, our officers, whom we thus appoint there in the said island, shall be ready and diligent to supply clerks to the said shippers, so that each shall carry one, as is required in each ship which goes there, according as is now done in the ships which go from our kingdoms to the said parts of Guiné.

The said customs officer or receiver shall thus be ready to collect the said dues, which are to accrue to us from the said ships which are equipped in the said island, as soon as they return from the said parts of Guiné. If the said officers are not thus ready to collect the said dues and to provide

3. Port on the west coast of Africa, near Cape Blanco.

the said clerks, in their absence he may collect and provide who has charge of the government and captaincy of the said island for my said brother, and he shall keep these dues himself until we send for them. When this happens, the said governor or captain shall advise us thereof by letter. . . .

Furthermore, it is our will and pleasure that, when the amount of our dues has been paid on all the said imported negroes and goods, the said inhabitants of the said island may sell on their own accounts what they have left to all persons, who want and desire them, not only in the said island but in all our kingdoms and abroad; and if they sell in the said island, the buyers shall not have to pay on the said goods, in these kingdoms when they are brought here, either the tenth or any other dues; and if they do not sell them in the said island but wish to bring them to our kingdoms or to carry them to other parts, they may do this, because they are exempt from having to pay us the said dues; and this, provided they carry certificates from our officers, whom we shall thus appoint in the said island, showing that they have already paid our dues upon them there. . . .

Should any desire to disobey this, we command them in no wise to permit it, forasmuch as this is our wish, notwithstanding any doubt or embargo which others may raise or impose. And for its security and our remembrance, we command them to be given this letter, signed by our hand and sealed with our pendent seal. Given in Beja. 12 June 1466. Pedro da Alcaçova made this.

The Conversion of Bemoym, Prince of the Jalofo, and the Attempt to Build a Fort at the Mouth of the River Senegal. 1488

In this year one thousand four hundred and eighty-eight, while the king [John II] was in Setuvel [Setubal], he made a Christian of Bemoym, a negro prince of the kingdom of Gelof [Jalofo], which is at the entrance of the Rio de Canaga [Senegal] in Guinee. His motives and reasons for this and the manner of doing it were briefly and truthfully as follows. During the previous year, while Gonçalo Coelho, a dependant of the king, was trafficking at the mouth of the said river, the said Bemoym, who at that time with prosperity and great power governed the said kingdom of Gelof, was informed through the interpreters of the royal perfection and the many virtues of the king, and, desiring to serve him, through the said Gonçalo Coelho he sent him a rich present of gold and one hundred slaves, all young men, with some other products of his land. With them as ambassador to the king came one of his nephews. This man, by virtue of a huge manilla of gold, which he gave the king as a letter of credence, according to his custom and being illiterate, sent to him to ask for arms and ships; to which the king refused consent with just reasons, based on the excommunications and the apostolic prohibitions, since he [Bemoym] was not a Christian. Then in this year, because the said Bemoym was treacherously driven out of his kingdom, he determined to embark on one of the caravels of the trade, which frequent the coast, and to come in person to seek aid, assistance and justice from the king, who was in Setuvel. Bemoym arrived in Lixboa,[4] accompanied by some negroes of his own royal blood and sons of persons closely related to men of importance. When the king had been informed of their arrival, he commanded that they should come to be entertained at Palmella, where he forthwith commanded his men to make abundant provision for him and to serve him with silver and attendants and every other civility which was proper to his station. Also he commanded all to be given rich and fine clothes to wear, according as the quality and merit of their persons demanded. And when they were in a condition to come to the court, the king sent horses and mules, very well apparelled, to them all; and on the day when they were to make their entrance, the king commanded that Bemoym should be received by Dom Francisco Coutinho, the count of Marialva, and with him all the lords and noblemen of the court, whom the king purposely ordered to be robed and adorned as well as possible. The king was lodged in the house of the exchequer of the said town, and the queen in other houses next to him, and both residences were all furnished and decorated with very expensive cloths of silk and serge and provided with a royal dais with a canopy of brocade. With the king was the duke Dom Manuel, accompanied by many titled lords and bishops and many other nobles, robed with much gentility and exact perfection. With the queen was the prince, her son, because it was ordained that one should forthwith visit the queen immediately after seeing and speaking with the king. The king and the duke adorned their persons with the very rich robes of their authority, all trimmed with gold and many precious stones. Bemoym appeared to be forty years old, and he was a man of great stature, very dark, with a very long beard, limbs all well proportioned and a very gracious presence; and being dressed, he entered the king's rooms, and the king came forward two or three paces from the dais to receive him, raising his cap a little. Then he led him to the dais, on which there was a throne; but the king did not sit thereon, and, leaning against it, thus on foot gave ear to him. Then the said Bemoym and all his men threw themselves at his feet to kiss them, and they made a show of taking the earth from under them and, in token of their subjection and his overlordship and of their great respect, threw it over their heads. But the king with much honour and courtesy made him rise, and through the negro interpreters, who were already present for this purpose, commanded him to speak. Thereupon, Bemoym with great ease, majesty and considerable gravity made a public speech, which lasted for a

4. Lisbon.

long time, and he used such notable words and sentences in support of his case that they did not seem to come from a savage negro but from Prince Grego, educated in Athenas. . . .

Then the king replied to him in a few words, and devoted great care and much wisdom to everything, expressing great pleasure at their meeting and even more pleasure at his final intention to be a Christian. Therefore he gave him hope in this world of assistance in his cause and of restoration to his kingdom, and in the other that of glory and eternal salvation. Thereupon, he dismissed him, and Bemoym went to speak to the queen and to the prince, before whom he made a short speech, in which with shrewd judgment and very natural dignity he asked them for favour and assistance with the king. The queen and the prince dismissed him, shewing him much honour and kindness. Then, on another day, Bemoym came to speak with the king, and, alone and apart, with an interpreter, they both conversed for a long time. Here Bemoym again recounted his affairs with great prudence; and he also replied very wisely and exactly to the questions which the king asked him, and the king remained very satisfied with this. In his honour the king ordered bull-fights and tournaments, and he held fancy-dress balls and dances, and in order that he might see them he gave orders for a chair to be placed at the upper end of the state room opposite the king. Moreover, it was the king's wish that Bemoym, before becoming a Christian, should first be instructed in matters of the faith; for Bemoym was of the sect of Mafamede in whom he believed, because of his being a neighbour of, and dealer with, the Azanegues, and he had some knowledge of the contents of the Bible. For this reason, theologians and learned men conversed with him and taught and advised him. Then it was decided that he should see and listen to a mass for the king, and this mass was said in pontifical and with great formality and ceremonial in the church of Santa Maria de Todolos Santos. Bemoym with his men and with learned Christians was in the choir, and, at the elevation of the body of Our Lord, when he saw all on their knees with their hands raised in the act of prayer, his hand went up to the cap which he had on his head; and thus, like everybody, with his knees on the ground and his head uncovered, he prayed. Then he said with many indications of truth that the remorse, which he experienced in his heart in that hour, he took as clear proof that this was the only true God of salvation. Then for two days the king proceeded to banquet publicly, for which purpose he put on his robes and he commanded that the house and the table were to be furnished with plate and tapestries, dishes and service, and there were to be minstrels and dances, all in great perfection; for the king was deliberately very particular and exact about ceremonial above all in matters touching his estate. At the second hour of the night of the third day of the month of November, the said Bemoym, and six of the principal persons who had come with him, became Christians in the chamber of the queen, which was decorated for the occasion with elaborate formality. His godfathers were the king, the queen, the prince, the duke, a commissary of the pope who was at the court, and the bishop of Tanger who at that time was the licentiate Calçadilha. Dom Justo, bishop of Cepta, who in pontifical performed the office, baptised them, and Bemoym received the name Dom Joham for love of the king. Moreover, on the seventh day of November, the king dubbed him a knight; and twenty-four others of his men were made Christians in the counting-house of the said town. The king gave him a coat-of-arms consisting of a golden cross on a red field surrounded by the escutcheon of the arms of Portugal. On this same day, in a solemn act and speaking as a great lord he rendered obedience and paid homage to the king. Also he sent another submission, written in Latin, to the pope, wherein he gave an account of his case and of his conversion to the faith in words of deep devotion and high praise to the king. The king determined to give him help and assistance, and gave him twenty armed caravels. The captain of the caravels was Pero Vaaz da Cunha, who carried orders to build at the entrance of the Rio de Çanaga [Senegal] a fortress, which was not to be given to the said Bemoym, but was always to belong to the king. For this purpose a great quantity of stones and planed timber was then prepared, and also priests were assembled and a great number of articles for churches and for the business of conversion; and Master Alvaro, preacher to the king, of the order of Sam Domingos, was selected to be the principal person. One of the very chief reasons which inspired the king to prepare this fleet, and especially to undertake the building of a fortress at the entrance of this river, was his conviction that the said river, penetrating far into the interior, flowed to the city of Tambucutu [Timbuktu] and by Mombare, where are the richest trades and markets of gold in the world, from which all Berberia[5] from east and west up to Jherusalem is supplied and provided. For he believed that the said fortress in order to free and safeguard the trade would provide great security in such a place for his men and the merchandise. This region up to the river and a little beyond was discovered in the time and by the command of the Ifante Dom Anrique,[6] the inventor and discoverer of this enterprise and the conquest of Guinee; and in his letters and records it appears that he called this river the Nillo,[7] not that which centers the Mar do Levante[8] at Alexandria, but another branch of it which the cosmographers say runs out to this ocean

5. The Barbary Coast.
6. Henry the Navigator.
7. Nile River.
8. Mediterranean Sea.

sea. But the real truth of this up to now—which is the time of our lord King Dom Manuel the First[9]—has yet to be learned. Nevertheless, all these works, expenses and plans of Bemoym were changed to deeds of evil; because, after the said Pero Vaaz had put to land and entered into the said river, by readily believing suspicions of disloyalty and treason against Bemoym, or more truthfully because he wanted to return to the kingdom, he slew the said Bemoym with a sword, and then returned to this kingdom; whereat the king, being in Tavilla, grew very sad; and he overlooked this crime by Pero Vaaz, seeing that he did not visit heavy punishment upon him or upon many others who deserved it for the same reason; yet the king strongly disapproved of their killing him, since, being accomplices in such an error, they ought to have been treated as they treated him, because they had had him freely in their power without offence or peril.

9. Manuel I (1495–1521).

III

Spain: From Crusade to Empire

Introduction

In many respects, the Spanish empire in the sixteenth century was the most elaborate and the best organized of all the colonial empires. A major reason for this was that the Spanish had been engaged in the process of empire building and imperial administration for a longer period and on a broader scale than any other people in Europe. Roger B. Merriman put it well when he entitled his great history of the Spanish empire, *The Rise of the Spanish Empire in the Old World and the New*, thus emphasizing the continuity of imperial development.[1] More recently, Charles Verlinden has demonstrated how many of the economic institutions of the Spanish empire in the New World were rooted in the experience of operating a colonial economy that the Spanish had acquired in the conquest and settlement of the islands in the Mediterranean and in the Atlantic.[2]

Strictly speaking, Spanish colonization in the Americas sprang from two separate but related traditions, reflecting the fact that until the marriage of Ferdinand of Aragon and Isabella of Castile in 1469 these two kingdoms were in competition for control of the Iberian peninsula. Even after this marriage, the union was only a personal one, and it was not until well into the reign of Philip II (1556–98) that institutional union began to develop. What Castile and Aragon shared was a history of crusading. Castile was the heir of the tiny Christian principalities that survived the Moslem invasion of the eighth century by withdrawing to the mountains of northwestern Spain. Aragon developed from a number of small principalities in northeastern Spain, which came under the domination of French crusaders who spilled over the Pyrenees from Aquitaine in the twelfth century. Each kingdom was composed not only of land recaptured from the Moslems but of lands that had formerly been independent Christian communities as well.[3]

Two distinct themes marked the expansion of the Spanish Christian kingdoms. The first, and the obvious one, was the crusade against the Moslems. The second characteristic, one that has been less appreciated,

---

1. Roger B. Merriman, *The Rise of the Spanish Empire in the Old World and the New*, 4 vols. (New York: 1918–34; reprint ed., New York: Cooper Square, 1962).
2. Verlinden, pp. 13–14, 20–21.
3. For the history of Spain in the Middle Ages, see Joseph F. O'Callaghan, *A History of Medieval Spain* (Ithaca: Cornell Univ. Press, 1975).

was the desire of the Spanish to reach an accomodation with the Moslems once the military reconquest of the peninsula was completed. These two themes reflect the fact that periods of enthusiastic crusading warfare were punctuated by periods of peaceful coexistence. Furthermore, the Christians did not perceive the Moslems as beings radically different from themselves and therefore deserving extermination or permanent bondage. To the Christians, the Moslems were Agarenes, descendants of Agar, the wife of the Patriarch Abraham and mother of Ishmael, from whom the desert nomads, such as Mohammed, were descended (doc. 14). Christians were descended from Abraham through his wife Sara, the mother of Isaac. Christians and Moslems, then, shared a common ancestry. Furthermore, both shared the Bible and therefore a number of common beliefs, so that some kind of accomodation seemed possible (see chapter 7, doc. 39).

In addition to these ties of religious kinship, there was another, more pragmatic, reason for seeking a harmonious relationship with the conquered Moslems. The Christians needed a supply of labor to till the lands which they had reconquered. Although Christian colonists were sometimes recruited to replace the Moslem inhabitants who had been killed or sold into slavery, it was not always feasible to rely on the supply of colonists (doc. 15). The Christians found it necessary to encourage Moslem farmers to remain. As a result, agreements were made authorizing the conquered Moslems to retain their own local rulers and to practice their religion without interference (doc. 16). Similarly, the security of Aragonese merchants trading in the Mediterranean necessitated the making of treaties with the Moslem rulers of North Africa that in turn led to increased diplomatic and merchantile relations with the Moslems (doc. 17). To a significant extent, the success of the Christian kingdoms in Spain depended upon the ability of the Christian kings to work with the Moslems. The crusading spirit was always tempered by economic and political realities.

Out of the experience of the *Reconquista* came a body of laws, theory rather than practice to a large extent, dealing with the status of slaves. In the *Siete Partidas*, a collection of laws that King Alfonso X of Castile (1252–84) issued, slaves were recognized as human beings who possessed certain rights and deserved protection (doc. 18). Basing their arguments on ancient Roman law, the Spanish jurists saw slavery as an unfortunate condition that could befall anyone. They did not see slavery as a result of biological or racial inferiority. The slave was a man, not an animal. Although slavery was widespread in the Iberian world, nevertheless there were attempts to insure reasonable treatment of the slaves and manumission was possible.

When the Aragonese moved into the Balearic Islands in the thirteenth century, and when the Castilians moved into the Canary Islands in the fourteenth century, they began to apply the tools of colonial government and the techniques of imperial economy that they had developed in the course of the *Reconquista* (doc. 19). In addition, just as the Canaries served as a stepping stone for sailing westward, so too these islands served as part of a transmission belt, bringing the techniques of colonial government and economy to the Americas.

Bibliography

The history of medieval Spain as a frontier society, a society that found it necessary to deal pragmatically with the Moslems, has been dealt with at length in the works of Robert I. Burns. His basic works on the theme of the Spanish frontier are: *The Crusader Kingdom of Valencia*, 2 vols. (Cambridge, Mass.: Harvard Univ. Press, 1967), and *Islam Under the Crusaders: Colonial Survival in the Thirteenth-Century Kingdom of Valencia* (Princeton: Princeton Univ. Press, 1973). The most famous missionary to the Moslems was Ramon Lull whose life and career are discussed in E. Allison Peers, *Fool of Love: The Life of Ramon Lull* (London: S. C. M. Press, 1946). Until recently, scholars had not appreciated the amount of contact that existed between Christian and Moslem societies during the Middle Ages. The extensive trading relations that existed between Christians and Moslems in the Mediterranean are the subject of S. D. Goitein, *A Mediterranean Society: The Jewish Communities of the Arab World as Portrayed in the Documents of the Cairo Geniza*, 2 vols. (Berkeley and Los Angeles: Univ. of California Press, 1967, 1971).

The implications of the medieval Spanish experience on the development of the Spanish empire in the Americas have been developed by J. H. Parry, *The Spanish Theory of Empire in the Sixteenth Century* (Cambridge, Mass.: Harvard Univ. Press, 1940), and C. J. Bishko, "The Iberian Background of Latin American History," *Hispanic American Historical Review* 36 (February 1956): 50–80. The development of Spanish law in the Middle Ages and its application to the overseas empire is the subject of E. N. van Kleffens, *Hispanic Law Until the End of the Middle Ages* (Edinburgh: Edinburgh Univ. Press, 1968). One area of medieval Spanish law, the law of slavery, has attracted interest in recent years because of the differences in the legal status of slaves in the Spanish world because of its Roman law heritage and in the English-speaking world which did not use the Roman tradition. The basic book on this topic is Frank Tannenbaum, *Slave and Citizen* (New York: Alfred A. Knopf, 1947).

Document 14

"Historia Compostelana," in *España Sagrada*, ed. F. H. Florez, 51 vols. (Madrid, 1754–79), 20: 350–51, 354–56. Translated by James Muldoon. Like a number of other medieval chronicles, the *History of Compostela* was a piece of propaganda designed to publicize a particular shrine in order to encourage pilgrims to visit the shrine of the saint buried there. In this case, Diego Gelmírez (d. 1139), bishop of Compostela, sought to spread the fame of the shrine dedicated to St. James. The *History* provides an illustration of the way in which Christians and Moslems came into regular contact and the resulting hopes that the Moslems would convert to Christianity under the influence of the saint.—*ed.*

A king of the Saracens, Ali by name, who ruled over the children of Agar of Spain on both sides of the Spanish Sea, sent Ishmaelite ambassadors, discreet and illustrious men, to Queen Urraca and her son as an embassy. When they took the road west, having heard that the queen and her son were dwelling at the remote end of Galicia, they saw many Christian pilgrims coming from and going to St. James for the sake of his intercession and, wondering at this, they inquired of the officer, a man named Peter, whom they had with them as their guide and aide among the Christians and who was sufficiently learned in their language, asking, "Who is that whom the great multitude of Christians honors with such great devotion? Who could be so significant, that innumerable Christians from across the Pyrenees and beyond visit for the sake of his intercession? There is such a multitude of people coming from and going to him that there seems to be scarcely an unencumbered path leading to the west." He answered them, saying that this was St. James, the apostle of our Lord and Savior, the brother of the apostle and evangelist John, both of them being sons of Zebedee. St. James's body was buried on the border of Galicia. He is venerated by the men of France, England, Italy, Germany, and all the other provinces of Christendom, especially Spain, as their patron and protector. Moreover, the stock of the Ishmaelites learned that James of Jerusalem suffered under Herod and was carried to Galicia.

When they, who were earlier struck with wonder concerning what they had heard, came to Compostela and saw the Apostle's basilica, they were struck speechless. They said, "This noble and glorious structure that belongs to your father James surpasses all others. We have not seen anything anywhere to compare with it. By Mohammed, great glory would accrue to him if there was such esteem shown to him in heaven as you

77

show him on earth! What help and protection does he bestow upon those who honor and venerate him?" To this, the officer replied in the Ishmaelite tongue, "He obtains much grace from our Lord Jesus Christ through his merits and intercession so that through the mercy of God sight is given to the blind, the lame walk, health is restored to lepers and those suffering other kinds of disease. He brings aid and assistance to all who seek it from him with devotion, and he has worked numerous miracles both in Spain and across the Pyrenees. . . . " The Ishmaelites were astonished and amazed at this and were silent. They acknowledged that their Mohammed could not do such things. The officer, a most eloquent and prudent man, diligently added to the incredulity of the gentiles and extolled the Christian faith with praises. He instructed those gentiles who were blinded by the cloud of ignorance and deluded by many errors with truthful assertions and strong arguments. Against this kind of argument they could not fight back because they had evidence of the truth with their own eyes and they saw the great glories of St. James rising up before them. . . .

After these things had happened, while the Ishmaelites indulged themselves staying longer at Compostela, an abscess that broke out on the neck of one of them swelled up, so that it seemed incurable and would kill him, for it was of such a kind that was normally deadly. There was, however, a certain widow who frequented the house where they were staying who visited the house of the Apostle daily with candles and gifts, often remaining there praying through the night. Observing this, the Ishmaelites asked where and why the widow offered the gifts with such devotion. They were informed that she besought the favor of St. James the Apostle for the healing of her own soul and those of her parents and others of the faithful by these and other deeds. Perhaps their wickedness caused them to be slow to believe and to laugh at the consecrated hosts, unless they saw the clearest evidence of a miracle of apostolic virtue in the discussion. . . . They did not presume to detract from the miracle or to diminish the Apostle's glory, but he whose neck was swollen from the abscess said, "I beg you to intercede in my behalf with your apostle whose blessings on those who seek his aid we see here before us, and to beg him that he look kindly upon me, since he is powerful through the grace of God. Bring a candle for me also to his altar and beg him to restore me safely from this festering growth." At this the widow, smiling with joy, said, "I give thanks to God and to St. James who revealed wonderous workings of his virtue to you. He did not, however, show you their fullness." Taking the candle, she touched the abscess on that man with the candle, making the sign of the cross over him. Then she left for the church, and, according to the usual custom, presented her offerings and prayed. Having finished praying, she offered the candle which she had accepted from the Ishmaelite, joining his prayer to her prayers, beseeching St. James to restore the Ishmaelite to a state of good health and to render him free from the curse of the deadly abscess. Scarcely had she finished the prayer when the diseased matter of the abscess drained. The Ishmaelite was restored to good health. There remained a scar, however, a sign of the sickness that had been drained away. Great and ineffable is the mercy of God which, through the sign of the cross, a sign which is foolishness to the gentiles according to the Apostle Paul, does not refuse to confer even on the gentiles the remedies of salvation. Great also is the mercy of the blessed apostle James who does not refuse to entreat his Lord on behalf of those who seek his aid and who does not refuse to succor them with the grace of salvation.

After the Ishmaelite realized the blessings which he had received from St. James and that the deadly poisonous abscess had drained, he and his associates rejoiced, overflowing with happiness. They were astounded at the unheard-of power of such a miracle. They showed the officer, Peter, and the other Christians who were present what had taken place. They shouted that the aid of the apostle preceded the power of the medicine. What more? St. James the Apostle praised and honored by both the faithful and the gentiles alike as the most merciful benefactor. Everyone among the people benefitted from the wonderous power of the Apostle James through the grace of God, and they praised him with loud cries. Then the Ishmaelites asked, "As his fame has brought home to us, we have seen the great mercy of this apostle in the solution of your archbishop, and we have seen his miraculous quality in the sickness of our associate, and we cite our personal testimony. The favor of his intercession is rightly sought by Christians from both sides of the Pyrenees. He is rightly worshipped by many Christians with great devotion and he is rightly called and revered as patron and protector by Christians."

Document 15

Ramon Muntaner, *The Chronicle of Muntaner*, ed. Lady Goodenough, 2 vols., Hakluyt Society Publications, series 2, nos. 47, 50 (London: The Society, 1920, 1921), 1: 35–37, 44; 2: 413–16.

Ramon Muntaner (1264-after 1328), a soldier who had fought in the wars of Aragonese expansion, wrote his chronicle during the years 1325–28. A native of Valencia, he served Peter III and his sons Alfonso III and James II, rising to high office in Sicily which came under Aragonese control during Peter III's reign (1276–85). The first excerpt from his chronicle describes the conquest of Murcia by James I of Aragon (1213–76). Murcia was a small Moslem kingdom in south-eastern Spain that became a vassal kingdom of Castile during the Reconquest, but rebelled periodically during the mid-thirteenth century. Although the Aragonese were interested in acquiring Murcia, it remained in Castilian hands with the military assistance of Aragon. The second excerpt deals with the reconquest of Minorca, one of the Balearic Islands in the Mediterranean, during the reign of Alfonso III (1285–91). The picture of the conquest contained in these excerpts, a picture of bloodshed and the enslavement of the losers, differs from the description provided in the dry diplomatic texts that follow. These differences reflect what the Christians desired, the resumption of peaceful, orderly government immediately after the conquest, and what actually took place, a constant series of battles.—*ed.*

From now onwards I shall leave the King of Castile, who is back in his territories and his dominions, and I shall turn to speak of the Lord King of Aragon, who was preparing to enter the Kingdom of Murcia. And to that end he held a council with his sons and his barons and all agreed that, as he had given that promise to the King of Castile (which he related to them fully), he must at once invade the Kingdom of Murcia; and they all offered to follow him at their own cost and provisioning and said they would never fail him whilst there was life in them and until he had completed the said conquest. And of this the said Lord King was very joyous and content and gave them great thanks and immediately ordained that the Lord Infante En Pedro should make an incursion into the kingdom of Murcia, in order to reconnoitre all that kingdom. The Lord Infante En Pedro had a battle arrayed of many richs homens[1] and knights of Catalonia and Aragon and of the kingdom of Valencia, and citizens and seamen and almugavars;[2] and, overrunning the said kingdom by land and sea, went about, sacking and laying waste the whole country. And in each place he remained until he had destroyed it quite. First he laid waste and destroyed all the country around Alicante and Nompot and Aquast, and then he destroyed Elche and the vale of Elda and of Novelda and Villena and Aspe and Petrel and Crevillente and Catral and Abanilla, and Collosa, and Guardamar, and Orihuela. And he went as far as up to the castle of Montagut, which is in the huerta[3] of Murcia, and that place he wasted and destroyed. And the Saracen king of Murcia came out to meet him with all his power of horse and foot. And the said Lord Infante was two days awaiting him in order of battle, but the king of Murcia dared not fight with him. And, assuredly, if it had not been for the acequias[4] which

1. Great nobles.
2. Foot soldiers.
3. Irrigated plain around a town.
4. Irrigation canals.

were between the two hosts, the Lord Infante would have attacked, but the acequias were so wide and the water in them so deep, that he could not do it. Nevertheless there were many fine feats of arms, and in one hand-to-hand fight the Lord Infante had, it was found that he had killed, with his own hand, ten jinetes[5] and, where he attacked, do not imagine they dared face him. What shall I tell you? For a whole month he remained in the said kingdom with his hosts, burning and sacking; and all who were with him became wealthy men and prosperous from the great spoils they carried away, as well of captives, male and female, as of goods, and of cattle they drove off. The Lord Infante sent to the Lord King, his father, full a thousand head of big cattle and full twenty thousand of small cattle, and full a thousand male Saracen captives, and full a thousand female Saracen captives. And of these captives the said Lord King gave and presented, of the males, some to the Pope, some to the cardinals and to the Emperor Frederick and to the King of France and to counts and barons and to friends of his own. And the female captives he gave to the Lady Queen of France, his daughter, and to countesses and to other noble ladies, so that he left none for himself, but rather distributed and gave them all away; of which the Holy Father and the cardinals and other powers of the Christian world were very joyous and content, and made processions in honour of Our Lord the true God, Who had given this victory to the Lord Infante. . . .

And when he had taken the said city he peopled it wholly with Catalans, and so he did Orihuela and Elche and Guardamar and Alicante and Cartagena and the other places. You may be sure that all who inhabit the city of Murcia and the aforesaid places are true Catalans and speak the most beautiful Catalan of the world, and are all good men of arms and expert in all matters. And it may well be said that that kingdom is one of the most fertile in the world. I tell you truly that in all the world not I, nor any other man, could know two provinces that are better and more fertile in all things than the Kingdom of Valencia and the Kingdom of Murcia. . . .

Now I shall turn to speak to you of the Lord King of Aragon who, after he had kept Christmas in the city of Mallorca, made every one embark and set his course for Minorca. And when he was twenty miles out at sea, near the island of Minorca, he encountered a great storm which scattered all his fleet, in such manner that he landed at the port of Mahon with only twenty galleys. And the almojarife of Minorca, who had prepared himself well for defence and had had great succours from Barbary, came to the stern of the galleys with all his forces, so that he was there with full five hundred horsemen and forty thousand afoot. And the Lord

5. Light cavalry.

King was with the galleys in echelon at Conejo Island. And that storm lasted full eight days during which none of his men could join him, and then the weather improved and soon they came to the port of Mahon, now two galleys, then three ships; thus all assembled as they could.

And when the Lord King of Aragon saw that two hundred armed horses had arrived, he landed the horses and all his followers landed. And the almojarife,[6] who saw what forces had arrived, went to the castle of Mahon and there assembled all his forces. And then the Lord King to whom full four hundred armed horses and a part of the almugavars had come, said to the admiral and to the other richs homens who were there that he would not await more of his followers, but the admiral and the others entreated him not to do that, but to await all his knights. But he said that the winter was very severe and the galleys were suffering great hardship and that he would not endure this on any account, so he went to where the almojarife was.

And the almojarife with all his forces came down in order of battle, to a fine plain which is near the said castle of Mahon. And when the hosts were near each other the Lord King attacked in good order with all his followers and the almojarife likewise attacked the King of Aragon. And the battle was cruel, for the men of the island were good men of arms, and there were Turks there, brave men whom the almojarife had in his pay. And the battle was so cruel that all had enough to do; but the Lord King, who was of the most expert knights of the world, attacked here and there and no knight escaped him whom he could reach with a blow, so that all his arms broke except the mace, with which he did so much that no man dared to stand up to him. And so, by the favour of God, and by his prowess and that of his followers, he won the battle; the almojarife fled into the castle with about twenty of his kinsmen, and all the others died.

And so the Lord King had the field searched by his followers and then went to beseige the castle to which the almojarife had retreated; and meanwhile the whole of the fleet of the Lord King had arrived. And when the almojarife saw the great forces of the Lord King, he sent him his messengers and begged him that, in his kindness and mercy, he let him go to Barbary with twenty of his kinsmen who were with him, and their wives and children, with only their clothes and with provisions to last them so far, and he would surrender the castle of Mahon and the town of Ciutadella.

And so the Lord King, in order to have the whole island without further hindrance, granted this; and so the almojarife surrendered the

6. Officer in charge of finances.

castle to him and the town of Ciutadella and all the other places in the island and gave him all the treasure he had. And the Lord King chartered for him a ship manned by Genoese, which had come to Mahon on account of the storm and was going to Ibiza to load up with salt. And on board that ship he put the almojarife with about a hundred persons, men, women and children, and he paid the ship and had many provisions put in. And they left the port at such a time that the ship encountered a storm and was destroyed off the coast of Barbary and not one person escaped. And so you see when Our Lord wishes to destroy a nation how easily He does it; wherefore everyone should beware of His wrath, for you see how the wheel of fortune turned suddenly against the almojarife and his race who had ruled that island for over a thousand years.

Then, when the Lord King had sent away the almojarife and his dependents, he went to Ciutadella and had all the women and children of the whole island taken, and the men who had remained alive, of whom there were very few, for all those in the battle had died. And when the women and children and men of the island were all taken, there were full forty thousand. And he had them bound, and made En Ramon Calbet, a franklin of Lérida, their chief and master for their sale. And En Ramon appointed other officials under himself, and sent the greater number of prisoners to Mallorca, and some to Sicily and to Catalonia and to other parts. And at each place there was a public auction of the people and of the goods which were found belonging to them.

And when this had been settled the Lord King ordained that a strongly walled town should be built at Mahon, by the harbour. And he left, as procurator of the island, En Pedro de Lebia, a burgess of Valencia, and gave him full powers to give all the island to Catalan inhabitants and to people it with worthy people. And he did so assuredly, for the island of Minorca is inhabited by as worthy Catalans as any place could be.

And when the Lord King had settled all his officials in the island and given orders to people it, leaving En Pedro de Lebia, who was a very worthy and wise man, as head and captain of all, he departed from Minorca and came to Mallorca where a great feast was made for him on the occasion of his arrival. And he visited all the island of Mallorca with the admiral and with Galceran de Anglesola and other richs homens who were with him. And then he departed from Mallorca and sent all the fleet to Catalonia with the admiral; and the Lord King, with four galleys, went to visit Ibiza where a great feast was made for him. And there he stayed four days and then went to Catalonia and landed at Salou; and from Salou he went to Barcelona, where he found the admiral who had already landed with all the fleet. And the admiral took leave of him and then returned to Sicily.

Document 16

M. L. de Mas Latrie, ed., *Traités de paix et de commerce et documents divers concernant les relations des Chretiens avec les Arabes de l'Afrique Septentrionale au moyen age*, 2 vols. (Paris: 1866; reprint ed., New York: Burt Franklin, n.d.), 2: 182–84. Translated by James Muldoon.

The expansion of the Aragonese empire during the reign of James I (1213–76) spread the Aragonese crown's power over an increasingly wide area, bringing the Aragonese into extensive and regular contact with Moslems. The conquest of the Balearic Islands brought them into contact with a large, organized native population. The Aragonese sought to come to an accomodation with them, working with the existing leaders of the people rather than replacing them. The fact that the Aragonese were merchants encouraged them to develop peaceful trading relations with the Moslems. The Aragonese were less interested in adding to their domains for the purpose of providing more land for colonization by Aragonese farmers.—ed.

This is a translation taken from a certain document sealed with the seal of the most illustrious James, by the grace of God king of the Aragonese, of good memory. The substance of the document is as follows:

1. In the name of the Creator, I Doctor Aboabdille Mafomet . . . commander of the fortress and mayor of the island of Minorca, along with all the old and wise men and the entire population, all the inhabitants, of the aforesaid island, both those now living and those yet to come, by the counsel and with the agreement of all, as is the usual practice, in the presence of [he lists 16 of the leading men of the island] we yield and we accept you, Lord James, King of Aragon and Majorca, Count of Barcelona, and Lord of Montpellier, and your heirs who hold the kingdom of Majorca, as our natural lord. We do homage to you, swearing oaths and becoming your faithful men. We withdraw ourselves from and renounce all other lordships, agreements, alliances, and oaths which previously we made with anyone else. And by recognizing your lordship and the alliance with you by which we are and will be bound to you, we give, grant, concede, and release to you in the present document power over the fortified town of Majorica, so that your badge or banner may be placed on the peak of the town by five of your men, and that your name and lordship might be proclaimed in a loud voice by your men from the summit. After this is down, the town may be handed over to the alfaqui[1] who is there at the time, or to him who shall replace him there, and who is confirmed by us and by you. This power we promise to give and to release to you, or to your agent, without any hesitation, for many years or for a single year, just as you wish it. The town having been restored to the

---

1. Teacher of the Koran.

alfaqui, as mentioned above, all the citizens are bound to return to their homes.

2. For the even greater recognition of your lordship, we promise you and your heirs or your agents, to give annually 90 almudinos of barley and 100 of wheat . . . 100 bullocks and cows . . . 300 goats . . . 200 sheep. . . . The tribute of animals shall be given to your representatives every year in the month of March, along the shore, in the presence of the official of the port of Minorca. Having handed over these animals to your agent, he will guard the tribute at his own cost and expense.

3. Also, we promise in good faith to aid and defend you and your men and your possessions, to the fullest of our ability, against all men, and on your behalf and at your command to make peace and war, but only on our island, and we may not receive any pirate or any enemy of yours either on land or on the sea.

4. Also, if any Christian vessel incur shipwreck on the island of Minorca, we promise to gather up all the goods and to protect them and to return them to their owner, or to you, if the true owner is not found. And if it was a Saracen ship, we can requisition those goods and place them in the service of the town. And the same may be done if one of our ships from Minorca reaches any land under your control.

5. Item: We promise that if a captive runs away or flees from the kingdom of Majorca and comes to Minorca, we will return him, unless he belongs in a special way on the island of Minorca. We will not keep him if he comes from any other place. . . .

6. And we James the aforementioned king, along with our heirs and men, promise you, each and every one of the inhabitants of Minorca, that we will defend and protect you and your goods on land and sea. And by the special grace and honor which we wish to render to you, we concede to you that no Christian or Jew can dwell continuously on the island of Minorca unless you authorize it. And because of this, we concede and confirm as alfaqui over you, to act in our place, the venerable and worthy alfaqui who is now there, Aboabdille Abenixem by name, that he remain alfaqui for the rest of his life. And after his death, you may elect as alfaqui anyone you wish from among yourselves. And the alfaqui, the alcayd,[2] the alcadi,[3] and the almoxariff[4] may always be drawn from among yourselves. And when you elect the alfaqui, you shall inform us through your ambassador and letters, so that we may confirm him; and we ought to send our messenger at that time to take the oath from him that he may observe all of the aforementioned matters for you. And if you fail to reach agreement among yourselves in the election, we can choose as alcayd one from among you and appoint him with the advice of your senior men.

2. Mayor.
3. Governor of a castle or fortress.
4. Royal tax collector.

7. Item: We concede and grant to you that whenever some or any of you wish to go into any part of our land for the sake of doing business, you shall be safe and secure, and free and exempt from toll and leçda and every other demand which can be levied on trade.

8. Item: We concede to you that whenever Saracen ships come to Minorca for the sake of trade, they shall not be seized by us nor harassed by our men while they are in the port or on shore; but after they have left port, we are no longer bound to do so.

9. Item: We concede that any inhabitants of Minorca, with the assent of the alfaqui who is there, can remove himself so that he may dwell wherever he wishes in the land of the Saracens or in the land of the Christians. . . .

10. Item: We promise that if, in the event of attacks by infidels or enemies, it shall be necessary to aid you, that when we have received your ambassador, we will aid you and we will assist and defend you as if you were our own people; and when it seems necessary to you to send a messenger seeking help and he comes to Majorca, we promise that he who holds our office will conduct and bring him safe and sound to us.

11. Finally, we promise that if any of our men seize a Saracen inhabitant of Minorca, or if one is captured in any other part of our lands, we will return him free and safe with all his possessions.

Document 17

M. L. de Mas Latrie, ed., *Traités de paix et de commerce et documents divers concernant les relations des Chretiens avec les Arabes de l'Afrique Septentrionale au moyen age*, 2 vols. (Paris: 1866; reprint ed., New York: Burt Franklin, n.d.), 2: 280–81. Translated by James Muldoon.

During the Middle Ages there existed an extensive trading network in the Mediterranean. Although ecclesiastical officials condemned those who sold arms and war materials to the Moslems, the trade flourished. In order to encourage this trade, Christian and Moslem rulers made treaties insuring the safety of their subjects who engaged in trade. The success of the Aragonese in their military and commercial ventures made them the dominant Christian power in the Mediterranean. As a result, the Castilians were forced to look to the Atlantic when they became interested in expanding beyond the Iberian peninsula.—ed.

Let all men to whom this charter shall come know that there will be peace and truce between us, James, by the grace of God, King of Aragon, Majorca and Valencia, Count of Barcelona and Urgel, and lord of Montpellier, on the one hand, and the noble and honorable Miramomeni

Aboabdille, King of Tunis on the other. Be it known that there will be peace on land and sea according to what is contained herein.

1. In the first place, let it be known that every Saracen of the land of the aforementioned Miramomeni, from any part of that land . . . who shall come to our lands . . . let him be safe and secure in both his person and his goods, so that no man will do him harm while this treaty is in effect.

2. And if any person or persons wish to leave any part of our land in order to go to some part of the land of the aforementioned Miramomeni, or to any of his parts, or his beaches, Saracens or any other men, . . . (let them be safe and secure) in their persons and their possessions. . . .

3. And if by chance any men from places in our lands already mentioned, or from other places in our land, go then to any of the parts of the land of the lordship aforementioned of Miramomeni, . . . we are bound to return and restore everything they lost there, if they swear truthfully that they have lost those things or can prove it.

4. And all those from the land of the aforementioned Miramomeni who come to our land, or to any of the islands we possess, or into any part of our lordship, shall be safe and secure, in both their persons and their possessions. . . .

5. Item: No man of our land shall do any harm to any persons from the land of the aforementioned Miramomeni of Tunis, nor to their possessions.

6. Item: If any vessel of the lordship of the aforementioned Miramomeni is lost in any part of our land, or if any Saracen from that lordship who goes in any Christian ship to any one of our islands, the men of that place shall guard and defend any and all Saracens and their goods and return anything the Saracens may have lost. . . .

7. Item: Every ship that is in any of the ports of Miramomeni, regardless of its place of origin, shall possess the rights of his own subjects.

Document 18*

Alfonso X, *Las Siete Partidas*, trans. Samuel P. Scott (Chicago: Commerce Clearing House, 1931), pp. 847, 901–3, 977–80, 1438–40.

Las Siete Partidas was one of the great legal codes of the Middle Ages. It represented the goals of King Alfonso X (1252–84) of Castile, though not the actual practice of Castilian political and legal life. Only in the sixteenth century did the code become fully enforced in both Spain and

* Reproduced with permission from *Las Siete Partidas*, translated by Samuel P. Scott, published and copyrighted by Commerce Clearing House, Inc., Chicago, Illinois.

in the Spanish empire overseas. Nevertheless the code had an impact on the shaping of legal thought in Spain before the sixteenth century because it was the chief vehicle for the spread of Roman law in Spain. The discussion of slavery in *Las Siete Partidas* was largely derived from Roman law, which saw slavery as a normal part of human existence but strove to mitigate it. As a result, the slave was a person, not an animal, and had to be treated within certain limits.

This code also dealt with the status of Moslems living among Christians, emphasizing that so long as Moslems and Jews did no harm to Christians, they in turn would not be harassed. This was not toleration in the modern sense so much as a recognition of the large non-Christian population of Spain.—*ed.*

TITLE V.

Concerning the Marriages of Slaves.

Servitude is the vilest and most contemptible thing that can exist among men, for the reason that man, who is the most noble and free among all the creatures that God made, is brought by means of it under the power of another, so that the latter can do with him what he pleases, just as he can with any of the rest of his property living or dead. And slavery is such a contemptible thing, that the party who is subjected to it not only loses the power of disposing of his property as he desires, but he has not even control of his own person, except under the orders of his master. Wherefore, since in the preceding Title we spoke of the impediments which exist in marriages and betrothals, by reason of the conditions which men impose on them, some promising others to give or to do something, and afterwards do not keep their promises; we intend in this Title to speak of other impediments which also arise, because of persons being of a servile condition. We shall show, in the first place, whether slaves can marry, with whom they can do so, and if the consent of their masters is required; and what law should be observed in a marriage contracted between a slave and a person who is free.

LAW I.

Whether Slaves Can Marry, Whom They Can Marry, and Whether the Consent of Their Masters Must Be Obtained.

It was a practice in ancient times, and one approved by the Holy Church, for slaves to marry one another; moreover, a slave can marry a free woman, and the marriage will be valid if she knew that he was a slave when she married him. A female slave can marry a freeman under the same circumstances, but they must be Christians for the marriage to be valid. Slaves can marry one another, and although their masters oppose it, the marriage will be valid, and should not be annulled for this reason if both give their consent, as stated in the Title concerning Marriages. Although they can marry against the will of their masters, they are nevertheless bound to serve them as they formerly did; and where several men own two slaves, who were married, and it becomes necessary to sell them, it should be done in such a way that they can live together, and serve those who purchase them. They cannot be sold, one in one country and one in another, because they would have to live apart, and where a slave belonging to one man marries a free woman, or a free man marries a female slave, and the master of either of them is present, or aware of it, and does not say at the time that he or she is his slave; by this act alone, which the master sees, or is aware of, but remains silent, the slave becomes free, and cannot afterwards be returned to slavery. And although it is stated above that a slave becomes free for the reason that his master sees him married, or knows of it, and conceals his ownership, nevertheless, the marriage will not be valid, because the woman did not know that the man was a slave when she married him, except where she afterwards gives her consent either by word or deed.

LAW II.

Under What Circumstances a Slave is Bound to Obey the Order of His Master, Rather Than That of the Woman Whom He Married.

Where a master calls his slave to order him to perform some service, and at the same time his wife calls him to perform his marital obligations, in a case of this kind, a slave should rather obey the order of his master than that of his wife; except where the husband thinks that if he does not comply with her request, she will be guilty of depravity with some one else. Where two slaves who are married have two masters, one in one country and the other in another, and they are so far apart that where they serve their masters they cannot join one another and live together, the church can then compel one of the masters to buy the slave of the other. Where they are unwilling to do this, whichever one of them the church may select can be compelled to sell his slave to some man who is a resident of the town or community where the master of the other slave resides, and if no one wishes to buy him, the church should do so, in order that the husband and wife may not be separated.

LAW III.

What Law Should Be Observed in a Marriage Contracted Between a Slave and a Freeman.

Where a female slave belonging to any person marries a freeman, and the party who married her was not aware that she was of the servile condition, the marriage in this way will not be valid, as stated in the Title concerning Marriages, in the law beginning. "A servile condition." Moreover, when a slave marries a free woman, thinking that she was a slave, he cannot separate from her by saying that he made a mistake, for, since he married a woman of superior condition to himself, he cannot allege that he was deceived. This is understood to apply where she desires to remain with him knowing that he is a slave. If, when she married him, she did not know that he was a slave, although she may have ascertained it afterwards she has the choice to remain with him, if she desires to do so, or to leave him. Nor can a slave, thinking that he is marrying a free woman when he marries a slave, leave her by saying that he made a mistake; for he should not consider himself deceived by such an error, nor should the marriage be annulled on account of it, since he married a woman of the same condition as himself.

LAW IV.

Concerning Men Who Marry Female Slaves, Thinking That They Are Free.

Men sometimes decide upon marriage, thinking that they are marrying free women, and marry slaves. Wherefore, when a man marries a woman of this kind, not knowing that she is a slave, and, her master subsequently sets her free, although some persons are of the opinion that the marriage is confirmed by an enfranchisement of this kind, it is not true. This is the rule on account of the mistake which was made in the marriage in the first place, where the party thought he was giving his consent to a free woman when he was not. If, however, after he learned that she was of such a condition he should give his consent by word or deed to accept her, the marriage will be valid, and the parties should not be separated. Where a freeman marries a female slave, not knowing that she is such, and her master brings a suit against her for her services, after her husband learns that she is of such a condition he should not have carnal intercourse with her, even though she requests it. For if he should lie with her after she has lost the suit, even though she should be returned to slavery, he cannot separate from her. The same rule applies where the wife is free, and proceedings are instituted against the husband, to prove that he was a slave. Where a husband knowingly becomes a slave, in order for having a reason for leaving his wife, his act is not valid, nor should the marriage be annulled on this account, but his wife can claim him and release him from servitude if she desires to do so; and this is the case because she has a right in him, and for the reason that great dishonor may result from this source to her and to her children, if she has any. The way in which a freeman can become a slave is explained hereafter in the Title concerning Slaves. . . .

TITLE XXI.

Concerning Slaves.

Slaves are another kind of men who are under obligations to those to whom they belong, by reason of the authority they have over them. Wherefore, since in the preceding Title, we spoke of the retainers that a man brings up in his house, who are free, we intend to speak here of slaves because they belong to the household. In the first place we shall explain what servitude is; where it originated and how many kinds there are; under what circumstances a slave is bound to protect his master from injury; and what authority masters have over their slaves.

LAW I.

What Servitude Is, Whence It Derived Its Name, and How Many Kinds There Are.

Servitude is an agreement and regulation which people established in ancient times, by means of which men who were originally free became slaves and were subjected to the authority of others, contrary to natural reason. The slave derived his name from a word called in Latin, *servare* which means, in Castilian, to preserve. This preservation was established by the emperors, for, in ancient times, all captives were put to death. The emperors, however, considered it proper, and ordered that they should not be killed, but that they should be preserved, and use made of them.

There are three kinds of slaves, the first is those taken captive in war who are enemies of the faith; the second, those born of female slaves; the third, when a person is free and allows himself to be sold. Five things are necessary, in the case of the third. First, the party must voluntarily consent to be sold; second, he must receive a part of the price; third, he must know that he is free; fourth, the party who purchases him must believe that he is a slave; fifth, he who permits himself to be sold must be more than twenty years of age.

LAW II.

To What Conditions Those Belong Who Are Born of a Female Slave and a Freeman

Persons born of a father who is free and a mother who is a slave are slaves, because they follow the condition of the mother, as respects both slavery and freedom. But where a woman of this kind, while pregnant, is set free, her child will be free also, although the said child may be born only an hour, or even less, after she was liberated. And, even if the mother should be subsequently returned to slavery, her child will always remain free, on account of the time during which his mother bore him after she was liberated, whether this be much, or little. Children born of a free mother and a father who is a slave are free, because they always follow the condition of the mother, as aforesaid. Although we stated above that children follow the condition of the mother, nevertheless, children who are born of a father and mother who are free, should follow the condition of the father, so far as secular honors and *fueros* are concerned. . . .

LAW IV.

Christians Who Provide the Enemies of the Faith with Iron, Wood, Arms, or Ships, Become Slaves by Reason of Such Acts.

There are some wicked Christians who give assistance or advice to the Moors, who are the enemies of the faith; as, for instance, when they give, or sell them arms of wood and iron, or galleys or ships already built, or the materials with which to build them; and this also includes those who pilot or navigate their ships in order to inflict injury upon Christians; and those who give or sell them wood for the purpose of making battering-rams or other engines. And, for the reason that such persons are guilty of great wickedness, the Holy Church deemed it proper that whoever could seize individuals guilty of acts of this kind, might reduce them to slavery, and sell them if they desired to do so, or make use of them as they would of their own slaves. In addition to this, such persons are excommunicated solely on account of their deeds, as stated in the Title concerning Excommunications, and they should lose everything they have, and become the property of the king. . . .

LAW VI.

What Authority Masters Have Over Their Slaves.

A master has complete authority over his slave to dispose of him as he pleases. Nevertheless, he should not kill or wound him, although he may give him cause for it, except by order of the judge of the district; nor should he strike him in a way contrary to natural reason, or put him to death by starvation; except where he finds him with his wife or his daughter, or where he commits some other offence of this kind, for then he has certainly a right to kill him. We also decree that, where a man is so cruel to his slaves as to kill them by starvation, or to wound or injure them so seriously that they cannot endure it, in cases of this kind said slaves can complain to the judge; and the latter in the discharge of his official duty should investigate and ascertain whether the charge is true, and if he finds that it is, he should sell the slaves, and give the price of them to their master; and he should do this in such a way that they never can be again placed in the power, or under the authority of the party through whose fault they were sold.

LAW VIII.

Neither a Jew Nor a Moor Can Hold a Christian as a Slave.

Neither a Jew, a Moor, a heretic, nor anyone else who does not acknowledge our religion, can hold a Christian as a slave. Anyone who violates this law, by knowingly holding a Christian in servitude, shall lose his life on that account, and forfeit all his property to the king. We also decree that if any of the persons aforesaid has a slave that does not acknowledge our religion, and said slave becomes a Christian, the latter will be free for that reason, as soon as he is baptized and accepts our faith; nor will he be required to pay anything for himself to the party to whom he belonged before he became a Christian; and even though the party who was his master may subsequently become a Christian, he will retain no rights in said person who was his slave and became a Christian before he did.

This is understood to apply where a Jew, or a Moor purchases a slave who becomes a Christian, with the intention of making use of his services and not for the purpose of disposing of him in trade. If, however, he buys him with the intention of selling him, he should do so within three months; and if, before the said three months have expired, and while his master was making an attempt to sell him, he should become a Christian, the said Jew or Moor should not, for that reason, lose all the price he paid for him, but we decree that the slave shall be required to pay for himself, or the party who caused him to become a Christian should pay for him, twelve maravedis of the money current in that locality; and where he has not the means to pay them, he should give his services instead of them, not as a slave but as a freeman, until he is entitled to that amount. If he should not be sold within the three months aforesaid, the party who was his master will retain no rights in him, even though he may subsequently become a Christian. . . .

TITLE XXV.

Concerning the Moors.

The Moors are a people who believe that Mohammed was the Prophet and Messenger of God, and for the reason that the works which he performed do not indicate the extraordinary sanctity which belongs to such a sacred calling, his religion is, as it were, an insult to God. Wherefore, since in the preceding Title we treated of the Jews and of the obstinacy which they display toward the true faith, we intend to speak here of the Moors, and of their foolish belief by which they think they will be saved. We shall show why they have this name: how many kinds of them there are; how they should live among Christians, and what things they are forbidden to do while they live there: how Christians should convert them to the Faith by kind words, and not by violence or compulsion: and what punishment those deserve who prevent them from becoming Christians, or dishonor them by word or deed after they have been converted, and also to what penalty a Christian who becomes a Moor, is liable.

LAW I.

Whence the Name of Moor Is Derived, How Many Kinds of the Latter There Are, and in What Way They Should Live Among Christians

Sarracenus, in Latin, means Moor, in Castilian, and this name is derived from Sarah, the free wife of Abraham, although the lineage of the Moors is not traced to her, but to Hagar, who was Abraham's servant. There are two kinds of Moors; some do not believe in either the New or the Old Testament; the others accept the five books of Moses, but reject the Prophets and do not believe them. The latter are called Samaritans because they first appeared in the city called Samaria, and these are mentioned in the Gospel where it is stated that the Jews and the Samaritans should not associate with one another or live together.

We decree that Moors shall live among Christians in the same way that we mentioned in the preceding Title that Jews shall do, by observing their own law and not insulting ours. Moors, however, shall not have mosques in Christian towns, or make their sacrifices publicly in the presence of men. The mosques which they formerly possessed shall belong to the king; and he can give them to whomsoever he wishes. Although the Moors do not acknowledge a good religion, so long as they live among Christians with their assurance of security, their property shall not be stolen from them or taken by force; and we order that whoever violates this law shall pay a sum equal to double the value of what he took.

LAW II.

Christians Should Convert the Moors by Kind Words, and Not by Compulsion.

Christians should endeavor to convert the Moors by causing them to believe in our religion, and bring them into it by kind words and suitable discourses, and not by violence or compulsion; for if it should be the will of Our Lord to bring them into it and to make them believe by force, He can use compulsion against them if He so desires, since He has full power to do so; but He is not pleased with the service which men perform through fear, but with that which they do voluntarily and without coercion, and as He does not wish to restrain them or employ violence, we forbid anyone to do so for this purpose; and if the wish to become Christians should arise among them, we forbid anyone to refuse assent to it, or oppose it in any way whatsoever. Whoever violates this law shall receive the penalty we mentioned in the preceding Title, which treats of how Jews who interfere with, or kill those belonging to their religion who afterwards become Christians, shall be punished.

LAW III.

What Punishment Those Deserve Who Insult Converts.

Many men live and die in strange beliefs, who would love to be Christians if it were not for the villification and dishonor which they see others who become converted endure by being called turncoats, and calumniated and insulted in many evil ways; and we hold that those who do this wickedly offend, and that they should honor persons of this kind for many reasons, and not show them disrespect. One of these is because they renounce the religion in which they and their families were born; and another is because, after they have understanding, they acknowledge the superiority of our religion and accept it, separating from their parents and their relatives, and abandoning the life which they have been accustomed to live, and all other things from which they derive pleasure. There are some of them who, on account of the dishonor inflicted upon them after they have adopted our Faith, and become Christians, repent and desert it, closing their hearts against it on account of the insults and reproaches to which they are subjected; and for this reason we order all Christians, of both sexes, in our dominions to show honor and kindness, in every way they can, to persons of other or strange beliefs, who embrace our religion; just as they would do to any of their own parents or grandparents, who had embraced the faith or become Christians; and we forbid anyone to dishonor them by word or deed, or do them any wrong, injury, or harm in any way whatever. If anyone violates this law we order that he be punished for it, as seems best to the judges of the district; and that the punishment be more severe than if the injury had been committed against another man or woman whose entire line of ancestors had been Christians.

LAW IV.

What Punishment a Christian Deserves Who Becomes a Moor.

Men sometimes become insane and lose their prudence and understanding, as, for instance, where unfortunate persons, and those who despair of everything, renounce the faith of Our Lord Jesus Christ, and become Moors; and there are some of them who are induced to do this through the desire to live according to their customs, or on account of the loss of relatives who have been killed or died; or because they have lost their property and become poor; or because of unlawful acts which they commit, dreading the punishment which they deserve on account of them; and when they are induced to do a thing of this kind for any of the reasons aforesaid, or others similar to them, they are guilty of very great wickedness and treason, for on account of no loss or affliction which may come upon them, nor for any profit, riches, good fortune, or pleasure which they may expect to obtain in this world, should they renounce the faith of Our Lord Jesus Christ by which they will be saved and have everlasting life.

Wherefore we order that all those who are guilty of this wickedness shall lose all their possessions, and have no right to any portion of them, but that all shall belong to their children (if they have any) who remain steadfast in our Faith and do not renounce it; and if they have no children, their property shall belong to their nearest relatives within the tenth degree, who remain steadfast in the belief of the Christians; and if they have neither children nor relatives, all their possessions shall be forfeited to the royal treasury; and, in addition to this, we order that if any person who has committed such an offense shall be found in any part of our dominions he shall be put to death.

Document 19

Alonso de Espinosa, *The Guanches of Tenerife*, trans. Clements Markham, Hakluyt Society Publications, series 2, no. 21 (London: The Society, 1907), pp. 84–86, 87–91.

Alonso de Espinosa, a Dominican friar, wrote the history of the conquest of the native population of the island of Tenerife in the Canary Islands between 1580 and 1590. Like the works of his fellow Dominican, Bartholomew de las Casas (1474–1566), which judged the Spanish conquest of the Americas to be unjust, Espinosa's writings denied the legitimacy of the conquest of these inhabitants of an island chain far removed from Spain and clearly posing no threat to the security of Spain. In his opinion, it was the greed and the pride of the Castilians that caused them to conquer these islands, and not any sincere desire to convert the natives.—*ed.*

In the year 1417, at the prayer and request of Moser Rubin de Bracamonte, Admiral of France, the King Don Juan II[1] granted the conquest of those seven islands to a French knight named Monsieur Jean de Betencourt, with the title of King of Canaria, and as Bishop of them he named Fray Mendo who went there and saw them all. The said Monsieur Jean de Betencourt, having easily subdued the islands of Lanzarote and Fuerteventura, made his abode in Lanzarote, whence he began the conquest of the other islands. He commenced with Gomera and Hierro, because they were less populous, and therefore easier to subdue.

On the death of this knight, his rights were inherited by a relation named Monsieur Menaut de Betencourt who illtreated his vassals, and they made a complaint against him to the King Don Juan, who, having received the information, sent Pedro Barba, with three armed vessels, to take the government from Menaut. After some trouble, they came to an agreement, and Pedro Barba bought the islands and the conquest of them, with the approval of the King Don Juan and of the Queen Doña Catalina, his mother.

---

1. John II of Castile (1406–54).

Pedro Barba sold them to Hernan Perez, a knight of Seville, from whom they say that the Duke of Medina Sidonia held them. They were next sold to Guillen de las Casas, from whom they were bought by Hernan Peraça, father of Doña Inez Peraça, who inherited them. She married Diego de Herrera, brother of the Marshal Lord of Ampudia, Don Diego de Ayala. The Herrera family being in possession, their vassals made complaints to the Royal Council of certain injuries they had received. Their petition having been considered by the Council, an order was sent to Doña Inez Peraça, as proprietary lady of the islands, to come personally to the court to defend herself. As she called herself Queen of the Canary Islands, and this was the first time she had been to court, she embarked at Lanzarote with the best company she could get together, and presented herself before the Kings Don Fernando[2] and Doña Isabel.[3] Having kissed hands, she presented her defence, and a law-suit was commenced in the Royal Council. During its course, the kings became aware that Diego de Herrera and Doña Inez did not possess the possibility or the means of conquering the remaining islands, which were Canaria, Tenerife, and Palma. Their Highnesses, therefore, decided to purchase the rights for 6 quentos de maravedis; and that the Herreras should sell and give up their rights they held in these islands to the royal crown of Castille, retaining the other islands of Gomera, Hierro, Lanzarote, and Fuerteventura, which are possessed by their descendants. The three best islands, of which we are about to treat, became the patrimony of the crown.

Some years having passed since the above purchase, the Governor of Canaria, a knight of Xeres, named Pedro de Vera, having subjugated that island in 1483, came to the conclusion that, in order that Canaria might continue quiet and in peace, it would be well to get the principal and most valiant of the natives out of that island by engaging them in the conquest of Tenerife. With this object he embarked, with the greater part of the Canarians and a force of Spaniards. He came to this island. I do not know at what port he landed, but he prepared his Canarians by telling them that if they fought like men, and were loyal, they would receive great benefits, and the king, their lord, would show them much favour. This was declared to them by Guillen Castellano, the interpreter. Seeing that the Governor showed them goodwill, they made an entry into the island, and captured many people with their flocks. For the object was not to found a colony, but to give employment to the Canarians. The Governor embarked with his captives, and ordered that all the Canarians should embark in another ship commanded by his son, Hernando de Vera, who, during the night, parted company and took the route to Spain, taking the

---

2. Ferdinand II of Aragon (1479–1516).
3. Isabella of Castile (1474–1504).

Canarians with him. But he did not reach Spain on that voyage, nor did he succeed in his intention, as will be seen in the history of Canaria.

Some years afterwards, owing to the death of Don Juan de Frias, Bishop of Canaria, Fray Miguel de la Serna was promoted to the See. The new Bishop looked upon it as a serious thing that Pedro de Vera should have sold and delivered as captives the people of Gomera, on the death of their Lord Hernan Peraça, husband of Doña Leonor de Bobadilla. He made a criminal accusation against the Governor before their Highnesses, that being Christians and not culprits, he had committed an offence against them. In consequence of this, the said Governor, Pedro de Vera, was recalled to Spain by the Catholic king. . . .

When peace was established in the Island of Canaria, several attacks were made on Tenerife, as has been mentioned: for it was seen that it was fertile and thickly inhabited, with a great number of flocks; for at the time that the Spaniards first came there were over 200,000 head of goats and sheep.

The knights of the conquests were anxious to win renown, and to see new lands; so they sought means for the conquest of Tenerife and of Palma. One of these was Alonso de Lugo, brother-in-law of the wife of Pedro del Algava, former Governor of Canaria, who was beheaded, on false accusations and information by the Captain Juan Rejon. This knight of whom I am treating, Alonso de Lugo, was in the conquest of Canaria almost from the very beginning, and, as a man renowned for his valour, he had the charge and tenancy of the tower of Agaete, that he might subdue that part. He was very dexterous in this war, and from the side of Agaete he had made several entries into Tenerife. Thus he had some knowledge of the people. Moved by the execution of the said Governor, although it was some time since it took place, Alonso de Lugo went to Court, to petition for justice against the said Juan Rejon. There he received the news that his enemy was dead, having been killed by Hernan Peraça. He, therefore, desisted from the prosecution. Alonso de Lugo then procured from their Majesties the conquests of Tenerife and Palma, which had been granted to Juan Rejon. It was at the time when the conquest of Granada had been completed, and so his affair was quickly despatched, for the Kings then had more leisure. Alonso de Lugo offered to undertake the said conquest at his own cost, and that of his friends, and their Majesties gave him the title of Governor of the Conquest and Captain-General of the parts of Africa from the Cape of Aguer to the Cape Bojador. The islands being conquered, he was to be partitioner of the lands jointly with another, who would be named by their Majesties. This was arranged then; but on the 5th of November 1496, power was sent to him to divide the land without a colleague, which he did.

Having obtained the concessions, Alonso de Lugo was joined by many persons of note. Among these were Hernando del Hoyo, of the royal household; Pedro de Vergara, Hieronimo de Valdes, son of Pedro de Algava, also of the royal household; Bartolomé Benitez, Pedro Benitez, the one-eyed, a man well disposed and most valiant, with many others. They came to Gran Canaria, where, having raised their banner, they were joined by many soldiers, as well among the Spanish conquerors as among the native Canarians. Among the latter were Guadarteme, Maninidra, Gonzalo Mendez Castellano, Pedro Mayor, Pedro de Eruas, Thomé de Armas, Juan Dara (whose former name was Dutindana), Juan Pascual, with many others. They made for the island of Palma, which, owing to the cowardice of the natives, was soon conquered. Leaving some of their people to settle there, they returned, after a prosperous voyage, to Gran Canaria. Troops and necessary stores were collected for the next enterprise, and they set out with more than a thousand soldiers in a small fleet for Tenerife.

They entered the port which is called Santa Cruz, and landed in May 1493, with little opposition on the part of those on shore, though not without some skirmishes and encounters. Thence they ascended the cuesta, marching to Laguna, where the camp was formed at the place where the hermitage called "Of Grace" was afterwards founded. It was in the lordship of Tegueste.

Acaimo, the Lord of Guimar, came to confirm the treaties he had made with Diego de Herrera and other captains; for this Lord (by reason of the image of Candelaria which he had in his possession) was always friendly to the Christians. He supplied the Governor of the Conquest, Alonso de Lugo, with information respecting the number of men that the Overlord of Taoro, named Quebihi Bencomo, had with him.

It was not long before the said Overlord Bencomo, being a courageous man, who had already gained experience of the Spanish forces in previous encounters, and not thinking much of them, came in person, with only 300 men, to see the Governor, and to ascertain the object of his coming; for he had remained longer than on former occasions.

The Governor said, through his interpreter, Guillen Castellano, that he came to obtain the Overlord's friendship, to require that he and his people should become Christians, as those of the other neighbouring islands had done, and that they should submit themselves as subjects to the King of Spain, that they might receive many benefits under his rule and protection. The Overlord replied, not like a barbarian, but like the man of discretion that he was—for this dignity of Sovereign brings discretion with it. As regards the request for friendship, he said that no one who was not provoked or irritated by another need fly or seek refuge, and that this was well understood; and that he would grant the request willingly if the Spaniards would depart and leave them in peace; in which case he would gladly serve them with what they needed. As for being Christians, he did not know what Christianity was, nor did he understand that religion. If he was informed respecting it, he could with more intelligence give an answer. As to being subject to the King of Spain, the proposal did not appear to him to be reasonable, for he had never acknowledged subjection to another man. After some other discussion between them, which settled nothing, the Overlord returned with his followers to Taoro, leaving our people in their camp.

It is an acknowledged fact, both as regards divine and human right, that the wars waged by the Spaniards against the natives of these islands, as well as against the Indians in the western regions, were unjust and without any reason to support them. For the natives had not taken the lands of Christians, nor had they gone beyond their own frontier to molest or invade their neighbours. If it is said that the Spaniards brought the Gospel, this should have been done by admonition and preaching— not by drum and banner; by persuasion, not by force.

IV

The Germans Push East

Introduction

Among the major powers of modern Europe, Germany stands out as the nation that had the least experience of overseas colonization. With the exception of some comparatively unproductive regions in Africa and a handful of islands in the Pacific, regions acquired in the last half of the nineteenth century, Germany missed the landrush that began in the late fifteenth century.[1] This does not mean that the Germans have historically not shown any interest in expansion beyond their borders. Rather, it means that German expansion has been devoted almost entirely to the conquest of those regions that bordered the original German kingdom. Furthermore, at the point at which the major European powers began to move overseas, Germany was wracked by the Reformation and the wars of religion which followed. The result was a badly fragmented German kingdom that lacked the resources to develop an overseas empire. Only after the unification of Germany in the nineteenth century was much attention paid to colonization and then more for reasons of national prestige than for economic reasons.[2]

During the reigns of the Saxon Emperors, beginning with that of Otto I (936–73), the effort to expand beyond the borders of Germany, specifically beyond the limits of the Duchy of Saxony, began. Saxony itself had originally been conquered and Christianized by the expanding Carolingian Empire in the late eighth century.[3] The Saxon emperors revived the imperial title, which Charlemagne and his immediate successors held, and attempted to emulate Charlemagne's imperial sway. Logically, they sought to combine missionary and colonizing efforts as the Carolingians had done. The great symbol of medieval German expansion was the frontier archbishopric with its network of suffragan bishoprics planted among the infidels.[4] When Otto I began the work of extending the borders of Saxony

---

1. Some of the small German principalities did establish trading stations overseas. The Brandenburg Company, for example, had a slaving station in West Africa from 1682 to 1717; see D. K. Fieldhouse, *The Colonial Empires* (New York: Delacorte, 1966), p. 134.
2. Mary Evelyn Townsend, *The Rise and Fall of Germany's Colonial Empire 1884–1918* (New York: Macmillan, 1930), pp. 1–28.
3. Stewart C. Easton and Helene Wieruszowski, eds., *The Era of Charlemagne* (Princeton: D. van Nostrand, 1961), pp. 117–22.
4. Geoffrey Barraclough, *The Origins of Modern Germany*, 2nd rev. ed. (Oxford: Blackwell, 1947), pp. 41–42.

north and east of the Elbe River, into Scandinavia and into the Slavic lands, two archbishoprics served as headquarters for the effort. The diocese of Hamburg-Bremen, which had been founded in 834 as an outpost of the Carolingian empire, was, under the Saxon emperors, turned into a center for the conversion of Scandinavia and the regions to the west. The archbishops were interested not only in neighboring Denmark, but in Christians as far away as Iceland, Greenland, and even Vinland (doc. 20).[5] Magdeburg served the same role in the conquest and conversion of the Slavs after its creation in 968. Eventually, the appearance of a series of independent Christian kingdoms to the north (Denmark, Norway, and Sweden) and to the east (Poland, Bohemia, and Hungary) blocked most further German expansion. The remaining effort was expended in the northeast, along the shores of the Baltic, where a number of infidel peoples, Pomeranians, Letts, Prussians, and others, remained (doc. 21). The Germans poured the same kind of crusading energy into northeastern Europe that the French poured into the lands at the eastern end of the Mediterranean. An order of crusading knights, the Teutonic Knights, was established along the lines of the orders of warrior-monks that developed during the crusades in the Holy Land.[6]

Once the lands of eastern Europe were open to German settlement, it was necessary to recruit settlers to occupy the land. Peasants were encouraged to abandon the overpopulated regions of Europe, such as Flanders, and migrate to the east (doc. 22). Those who came received land and in return promised to perform military service. In many cases they held their land from ecclesiastical officials, as fiefs of a diocese or of a religious order (docs. 23 and 24). The work of conquest was a continuing one. Converts apostatized and seemingly peaceful infidels rebelled (docs. 25 and 26). The frontier was constantly in need of new recruits. Because the settlers were expected to work the land themselves, not simply supervise the work of a class of conquered Slavs, the status of the peasant who moved to the east was that of a freeman. Serfdom did not take hold in eastern Germany until the sixteenth century when, paradoxically, it had largely ended in western Europe.[7]

5. Adam of Bremen's History contains the oldest reference to Vinland in European geographical literature: see R. A. Skelton, Thomas E. Marston and George D. Painter, The Vinland Map and the Tartar Relation (New Haven: Yale Univ. Press, 1965), p. 172. If the Vinland map is authentic, something many experts doubt, it would provide another small link between medieval and modern exploration. For a discussion of the map's authenticity, see Armando Cortesão, "Is the Vinland Map Genuine?", Proceedings of the Vinland Map Conference, ed. Wilcomb E. Washburn (Chicago: Univ. of Chicago Press for the Newberry Library, 1971), pp. 15-18.

6. A convenient introduction to the History of the Knights is provided in Alexander Bruce-Boswell, "The Teutonic Order," in The Cambridge Mediaeval History, eds. H. M. Gwatkin and J. P. Whitney, 8 vols., vol. 7, Decline of Empire and Papacy (Cambridge, Eng.: Cambridge Univ. Press, 1932), pp. 248-69.

7. Barraclough, pp. 392-94.

During the fourteenth century, German eastward expansion was slowed and finally stopped. The union of Poland and Lithuania under Jagiello in 1386 marked the beginning of the end.[8] The Teutonic Knights lost a number of battles to the army of the combined kingdom. The climax came at the battle of Tannenberg in 1410 when the Knights were decisively beaten.[9] The signing of the Second Peace of Thorn in 1446 signaled the end of German expansion in the Baltic region.

German expansion was justified in the same terms as expansion elsewhere. The conversion of the infidel was given high priority, at least on paper. At the same time, trade was a much more important motive. The Hanseatic League, an association of trading cities headed by Lübeck, was anxious to develop trade so that merchants as well as peasants migrated to the east, setting up towns to serve as marketplaces.[10] The conflicting interests of peasants, merchants, and missionary clergy led to different opinions about the native population. Henry of Livonia, for example, who saw baptism as radically transforming the barbarous natives, feared that the influx of farmers and merchants would scandalize the converts, so he favored having priests rather than laymen rule them. This suggestion anticipated the Reductions (ecclesiastically directed estates), which the Jesuits created in sixteenth century Paraguay in order to protect their converts from contact with the Conquistadors. Helmold of Bosau saw the natives in kinder terms, as men possessing important natural virtues. His description of the Prussians as being disinterested in riches was probably an indirect slap at the greed of his countrymen who were devouring the lands of the conquered infidels. Like Thomas More and many other later critics of their own times, Helmold used an idealized portrait of an primitive people in order to criticize his contemporaries. For the settlers actually living on the frontier and in constant fear of uprisings that could wipe out an entire settlement, the native population would have appeared in a much harsher light.

8. Ibid., 270–71.
9. Ironically, the Germans defeated the Russians in this same area at the outset of World War I.
10. On the role of the League in the conquest, see Philippe Dollinger, *The German Hansa*, trans. and ed., D. S. Ault (Stanford: Stanford Univ. Press, 1970), pp. 19–44.

Bibliography

An old but still useful history of Germany in the Middle Ages that gives special emphasis to the expansion of Germany is James Westfall Thompson, *Feudal Germany*, 2 vols. (Chicago: Univ. of Chicago Press, 1928). The continuous nature of German interest in eastern Europe is discussed in Hermann Schreiber, *Teuton and Slav: The Struggle for Central Europe*, trans. James Cleugh (New York: Alfred A. Knopf, 1965). The rise of the independent kingdoms of eastern and central Europe that blocked German expansion is dealt with in Oscar Halecki, *Borderlands of Western Civilization* (New York: Ronald Press, 1952). In recent years, interest in the lands along the Baltic has given rise to a scholarly journal devoted to the history of the region that contains articles on the medieval period: *The Journal of Baltic Studies* (1970–). For the relations of the Germans with their neighbors to the north, see Halvdan Koht, "The Scandinavian Kingdoms During the Fourteenth and Fifteenth Centuries," *Cambridge Mediaeval History*, vol. 8, *The Close of the Middle Ages* (Cambridge, Eng.: Cambridge Univ. Press, 1936), pp. 533–55.

Document 20

Adam of Bremen, *History of the Archbishops of Hamburg-Bremen*, ed. Francis J. Tschan, Records of Civilization, Sources and Studies, no. 53 (New York: Columbia Univ. Press, 1959), pp. 61–63, 83–85, 105–6, 179–81, 218–19.

For Adam of Bremen, the story of German expansion was the story of conversion of the infidel to Christianity. During his career as a canon of the cathedral at Bremen (ca. 1066–ca. 1085), Adam penned the glories of his church and its bishops in the work of bringing Christianity to the Scandinavians to the North and the Slavs to the East. The work began with the conversion of Saxony itself during the eighth century by English missionaries. Then the work advanced under the sponsorship of Charlemagne and his sons. The diocese of Hamburg-Bremen came into its own with the emergence of the line of great Saxon emperors of Germany that began with Otto I (936–73). Founded by the forced union of two separate dioceses in 864, the combined diocese became responsible for suffragan bishops established in Denmark after Otto I had defeated the Danish king. Like the Carolingians, the Ottonians used ecclesiastical institutions to organize and consolidate their conquests. Adam, however, like many other missionaries, believed that the colonists and adventurers who entered the newly converted regions scandalized the converts and caused them to fall away from the Faith.—ed.

When in those days Otto the Great had subjugated the Slavic peoples and bound them to the Christian faith, he built on the banks of the Elbe River the renowned city of Magdeburg and, designating it as the metropolitan see for the Slavs, had Adalbert, a man of the greatest sanctity, consecrated as its archbishop. This man was the first prelate to be consecrated in Magdeburg, and he administered his episcopal office with untiring energy for twelve years. By his preaching he converted many of the Slavic peoples. His consecration took place in the thirty-fifth year of the emperor and of our archbishop, and one hundred and thirty-seven years had passed since the consecration of Saint Ansgar.[1]

To the archbishopric of Magdeburg was subjected all Slavia as far as the Peene River. There were five suffragan bishoprics. Of these Merseburg and Zeitz were established on the Saale River, Meissen on the Elbe

1. The year 969.

Brandenburg and Havelberg farther inland. The sixth bishopric of Slavia is Oldenburg. Because it is nearer to us, the emperor put it under the jurisdiction of the archbishopric of Hamburg. For it our archbishop consecrated as the first bishop Ebrachar or Egward, whom in Latin we call Evagrius.

And because occasion has presented itself here, it seems proper to set forth what peoples across the Elbe belong to the diocese of Hamburg. The diocese is bounded on the west by the British Ocean;[2] on the south by the Elbe River; on the east by the Peene River, which flows into the Barbarian Sea; on the north by the Eider River, which divides the Danes from the Saxons. There are three Transalbingian Saxon peoples. The first, along the ocean, are the Ditmarshians and their mother church is at Meldorf. The second are the Holzatians, named from the woods near which they dwell. The Stör River flows through their midst. Their church is at Schenefeld. The third and best-known are called Sturmarians because they are a folk frequently stirred up by dissension. Among them the metropolis Hamburg lifts up its head, at one time mighty in men and arms, happy in its fields and crops; but now, suffering vengeance for its sins, turned into a wilderness. Although this metropolis has lost its urban attraction, it still retains its strength, consoled for the misfortune of its widowhood by the progress of its sons, whom it sees daily enlarging its mission throughout the length and breadth of the north. They seem to justify one in crying out with much joy, "I have declared and I have spoken; they are multiplied above number."

We have also found that the boundaries of Saxony across the Elbe were drawn by Charles and other emperors as follows: The first extends from the east bank of the Elbe up to the rivulet which the Slavs call Boize. From that stream the line runs through the Delvunder wood up to the Delvenau River. And so it goes on to the Hornbecker Mühlen-Bach and to the source of the Bille, thence to Liudwinestein and Weisbirken and Barkhorst. Then it passes on through Süderbeste to the Trave woods and again through this forest to Blunk. Next it goes to the Tensfelder Au and ascends directly up to the ford called Agrimeswidil. At that place, too, Burwid fought a duel with a Slavic champion and slew him; and a memorial stone has been put in that spot. Thence the line runs up, going to the Stocksee, and thus on to the Zwentifeld. . . .

In the meantime the thousandth year since the incarnation of our Lord was happily completed and this was the archbishop's twelfth year. The following year the most valiant emperor Otto,[3] who had already conquered the Danes, the Slavs, likewise also the Franks and Italians, succumbed,

2. The North Sea.
3. Otto III (983–1002).

overtaken by an untimely death, after he had thrice entered Rome as victor. After his death the kingdom remained in confusion. Then, indeed, the Slavs, more than fairly oppressed by their Christian rulers, at length threw off the yoke of servitude and had to take up arms in defense of their freedom. Mistivoi and Mizzidrag were the chiefs of the Winuli under whose leadership the rebellion flared up. Under these leaders the rebel Slavs wasted first the whole of Nordalbingia with fire and sword; then, going through the rest of Slavia, they set fire to all the churches and tore them down to the ground. They also murdered the priests and the other ministers of the churches with diverse tortures and left not a vestige of Christianity beyond the Elbe.

At Hamburg, then and later, many clerics and citizens were led off into captivity, and even more were put to death out of hatred for Christianity. The long-to-be-remembered king of the Danes who held in memory all the deeds of the barbarians as if they had been written down told us how Oldenburg had been a city heavily populated with Christians. "There," he said, "sixty priests—the rest had been slaughtered like cattle—were kept for mockery. The oldest of these, the provost of the place, and our kinsman, was named Oddar. Now, he and others were martyred in this manner: after the skin of their heads had been cut with an iron in the form of a cross, the brain of each was laid bare; with hands tied behind their backs, the confessors of God were then dragged through one Slavic town after another, harried either with blows or in some other manner, until they died. After having been thus made "a spectacle . . . to angels and to men," they breathed forth their victorious spirits in the middle of the course." Many deeds of this kind, which for lack of written records are now regarded as fables, are remembered as having been done at this time in the several provinces of the Slavs. When I questioned the king further about them, he said, "Stop, son. We have so many martyrs in Denmark and Slavia that they can hardly be comprehended in a book."

And so all the Slavs who dwell between the Elbe and the Oder and who had practiced the Christian religion for seventy years and more, during all the time of the Otto's, cut themselves off from the body of Christ and of the Church with which they had before been joined. Oh, truly the judgments of God over men are hidden, "Therefore He hath mercy on whom He will; and whom He will He hardeneth." Marveling at His omnipotence, we see those who were the first to believe fall back into paganism; those, however, who seemed to be the very last, converted to Christ. But He, the "just judge, strong and patient," who of old wiped out in the sight of Israel the seven tribes of Canaan, and kept only the strangers, by whom the transgressors might be punished—He, I say, willed now to harden a small part of the heathen through whom He might confound our faithlessness. . . .

While he left these monuments of his activity at Bremen, he forthwith addressed himself with all the love of his heart to the building up of the church at Hamburg. There, indeed, after the Slavic cataclysm of which we have given an account above, Archbishop Unwan and along with him Duke Bernhard had built a stately fortress from the ruins of the old city and erected a church and dwelling places, all of wood. Archbishop Alebrand, however, thought a somewhat stronger defense against the frequent incursions of enemies was necessary for an unprotected place, and first of all rebuilt of squared stone the church that had been erected in honor of the Mother of God. Then he constructed for himself another stone house, strongly fortified with towers and battlements. In emulation of this work the duke was roused to provide lodging for his men within the same fortified area. In a word, when the city had thus been rebuilt, the basilica was flanked on one side by the bishop's residence, on the other by the duke's palace. The noble archbishop also planned to have the metropolis of Hamburg girded with a wall and fortified with towers, had his swift death not interfered with his desires.

Across the Elbe and throughout the realm there was a firm peace at that time. The princes of the Slavs, Anadrag and Gneus and Ratibor, came peacefully to Hamburg and rendered military service to the duke and prelate. But then as now the duke and bishop worked at cross purposes among the Winuli people; the duke, indeed, striving to increase the tribute; the archbishop, to spread Christianity. It is clear to me that because of the efforts of the priests the Christian religion would long ago have become strong there if the avarice of the princes had not hindered the conversion of the folk.

The archbishop was also, in the manner of his predecessors, solicitous about the mission among the heathen with which he had been entrusted, and he consecrated as coadjutors in the preaching bishops Rudolf, one of his chaplains, for Schleswig; Abhelin for Slavia; Wal, of the chapter at Bremen, for Ribe; while the others, who were mentioned above, still lived and were not idle in the vineyard of God. . . .

Although our great archbishop Adalbert knew that all his predecessors had worked zealously in the mission which the Church at Hamburg traditionally carried on among the heathen, he extended the archiepiscopal sway far and wide over the farther nations ever more magnificently than the others had done. On this account he sedulously set about undertaking that mission himself, to see if he could bring the tidings of salvation to peoples not yet converted or impart perfection to those already converted. With his usual ostentation he began to boast about the laborious tour he would have to make: that the first evangelist had been Ansgar, then Rimbert, after that Unni; but he, the fourth evangelist, was called for because he had noticed the rest of his predecessors had toiled at the burdensome task through their suffragans and not in person. When he was certain of going, he decided to arrange his itinerary in a manner that would enable him to cover in his travels the expanse of the north, that is, Denmark, Sweden, and Norway, and cross thence to the Orkneys and to Iceland, the farthermost land of the earth. For these peoples had in his time and by his efforts been converted to the Christian faith. He was duly dissuaded from setting out on this journey, with which he already was publicly busied, by the very prudent king of the Danes, who told him that the barbarian peoples could more easily be converted by men like them in language and customs than by persons unacquainted with their ways and strange to their kind. And further, that there was nothing for him to do except by his generosity and affability to gain the good will and fidelity of those whom he found prepared to preach the Word of God to the heathen. In respect of this exhortation our metropolitan was in accord with the orthodox king and began to extend the liberality with which he treated all much more indulgently to the bishops of the heathen and to the legates of the eastern kings. Each one of them he received, entertained, and dismissed with such good cheer that, after the pope, they all sought him of their own accord as the father of many peoples, offering him extraordinary gifts and bringing back his blessing for a favor.

In respect of his mission the archbishop was, therefore, such as both the times and the manners of men would have him be—so affable, so munificent, so hospitable toward everyone that little Bremen was, because of his greatness, widely spoken of as the equal of Rome and sought by people in troops from all parts of the world, especially by the northern peoples. Of these the Icelanders and Greenlanders and the legates of the Goths and Orkney Islands came the farthest, entreating him to send preachers thither, as indeed he immediately did. For Denmark, Sweden, Norway, and the islands of the sea he also consecrated many bishops, of whom he himself used to say joyfully, "The harvest, indeed, is great, but the laborers are few. Pray ye therefore the Lord of the harvest, that he send forth laborers into his harvest." . . .

In the ocean there are very many other islands of which not the least is Greenland, situated far out in the ocean opposite the mountains of Sweden and the Rhiphaean range. To this island they say it is from five to seven days' sail from the coast of Norway, the same as to Iceland. The people there are greenish from the salt water, whence, too, that region gets its name. The people live in the same manner as the Icelanders except that they are fiercer and trouble seafarers by their piratical attacks. Report has it that Christianity of late has also winged its way to them.

The third island is Helgeland, nearer to Norway but in extent not unequal to the rest. That island sees the sun upon the land for fourteen days continuously at the solstice in summer and, similarly, it lacks the sun for the same number of days in the winter. To the barbarians, who do not know that the difference in the length of days is due to the accession and recession of the sun, this is astounding and mysterious. For on account of the rotundity of the earth, the sun in its course necessarily brings day as it approaches a place, and leaves night as it recedes from it. While the sun is approaching the summer solstice, the day is lengthened for those who live in the northern parts and the nights shortened; when it descends to the winter solstice, that is for the same reason the experience of southerners. Not knowing this, the pagans call that land holy and blessed which affords mortals such a wonder. The king of the Danes and many others have attested the occurrence of this phenomenon there, as in Sweden and in Norway and on the rest of the islands in those parts.

He spoke also of yet another island of the many found in that ocean. It is called Vinland because vines producing excellent wine grow wild there. That unsown crops also abound on that island we have ascertained not from fabulous reports but from the trustworthy relation of the Danes. Beyond that island, he said, no habitable land is found in that ocean, but every place beyond it is full of impenetrable ice and intense darkness.

Document 21

Helmold, The Chronicle of the Slavs, ed. Francis J. Tschan, Records of Civilization, Sources and Studies, no. 21 (New York: Columbia Univ. Press, 1935), pp. 46–47, 220–21, 235–36, 254–55
Helmold of Bosau (ca. 1118–ca. 1172) was a German priest closely connected with the expansion of German Christianity into the Slavic lands. He had first-hand knowledge of the progress of Christianization in the east, having accompanied a newly installed bishop of Oldenburg on his first visitation of his diocese. The diocese was the fundamental tool of German eastward expansion, bringing the Slavs not only into the Christian Church, but bringing them under German political domination as well. Although Helmold seems to have been optimistic about the conversion of the peoples of eastern Europe, he also pointed out the dangers of living on the frontier. Constant warfare with the Slavs and the pressure of the German push eastward, pressure supported by settlers brought in from overcrowded parts of northern Europe, led to the subjugation of the native population.—ed.

Although the Prussians do not yet know the light of the faith, [they are, nevertheless] men endowed with many natural gifts. Most humane toward those in need, they even go out to meet and to help those who are in danger on the sea or who are attacked by pirates. Gold and silver they hold in very slight esteem. They have an abundance of strange furs, the odor of which has inoculated our world with the deadly poison of pride; but these, indeed, they regard as dung, to our condemnation, I believe, for we hanker after a marten-skin robe as much as for supreme happiness. Therefore, they offer their very precious marten furs for the woolen garments which we call *faldones*. Many praiseworthy things could be said about this people with respect to their morals, if only they had the faith of Christ whose missionaries they cruelly persecute. At their hands Adalbert, the illustrious bishop of Bohemia, received the crown of martyrdom. Although they share everything else with our people they prohibit only, to this very day, access to their groves and springs which, they aver, are polluted by the entry of Christians. They take the meat of their draft animals for food and use their milk and blood as drink so freely that they are said to become intoxicated. These men have blue eyes, ruddy faces, and long hair. Living, moreover, in inaccessible swamps they will not endure a master among them. . . .

The following Lord's day all the people of the land convened in the market place at Lübeck and the lord bishop came and exhorted the assemblage to give up their idols and worship the one God who is in heaven, to receive the grace of baptism and renounce their evil works; namely, the plundering and killing of Christians. And when he had finished speaking to the congregation Pribislav, with the consent of the others, said:

> Your words, O venerable prelate, are the words of God and are meet for our salvation. But how shall we, ensnared by so many evils, enter upon this way? In order that you may understand our affliction, hear patiently my words, because the people whom you see are your people, and it is proper for us to make known to you our need. Then it will be reasonable for you to pity us. Your princes rage against us with such severity that, because of the taxes and most burdensome services, death is better for us than life. Behold, this year we, the inhabitants of this tiny place, have paid the duke in all a thousand marks, so many hundred besides to the count, and yet we are not through but every day we are outdone and oppressed even to the point of exhaustion. How, therefore, shall we, for whom flight is a matter of daily consideration, be free to build churches for this new religion and to receive baptism? Were there but a place to which we could flee! On crossing the Trave, behold, like ruin is there; on coming to the Peene River, it is not less there. What remains, therefore, but to leave the land and take to the sea and live with the waves? Or what fault is it of ours, if, driven from our fatherland, we have troubled the sea and got our livelihood by plunder of the Danes or the merchants who fare the sea? Will not this be the fault of the princes who are hounding us?

To these words the lord bishop replied:

> at, for they do not think that they do much wrong to those who are
> That our princes have hitherto used your people ill is not to be wondered

worshipers of idols and to those who are without God. Nay, rather return to the Christian worship and subject yourselves to your Creator before Whom they stoop who bear up the world. Do not the Saxons and the other peoples who bear the Christian name live in tranquillity, content with what is legitimately theirs? Indeed, as you alone differ from the religion of all, so you are subject to the plundering of all.

And Pribislav said, "If it please the lord duke and you that we have the same mode of worship as the count, let the rights of the Saxons in respect of property and taxes be extended to us and we shall willingly be Christians, build churches, and pay our tithes." . . .

At that time Albert, the margrave whose by-name is the Bear, held eastern Slavia. By the favor of God he also prospered splendidly in the portion of his lot; for he brought under his sway all the country of the Brizani, the Stoderani, and the many tribes dwelling along the Havel and the Elbe, and he curbed the rebellious ones among them. In the end, as the Slavs gradually decreased in number, he sent to Utrecht and to places lying on the Rhine, to those, moreover, who live by the ocean and suffer the violence of the sea—to wit, Hollanders, Zeelanders, Flemings—and he brought large numbers of them and had them live in the strongholds and villages of the Slavs. The bishopric of Brandenburg, and likewise that of Havelberg, was greatly strengthened by the coming of the foreigners, because the churches multiplied and the income from the tithes grew enormously. At the same time foreigners from Holland also began to settle on the southern bank of the Elbe; the Hollanders received all the swamp and open country, the land which is called Balsamerlande and Marscinerlande, together with very many cities and villages from the city of Salzwedel clear to the Bohemian woodland. These lands, indeed, the Saxons are said to have occupied of old—namely in the time of the Ottos—as can be seen from the ancient levees which had been constructed in the lowlands of the Balsami along the banks of the Elbe. But afterwards, when the Slavs got the upper hand, the Saxons were killed and the land has been held by the Slavs down to our own times. Now, however, because God gave plentiful aid and victory to our duke and to the other princes, the Slavs have been everywhere crushed and driven out. A people strong and without number have come from the bounds of the ocean, and taken possession of the territories of the Slavs. They have built cities and churches and have grown in riches beyond all estimation. . . .

The same day that the ocean coastlands were overwhelmed by this terrible calamity there occurred a great massacre in Mecklenburg, the city of the Slavs. Vratislav, the younger son of Niclot, who was held in chains at Brunswick, through messengers upbraided his brother Pribislav, as the report goes, saying:

Behold, I am held, locked in everlasting chains, and you act indifferently. Watch and endeavor, act manfully and extort by arms what you cannot obtain by peace. Do you not remember that when our father Niclot was held in custody at Lüneburg, he could be ransomed neither by prayer nor with money? However, after we with valorous instinct seized our arms and set fire to and demolished the strongholds, was he not released?

On hearing these words, Pribislav secretly collected an army and came unexpectedly to Mecklenburg. Henry of Scathen, prefect of the castle, happened to be away at the time and the people who were in the castle were without a leader. Pribislav, therefore, went up and said to the men who were in the fortress:

Great violence, O men, has been done both me and my people who have been expelled from the land of our nativity and dispossessed of the inheritance of our fathers. You also have increased this wrong, who have invaded our confines and possessed the strongholds and villages which ought to be ours by hereditary succession. We set before you, therefore, the choice of life or death. If you are willing to throw the fortress open to us and to return the land which belongs to us, we shall lead you out in peace, with your wives and children and all your household goods. If any one of the Slavs takes anything that belongs to you, I shall restore it twofold. If, however, you are unwilling to go out, nay, if you rather obstinately choose to defend this stronghold, I swear to you that, if God favor us with victory, I shall kill you all with the edge of the sword.

In answer to these words the Flemings began to throw spears and to inflict wounds. The host of the Slavs, stronger in men and arms, thereupon broke into the fortress with a fierce attack and slew every male in it; and they left of the foreign people not one. They set fire to the fortress and led into captivity the wives and little ones of the Flemings.

Document 22*

The Chronicle of Henry of Livonia, ed. James A. Brundage (Madison: Univ. of Wisconsin Press, 1961), pp. 25–26, 27–28, 38–39, 67.

Livonia was the region that, between World Wars I and II, held the small republics of Estonia and Latvia. The land-owning aristocracy of these states spoke German, a reminder of the fact that German expansion into the eastern Baltic regions during the thirteenth and fourteenth centuries saw the imposition of a German ruling class over the native population in those areas where such a population survived the conquest. Henry of Livonia (ca. 1188–after 1259) was a German (probably

Saxon) priest who chronicled the story of the missionary work in
Livonia, which began in 1181 when a priest named Meinhard travelled
there to preach the Gospel. Henry was basically sympathetic toward the
inhabitants of the region, and, like many other missionaries, he ex-
pressed distaste for the greedy colonizers whose actions scandalized the
newly converted infidels.—ed.

Divine Providence, by the fire of His love, and mindful of Raab and
Babylonia, that is, of the confusion of paganism, aroused in our modern
times the idolatrous Livonians from the sleep of idolatry and of sin in the
following way.

In the monastery of Segeberg there was a man of worthy life, and with
venerable gray hair, Meinhard by name, a priest of the Order of Saint
Augustine. He came to Livonia with a band of merchants simply for the
sake of Christ and only to preach. For German merchants, bound together
through familiarity with the Livonians, were accustomed to go to Livonia,
frequently sailing up the Dvina River.

After receiving, therefore, the permission of King Vladimir of Polozk,
to whom the Livonians, while still pagan, paid tribute, and, at the same
time, after receiving gifts from him, this priest boldly set out upon the
divine work, preaching to the Livonians and building a church in the
village of Uexküll. And in the same village Ylo, the father of Kulewene,
and Viezo, the father of Alo, were the first to be baptized, while the
others followed in their turn. . . .

As a co-worker in the gospel the bishop had Brother Theodoric of the
Cistercian order, subsequently a bishop in Esthonia. Because the crops in
his fields were quite abundant and in their own fields dying because of a
flooding rain, the Livonians of Treiden prepared to sacrifice him to their
gods. The people were collected and the will of the gods regarding the
sacrifice was sought after by lot. A lance was placed in position and the
horse came up and, at the signal of God, put out the foot thought to be
the foot of life. Brother Theodoric prayed aloud and gave blessings with
his hand. The pagan priest asserted that the Christian God was sitting on
the back of the horse and was moving the horse's foot forward; that for
this reason the back of the horse had to be wiped off so that the God
might slide off. When this was done, the horse again put forth the foot
of life, as before, and Brother Theodoric's life was saved. When Brother
Theodoric was sent into Esthonia, he likewise endured from the pagans a
great many dangers to his life. Because of an eclipse of the sun which
took place on the day of John the Baptist, they said that he was eating the
sun. At that same time, a certain wounded Livonian from Treiden begged
Brother Theodoric to cure him and promised to be baptized if he were

cured. The brother pounded herbs together, therefore, and, not knowing the effects of the herbs, called upon the name of the Lord. The Livonian was thus healed in body and, by baptism, in soul. He was the first to accept the faith of Christ in Treiden. A certain sick man called Brother Theodoric and asked to be baptized. He was kept from his holy purpose by the violent stubbornness of the women; but when his illness grew worse, the incredulity of the women was overcome and he was baptized and commended by prayers to God. When he died a certain convert saw his soul being carried into heaven by the angels and recognized him from a distance of seven miles.

In the third year of his consecration [1201], the bishop left the hostages in Germany and returned to Livonia with the pilgrims whom he was able to get. The city of Riga was built in the next summer in a spacious field, next to which there was a potential harbor for ships. At that time the bishop, binding to himself Daniel, a noble person, and Conrad from Meiendorf, enfeoffed them with two forts, Lennewarden and Uexküll.

In the meantime, the Kurs, having heard of the coming of the bishop and the beginning of the city, not for fear of war, but rather at the call of Christ, sent messengers to the city to make peace. With the consent of the Christians, they confirmed the peace with the effusion of blood, as is the pagan custom. The Lithuanians also, God so disposing, came to Riga that same year asking for peace. When peace had been made, they at once entered into a friendly alliance with the Christians. In the following winter they went down the Dvina with a great army and made for Semgallia. Before entering the country, however, they heard that the king of Polozk was entering Lithuania with an army. Leaving the Semgalls, they returned in haste and, finding as they went up country two fishermen of the bishop's by the Rummel, like ravening wolves they raged against them and took away the clothes they were wearing. And thereupon the naked fishermen fled to Riga and exposed the injury they had suffered. The pilgrims then learned the truth of the matter, seized certain Lithuanians who were living in Riga at that time, and detained them in chains until the things stolen from the fishermen were returned. . . .

The people of Treiden, indeed, after they had accepted the mysteries of holy baptism and, with it, the whole spiritual law, asked their priest, Alabrand, just as he administered spiritual law for them, likewise to administer civil cases according to the law of the Christians, which by us is called secular law. The people of Livonia were formerly most perfidious and everyone stole what his neighbor had, but now theft, violence, rapine, and similar things were forbidden as a result of their baptism. Those who had been despoiled before their baptism grieved over the loss of their goods. For, after baptism, they did not dare to take them back by violence and accordingly asked for a secular judge to settle cases of this kind.

Hence the priest Alabrand was the first to receive the authority to hear both spiritual and civil cases. He, administering quite faithfully the office enjoined on him, both for the sake of God and because of his sins, exercised his authority in cases of rapine and theft, restored things unjustly seized, and so showed the Livonians the right way of living. This Christian law pleased the Livonians the first year because the office of magistrate was administered by faithful men of this kind. Afterwards, however, this office was very much degraded throughout all Livonia, Lettgallia, and Esthonia at the hands of divers lay, secular judges, who used the office of magistrate more to fill their own purses than to defend the justice of God.

Document 23

The settlement of Livonia (1225) in *Urkunden und Erzählende Quellen zur Deutschen Ostsiedlung im Mittelalter*, eds. Herbert Helbig and Lorenz Weinrich, 2 vols. (Darmstadt: Wissenschaftliche Buchgesellschaft, 1968, 1970), 1: 540. Translated by James Muldoon.

The documents that follow (docs. 23–26) reflect the difficulties of frontier life in the thirteenth century. There are constant calls for more men to join the crusade against the Slavs along the edge of the Baltic. The creation of a principality headed by the bishop of Livonia shows one aspect of the German advance, the use of bishops as administrators in the newly won lands. Those who came to settle in these regions were rewarded with lands proportionate to their contribution to the military effort. In the long run, Christians from the west seem to have been attractive as settlers because of the constant threat of revolt by the newly baptized natives who often waited until their German overlords felt secure and then rebelled against their masters.—ed.

Henry, by the grace of God, King of the Romans and ever August, to all the faithful men of the empire to whom these letters shall come, his grace and every blessing.

At the request of Albert, the venerable bishop of Livonia, we have established a single march consisting of his entire diocese, that is covering the land of the Letts, Leal, and the lands along the sea, and, by virtue of our royal munificence, we concede and grant that principality to him with all the rights pertaining to princes, giving him the power of coining money and of establishing a city in Riga and in other places where it would be proper to do so. If, however, a vein of any kind of metal or any other hidden treasure is discovered, we commit to that faithful man our special right in such matters with the counsel of our princes. We also declare and command firmly under threat of the loss of our favor that you answer to the aforementioned bishop for all justice and for every sort of proceeding pertaining to the royal jurisdiction and that you strive to do everything knowing that we love him sincerely as a beloved prince of the empire. And since the imperial boundaries will have been extended by him and the unbelief of the barbarians, the Lord willing, will have been subjected to the Christian religion, we do not wish to omit any of those things which aid and honor him. . . . Given at Nürnberg, on December 1 (1225). . . .

Document 24

The Teutonic Knights in Prussia (1236), in *Urkunden und Erzählende Quellen zur Deutschen Ostseidlung im Mittelalter*, eds. Herbert Helbig and Lorenz Weinrich, 2 vols. (Darmstadt: Wissenschaftliche Buchgesellschaft, 1968, 1970), 1: 448–50. Translated by James Muldoon.

In the name of the Lord, Amen. Brother Herman, superior of the German House in Prussia, to all the faithful in Christ who shall see this letter, perpetual greetings.

We desire that it be known to all now and in the future, that with the consent of our chapter, we conveyed to the noble gentleman, lord Theoderic of Tiefenau, that settlement which is called Little Queden. He may also measure off 300 Flemish hides[1] of the adjacent uncultivated land which is suitable for cultivation. He shall begin from the boundaries of the farms, which stretch toward the Island of St. Mary opposite the aforementioned settlement and then go downstream along the river Nogat until it reaches the pine forest. The other boundary shall begin at the initial measuring point and go straight to the previously cultivated land of Resien. At the lower end the boundary line will parallel the line to Resien. If indeed the stated amount is not to be found within these boundaries, we will make up the deficit in the region of Resien, to be sure, in the part that has not thus far been cultivated by the Prussians but which is suitable for cultivation in the future; and he shall likewise measure off this area. Also, we add that if within those limits there is included a pine forest about one hide in size, this is to be included but not counted with the above mentioned amount. Also we add the land from the lower boundary along the Nogat to the boundary of the pine forest, an area half mile in length and breadth. We also add the free right to the fishery across the Nogat in the pools of the island and in the Nogat

1. A hide may be defined as enough land for one family, an amount that varied according to the quality of the soil in various regions. In eastern Europe it ranged from 42 to 60 acres.

itself so that there is enough to provision him. We also add a tenth of the fish hooks from the three following villages, Watkowitz, Sercoy, and Myrowicz, in the quantity and the quality as they now have or shall have in the future, saving however the right of the parish of Pestlin. All this we convey to him and to his heirs of both sexes that they might hold them in perpetuity. And he and his successors will give to our house as an annual tax a talent of wax that is two pounds in weight and a penny of Cologne for the tithe, but from every German plowland an amount that is called a bushel of wheat flour and another of wheat annually; and because we have determined that it would detract from his noble status, we have not indicated any kind of service [to be performed] by him and his heirs. We also add this, that if he or his heirs wish to sell these lands that belong to them, they can do so freely, to whomever they wish, except to a Pole or a Pomeranian. The buyer, along with his successors, is bound not only to the aforementioned tax. He is also bound to come armed along with two knights and a squire outfitted as knights are customarily equipped against all who rise up against our house. And it should not be overlooked that all the farmers of those lands we have mentioned are bound to defend our land and to go on the offensive on our behalf just as the other farmers are bound to do.

Done on the island of St. Mary, in the year of grace 1236. . . .

Document 25

The Settlement of Livonia, in *Urkunden und Erzählende Quellen zur Deutschen Ostseidlung im Mittelalter*, eds. Herbert Helbig and Lorenz Weinrich, 2 vols. (Darmstadt: Wissenschaftliche Buchgesellschaft, 1968, 1970), 1: 544–46. Translated by James Muldoon.

To the honored and beloved citizens, magistrates, and municipality of Lübeck, Brother George, vice master of the Brothers of the House of St. Mary of the Germans in Livonia, and all his brothers send their prayers and every kind of friendship and favor. Anyone can easily see from the results of our activities that the prosperity that we now enjoy grew out of many great adversities, crises and turmoils.

We therefore do not doubt that it has come to your attention how much injury we the Brothers and the other Christians who dwell in the land of Livonia have received recently in terms of lost horses, arms and other goods. Because of this, the Catholic faith was greatly harmed so that many who had withdrawn from the error of their infidel ways and worshipped the name of the Lord, now spurning that name, become backsliders worshipping false idols. What Christian does not lament this? Therefore, let all lament and recall to mind that the Catholic faith was developed through your efforts in these regions, as is well known, and then watered by the blood of your fathers, brothers, sons, and friends, so that the garden of the elect might be irrigated. You can lead others to perform this task. You have the necessary qualities of leadership. We allow you to share your aid and advice with us so that the Catholic faith might be strong in those lands, the Lord aiding us to maintain it.

Therefore, we inform you that with the advice of our brothers we propose to draw the Germans to us, with the help of whom we wage the Lord's battle more forcefully. We will grant them fiefs in the lands which were abandoned when the apostate Kurlands had been killed or driven off, where the sea ports are open to them, where they think that settlement will be most suitable. For a knight or an honest burgher who comes there with a well-armed charger, there will be a fief of 60 Saxon hides; for a doughty squire with a heavy-armed war-horse, 40 hides; for a serf with horse and armor, 10 hides; for a farmer, we grant him free for six years whatever amount of land he wishes to farm, and afterwards he will pay to us a tenth from his lands. We cheerfully encourage all who come. All who wish to come should come before winter and they ought to come to Memel with their ships. . . . Given at Riga, in the year of our Lord, 1261. . . .

Document 26

The Settlement of Ermland (1289), in *Urkunden und Erzählende Quellen zur Deutschen Ostseidlung im Mittelalter*, eds. Herbert Helbig and Lorenz Weinrich, 2 vols. (Darmstadt: Wissenschaftliche Buchgesellschaft, 1968, 1970), 1: 480–83. Translated by James Muldoon.

In the name of the Lord, Amen. We Henry, by the grace of God Bishop of the Church of Ermland, wish that it be brought to the attention of all those to whom these writings come that:
—being as desirous as we can be for the rebuilding of our church, which has been completely destroyed by the enemies of the cross of Christ and of the Christian name, that is, by the Prussians, the Lithuanians, and by other infidels,
—and not having found any more useful means by which we would be able to assist the aforementioned decayed church, except to invite men to that deserted location who can defend and protect the aforementioned church against the enemies of Christ,
—and believing also that the honorable man Albert the Fleming, our brother, is willing and able to be of assistance in aiding the said church,

—weighing, not unsuitably, the fact that he brought us his own money acquired in remote parts of the world with great effort to the Roman court at the time of our greatest need, without which the business of our church could not have been satisfactorily completed,

—and taking notice of other welcome and faithful services toward us and our church which he has shown and will show in the future,

—[we grant] to him and to his legitimate heirs 34 hides in the aforementioned field of Schalmey along with a third part of the mountain, called in praise of God, Grunenberg,

—of which mountain C. Wendepfaffe has another third and John the Fleming has the other third, with the fields or woods adjacent to each, each man holds and shall hold his third by similar law as they have agreed,

—and to those 34 hides we grant possession in perpetuity according to Culman law, 110 hides in the fields of Basien, Sigdus, and Naglandithin as they are popularly called, with every right, with pastures, meadows, thickets, woods, and hunting grounds, waters, fishing spots, and each and every other useful appurtenance within the aforementioned 134 [sic] hides so included, with high and low justice extending to hand and neck, on the highways and off, adding that if God's grace is favorable, that a church be established in that same place, for which church Albert and his heirs, and C. Wendepfaffe and his legitimate heirs, and also John the Fleming and his heirs shall have the right of presentation without any opposition. That same Albert, however, or one of his heirs who holds the said lands shall serve us and our church of Ermland for these benefits against whatever attackers of our church with three geldings and as many armed men according to the custom of this land within the boundaries of our diocese when we or our successors request such service. Moreover, the oft-mentioned Albert and his legitimate heirs shall pay and give to us and our church annually at the feast of St. Martin a bushel of wheat and a bushel of rye from each of the plowlands of the 110 hides located in the fields of Basien, Sigdus, and Naglandgten, [he shall pay] a bushel of wheat for the fishhooks, and, in addition, [he shall pay] a talent of wax weighing two marks, and a penny of Cologne or six Culmen pennies without any excuse. The 34 hides which are in Schalmey, Albert and his legitimate heirs shall hold forever free of taxes; from service with horses and other payments the oft-mentioned Albert and his heirs shall be free for 12 years from this date. . . . Given in the year of the Lord, 1289. . . .

V

The Conquest of the Wild Irish

Introduction

From the twelfth to the sixteenth centuries various English kings considered conquering and colonizing Ireland. Interest in Ireland fluctuated considerably, however, because of English involvements elsewhere. The Welsh and the Scottish borders presented immediate military threats, and the Hundred Years war with France for control of English possessions in France was potentially more profitable. For the most part, the English in Ireland remained restricted during the later Middle Ages to a small area around Dublin known as the Pale. It was only in the sixteenth century, when the Welsh and Scottish borders had been pacified, when the English possessions on the continent were irrevocably lost, and when the War of the Roses was over, that the English government concentrated its attention on Ireland as a field for colonization.

The initial justification for the conquest had been that the Christian Church in Ireland was in need of reform. The Irish had been cut off from the mainstream of European society from the eighth to the eleventh centuries, and the Irish Church had not been affected by the Gregorian reform movement that had undertaken to reform the Church everywhere.[1] The first important document dealing with the English invasion of Ireland was therefore the papal bull, *Laudabiliter*, which Pope Adrian IV (1154–59) issued in 1155. The bull authorized Henry II (1154–89) to invade Ireland for the purpose of reforming the Church in Ireland along the lines of the Gregorian movement (doc. 27).

If the reasons for the invasion were only those advanced by the pope in *Laudabiliter* then the conquest of Ireland might not appear to be a part of European expansion overseas. The Irish were Christians and had been influenced by the classical cultural tradition. On the other hand, Irish society was very different from English society and both Christianity and the classical tradition had taken on distinctively Irish forms.[2] Furthermore, between the eighth and the eleventh centuries a series of invasions from Scandinavia had reduced Irish society to something approaching anarchy.

1. John A. Watt, *The Church and the Two Nations in Medieval Ireland*, Cambridge Studies in Medieval Life and Thought, series 3, no. 3 (Cambridge, Eng.: Cambridge Univ. Press, 1970), pp. 1–34.
2. A. J. Otway-Ruthven, *A History of Medieval Ireland* (London: Benn, 1968), pp. 22–24.

Even after the final defeat of the invaders at Clontarf in 1014, Irish society never fully recovered. By the twelfth century, to a foreign observer like Gerald the Welshman, an Englishman in spite of his name, Irish society was a very strange, not to say uncivilized affair (doc. 28). Gerald's picture of Ireland is that of a society unlike that found elsewhere in Europe. It was a pastoral, not an agricultural society, organized along tribal rather than territorial lines. Although much of what Gerald condemned in Irish society—the constant wars and the poor quality of the clergy—can be traced in large measure to the period of invasions, many of the qualities of the Irish he disliked stemmed from the nature of Irish society itself. Being a pastoral people who were accustomed to living largely off of the produce of their flocks, the Irish were not farmers. As a result, Gerald condemned them as being lazy, a complaint constantly re-echoed in English descriptions of the Irish for the next four hundred years. To the English, the conquest of the Irish meant the transformation of Irish society from a pastoral to an agricultural society and, eventually, the replacement of Irish cultural values and language with the values and language of the English.[3]

In the Remonstrance of the Irish princes (1317) we have an evaluation of the conquest through the eyes of the conquered (doc. 29). In their opinion, Laudabiliter had authorized the English conquest on the basis of allegations about the Irish that were not true. Furthermore, the invaders had not reformed the Church and were engaged in a policy of exterminating the native population.

The view that the Irish were so culturally different from the English was reflected in a series of laws the English made for dealing with the Irish. In 1321 the government sought to improve relations with the Irish by reasserting that those natives who were admitted to the protection of English law, that is, who had submitted to English rule, were not to be abused in ways that were contrary to the law. They were to be treated as Englishmen because legally they were Englishmen. The most famous compilation of such laws, the Statutes of Kilkenny issued in 1366, summed up the English view of the Irish (doc. 30). The benefits of English protection of the lives and possessions of the Irish were restricted to those who spoke English and lived in English fashion. The natives who chose to retain their traditional ways were essentially outlaws who lacked legal protection. In addition, the statutes forbade Englishmen from adopting the Irish style of life and from intermarrying with the Irish. These laws reflected the fact that a comparatively small number of Englishmen went

3. "From Gerald's charge of barbarism the Irish may be defended. Much of his evidence would, however, support a just claim for the archaism of their civilization." Ibid., p. 1.

to Ireland and a number of them had married into families of powerful Irish chiefs. The government feared that if the practice continued, there might emerge a society combining the strengths of Irish and English societies that would throw off English rule and create an independent Anglo-Irish kingdom.

Throughout the history of English expansion and colonization, the problem of what to do about the conquered, to exterminate them or to assimilate them, remained a constant. In the modern world, the Anglicized Pakistani or the Nigerian army officer with his moustache and Sandhurst manners reflect one result of the problem. The attempts to exterminate the American Indians may be seen as the other.[4]

Bibliography

The unique nature of Celtic Christian society is discussed in Ludwig Bieler, *Ireland—Harbinger of the Middle Ages* (London: Oxford Univ. Press, 1963), and Kathleen Hughes, *The Church in Early Irish Society* (London: Methuen, 1966). The way in which the English ruled Ireland is dealt with in H. G. Richardson and G. O. Sayles, *The Administration of Ireland, 1172–1377* (Dublin: Stationery Office for the Irish Manuscripts Commission, 1963).

In recent years a number of books and articles on the links between English colonization in Ireland during the Tudor era and the subsequent colonization of North America have appeared. Among the most important of these works are, David B. Quinn, *The Elizabethans and the Irish* (Ithaca: Cornell Univ. Press), and also his "Ireland and Sixteenth Century Expansion," *Historical Studies* 1(1958):20–32; Nicholas Canny, *The Elizabethan Conquest of Ireland* (Hassocks: Harvester Press, 1976), and his "The Ideology of English Colonization: From Ireland to America," *William and Mary Quarterly* 30 (October 1973):575–98.

The English stereotype of the barbarous Irish is discussed in William R. Jones, "England Against the Celtic Fringe: A Study in Cultural Stereotypes," *Journal of World History* 13 (1971): 155–71. For the role of Gerald the Welshman in shaping English attitudes about the Irish, see William R. Jones, "Giraldus Redivivus—English Historians, Irish Apologists, and the Works of Gerald of Wales," *Eire-Ireland* 9 (Autumn 1974): 3–20.

4. James Muldoon, "The Indian as Irishman," *Essex Institute Historical Collections* 111 (October 1975): 267–89.

Document 27

Adrian IV, *Laudabiliter*, in *Select Historical Documents of the Middle Ages*, ed. Ernest F. Henderson (London: G. Bell and Sons, 1925), pp. 10–11. The authenticity of this papal letter was long the subject of scholarly debate because it does not appear in the register of letters from the reign of Adrian IV (1154–59). The text usually cited is found in Giraldus Cambrensis's history of the English invasion of Ireland, the *Expugnatio Hibernica*, which is very favorable to the English and very critical of the Irish, as the next selection indicates. As a result, Irish scholars argued that the document had been forged, not an uncommon phenomenon in the Middle Ages, to justify English aggression in Ireland. Modern scholarship, however, has generally accepted the document as authentic. Adrian, the only English pope, was responding to a request that originated with Henry II (1154–89) to authorize an English invasion of Ireland, using as a justification the argument that the Church in Ireland was unreformed and that the English would impose the Gregorian reform of the Church on the Irish. As usual, papal involvement in expansion was linked with ecclesiastical matters.—ed.

Bishop Adrian, servant of the servants of God, sends to his dearest son in Christ, the illustrious king of the English, greeting and apostolic benediction. Laudably and profitably enough thy magnificence thinks of extending thy glorious name on earth, and of heaping up rewards of eternal felicity in Heaven, inasmuch as, like a good catholic prince, thou dost endeavour to enlarge the bounds of the church, to declare the truth of the Christian faith to ignorant and barbarous nations, and to extirpate the plants of evil from the field of the Lord. And, in order the better to perform this, thou dost ask the advice and favour of the apostolic see. In which work, the more lofty the counsel and the better the guidance by which thou dost proceed, so much more do we trust that, by God's help, thou wilt progress favourably in the same; for the reason that those things which have taken their rise from ardour of faith and love of religion are accustomed always to come to a good end and termination.

There is indeed no doubt, as thy Highness doth also acknowledge, that Ireland and all other islands which Christ the Sun of Righteousness has illumined, and which have received the doctrines of the Christian faith, belong to the jurisdiction of St. Peter and of the holy Roman Church. Wherefore, so much the more willingly do we grant to them that the

131

right faith and the seed grateful to God may be planted in them, the more we perceive, by examining more strictly our conscience, that this will be required of us.

Document 28

Giraldus Cambrensis, *The Historical Works*, trans. Thomas Forester and Richard C. Hoare, rev. and ed., Thomas Wright (London: Bell, 1905), pp. 134–35, 136–43, 184–86, 323–24.

Giraldus Cambrensis or Gerald of Wales (ca. 1146–ca. 1220) was a clergyman associated with the court of Henry II. He visited Ireland twice, in 1183 and again in 1185, so that his descriptions of Ireland and of the Irish are those of an eyewitness. He described the Irish as lazy and undisciplined, a judgement often made by European observers of societies different from their own. Interestingly enough, although it was Giraldus who provided us with the text of *Laudabiliter*, he also indicated that the actual invasion of Ireland resulted not from the bull but from the desire of a defeated Irish prince to obtain support in his bid to regain his throne. Seen in this light, the invasion was initiated by one Irish chief against another without any serious thought for the long term consequences. The attraction for the English knights who went to Ireland was the possibility of acquiring land. The practice of a defeated party calling in what turned out to be his conquerors was not unique to the twelfth century. In the modern era, small parties of Europeans found themselves able to conquer large kingdoms by playing off one faction against another in similar fashion.—*ed.*

Selections from the Topography of Ireland

The faith having been planted in the island from the time of St. Patrick, so many ages ago, and propagated almost ever since, it is wonderful that this nation should remain to this day so very ignorant of the rudiments of Christianity. It is indeed a most filthy race, a race sunk in vice, a race more ignorant than all other nations of the first principles of the faith. Hitherto they neither pay tithes nor first fruits; they do not contract marriages, nor shun incestuous connections; they frequent not the church of God with proper reverence. Nay, what is most detestable, and not only contrary to the Gospel, but to everything that is right, in many parts of Ireland brothers (I will not say marry) seduce and debauch the wives of their brothers deceased, and have incestuous intercourse with them; adhering in this to the letter, and not to the spirit, of the Old Testament; and following the example of men of old in their vices more willingly than in their virtues. . . . They are given to treachery more than any other nation, and never keep the faith they have pledged, neither shame nor fear withholding them from constantly violating the most solemn obligations, which, when entered into with themselves, they are above all things anxious to have observed. So that, when you have used the utmost precaution, when you have been most vigilant, for your own security and safety, by requiring oaths and hostages, by treaties of alliance firmly made, and by benefits of all kinds conferred, then begins your time to fear; for then especially their treachery is awake, when they suppose that, relying in the fulness of your security, you are off your guard. That is the moment for them to fly to their citadel of wickedness, turn against you their weapons of deceit, and endeavour to do you injury, by taking the opportunity of catching you unawares. . . .

Among many other inventions of their abominable guile, there is one which especially proves it. When they wish to take off any one, they assemble in company with him at some holy place, under the guise of religious and peaceful meeting; then they go in procession round the church, and afterwards, entering within its walls, they confederate themselves in an indissoluble alliance before the altar, with oaths prodigally multiplied upon the relics of the saints, and confirmed by the celebration of the mass and prayers of the holy priests, as if it were a solemn affiance. At length, as a still stronger ratification of their league, and, as it were, the completion of the affair, they drink each others' blood, which is shed for the purpose. This custom has been handed down to them from the rites of the heathens, who were wont to seal their treaties with blood. How often, in the very act of such an alliance being made by bloody and deceitful men, has so much blood been fraudulently and iniquitously split, that one or other of them has fainted on the spot! How often has the same hour which witnessed the contract, or that which followed it, seen it broken in an unheard-of manner by a bloody divorce! . . .

Woe to brothers among a barbarous race! Woe also to kinsmen! While alive, they pursue them to destruction; and even when dead they leave it to others to avenge their murder. If they have any feeling of love or attachment, it is all spent on their foster-children and foster-brothers. . . .

Thus it appears that every one may do just as he pleases; and that the question is not what is right, but what suits his purpose: although nothing is really expedient but what is right. However, the pest of treachery has here grown to such a height—it has so taken root, and long abuse has so succeeded in turning it into a second nature—habits are so formed by mutual intercourse, as he who handles pitch cannot escape its stains—that the evil has acquired great force. A little wormword, mixed with a large quantity of honey, quickly makes the whole bitter; but if the mixture contains twice as much honey as it does wormwood, the honey fails to sweeten it. Thus, I say, "evil communications corrupt good manners"; and even strangers who land here from other countries become generally imbued with this national crime, which seems to be innate and very contagious. It either adopts holy places for its purposes, or makes them; for, as the path of pleasure leads easily downwards and nature readily imitates vice, who will doubt the sacredness of its sanctions who is predisposed and foretaught by so many sacrilegious examples, by so many records of evil deeds, by such frequent forfeitures of oaths, by the want of all obligations to honesty? . . .

Moreover, though the faith has been planted for so long a period in this country that it has grown to maturity, there are some corners of the land in which many are still unbaptized, and to whom, through the negligence of their pastors, the knowledge of the truth has never penetrated. I heard some sailors relate that, having been once driven by a violent storm, during Lent, to the northern islands and the unexplored expanse of the sea of Connaught, they at last took shelter under a small island. Here they could hardly hold their ground, by the help of their anchor, though they had three cables out, or more. After three days, the storm abating, the sky becoming again clear, and the sea calm, they beheld at no great distance the features of a land which was before entirely unknown to them. From this land not long afterwards they saw a small boat rowing towards them. It was narrow and oblong, and made of wattled boughs, covered and sewn with the hides of beasts. In it were two men, stark naked, except that they wore broad belts of the skin of some animal fastened round their waists. They had long yellow hair, like the Irish, falling below the shoulders, and covering great part of their bodies. The sailors, finding that these men were from some part of Connaught, and spoke the Irish language, took them into the ship. All that they saw there was new to them, and a subject of wonder. They said that they had never seen before a large ship, built of timber, or anything belonging to civilized man. Bread and cheese being offered to them, they refused to eat them, having no knowledge of either. Flesh, fish, and milk, they said, were their only food. Nor did they wear any clothes, except sometimes the skins of beasts, in cases of great necessity. Having inquired of the sailors whether they had on board any flesh with which they could satisfy their hunger, and being told in reply, that it was not lawful to eat flesh during Lent, they were utterly ignorant what Lent was. Neither did they know anything about the year, the month, or the week; and by what names the days of the week were called was entirely beyond their conception. Being asked whether they were Christians, and had been baptized, they replied that to the present hour they had never heard of the name of Christ, and knew nothing about him. On their return, they carried back a loaf and a cheese, that they might be able to astonish their countrymen by the sight of the provisions which the strangers ate. . . .

We now come to the clerical order. The clergy, then, of this country are commendable enough for their piety; and among many other virtues in which they excel, are especially eminent for that of continence. They also perform with great regularity the services of the psalms, hours, lessons, and prayers, and, confining themselves to the precincts of the churches, employ their whole time in the offices to which they are appointed. They also pay due attention to the rules of abstinence and a spare diet, the greatest part of them fasting almost every day till dusk, when by singing complines they have finished the offices of the several hours for the day. Would that, after these long fasts, they were as sober as they are serious, as true as they are severe, as pure as they are enduring, such in reality as they are in appearance. But among so many thousands you will scarcely find one who, after his devotion to long fastings and prayers, does not make up by night for his privations during the day by the enormous quantities of wine and other liquors in which he indulges more than is becoming. . . .

There are, however, some among the clergy who are most excellent men, and have no leaven of impurity. Indeed this people are intemperate in all their actions, and most vehement in all their feelings. Thus the bad are bad indeed—there are nowhere worse; and than the good you cannot find better. But there is not much wheat among the oats and the tares. Many, you find, are called, but few chosen; there is very little grain, but much chaff. . . .

I find it especially worthy of reproach in the bishops and prelates, that they are very slothful and negligent in their duty of correcting a people guilty of such enormous delinquencies. As they neither preach nor correct, I predict that they will be corrected themselves; as they do not reprove others, I reprove them; as they neglect to censure others, I censure them. For, as St. Gregory says, whosoever is raised to the priesthood takes on himself the office of a preacher. . . .[1]

Thus the prelates of this country, secluding themselves according to ancient custom within the inclosures of their churches, are generally content with indulging in a contemplative life, and are so smitten with delight in the beauty of Rachel, that they turn away from the blear-eyed Leah. Hence it happens that they neither preach to the people the word of the Lord, nor tell them of their sins; neither extirpate vices nor implant virtues in the flock committed to their charge. . . .

1. Pope Gregory I (590–604), whose book on the responsibilities of the clergy, *The Pastoral Rule*, was the basic guide for parish clergy during the Middle Ages.

For as nearly all the prelates of Ireland are elected from the monasteries over the clergy, they scupulously perform all the duties of a monk, but pass by all those which belong to the clergy and bishops. An anxious care for the good of the flock committed to them is little cultivated, or made a secondary concern. . . .

Selections from the Conquest of Ireland

Dermitius, the son of Murchard, and prince of Leinster, who ruled over that fifth part of Ireland, possessed in our times the maritime districts in the east of the island, separated only from Great Britain by the sea which flowed between. His youth and inexperience in government led him to become the oppressor of the nobility, and to impose a cruel and intolerable tyranny on the chiefs of the land. This brought him into trouble, and it was not the only one; for O'Roric, prince of Meath, having gone on an expedition into a distant quarter, left his wife, the daughter of Omachlacherlin, in a certain island of Meath during his absence; and she, who had long entertained a passion for Dermitius, took advantage of the absence of her husband, and allowed herself to be ravished, not against her will. As the nature of women is fickle and given to change, she thus became the prey of the spoiler by her own contrivance. For as Mark Anthony and Troy are witnesses, almost all the greatest evils in the world have arisen from women. King O'Roric being moved by this to great wrath, but more for the shame than the loss he suffered, was fully bent on revenge, and forthwith gathered the whole force of his own people and the neighboring tribes, calling besides to his aid Roderic, prince of Connaught, then monarch of all Ireland. The people of Leinster, considering in what a strait their prince was, and seeing him beset on every side by bands of enemies, began to call to mind their own long-smothered grievances, and their chiefs leagued themselves with the foes of Mac Murchard, and deserted him in his desperate fortunes.

Dermitius, seeing himself thus forsaken and left destitute, fortune frowning upon him, and his affairs being now desperate, after many fierce conflicts with the enemy, in which he was always worsted, at length resolved, as his last refuge, to take ship and flee beyond the sea. . . .

Meanwhile, Mac Murchard, submitting to his change of fortune, and confidently hoping for some favourable turn, crossed the sea with a favourable wind, and came to Henry II., king of England, for the purpose of earnestly imploring his succour. Although the king was at that time beyond the sea, far away in Aquitaine, in France, and much engaged in business, he received Murchard with great kindness, and the liberality and courtesy which was natural to him; and having heard the causes of his exile and coming over, and received his bond of allegiance and oath of fealty, granted him letters patent to the effect following: "Henry, king of England, duke of Normandy and Aquitaine, and count of Anjou, to all of his liegemen, English, Normans, Welsh, and Scots, and to all other nations subject to his dominion, Sendeth greeting, Whensoever these our letters shall come unto you, know ye that we have received Dermitius, prince of Leinster, into our grace and favour,—Wherefore, whosoever within the bounds of our territories shall be willing to give him aid, as our vassal and leigeman, in recovering his territories, let him be assured of our favour and licence on that behalf." . . .

As this people are easily moved to rebel, and are as lightminded as they are light of foot, when they have been subjugated and reduced to submission, they will have to be ruled with great discretion. The government should be entrusted to men of firm and equitable minds, who in times of peace, when the people obey the laws and are content to be loyal subjects, will win their hearts by keeping good faith, and treating them with respect; but if, through their natural levity, they presume to break into revolt, the governor should then divest himself of all gentleness, and instantly bring the offenders to condign punishment. Peace being again restored, and due satisfaction made for their misdeeds, as it is a bad thing to keep in memory wrongs that are passed, as long as they behave well their misconduct should be buried in oblivion, and they enjoy the same security, and be treated with the same consideration, as before. Thus, obedience to the laws, and the beneficial pursuits of peace, would meet with reward, while the certainty of punishment would deter the rebellious from rash attempts at insurrection.

But governors who throw all things into confusion by being slow to punish the rebellions, while they oppress the humble, by fawning on insurgents while they plunder peaceable subjects, robbing the weak and truckling to the refractory, as we have seen many do; such governors in the end bring disgrace on themselves. Besides, as evils foreseen are less hurtful, a prudent governor will take measures in time of peace, by erecting fortresses and opening roads through the woods, to be in constant preparation to meet the dangers of war. For this people are always plotting hostilities under colour of peace. And as it is wise to take warning from the mishaps of others, and avoid their errors, and the blow falls less heavily when it is anticipated from past experience, the examples of such men as Milo de Cogan, Ralph Fitz-Stephen, that gallant youth, Hugh de Lacy, and I may add Roger Poer, may teach that there is never any security from the weapons of the Irish. For, as I have said in my Topography, the craft of this people is more to be feared than their prowess in arms, their show of peace than their fire-brands, their honey than their gall, their secret malice than their open warfare, their treachery than their attacks, their false friendship than their contemptible hostility.

. . . this people when finally subjected should, by a public proclamation, like the Sicilians, be entirely prohibited from carrying arms under the severest penalties. In the meantime, they ought not be allowed in time of peace, on any pretence or in any place, to use that detestable instrument of destruction [the broad-axe], which, by an ancient but accursed custom, they constantly carry in their hands instead of a staff. Finally, forasmuch as the kings of Britain have on many grounds already set forth a just title to Ireland, and the people of that island cannot subsist without the benefits conferred by commercial intercourse, it seems reasonable that it should be subjected to some tribute to England, either in money, or in the birds with which it abounds, in order that all occasions of dispute or opposition may be obviated for the future. Thus, as time proceeds on its course, and the regular line of descent is perpetuated to the farthest degree, this annual tribute should be retained, as a lasting acknowledgment of this conquest, in the place of a written instrument, to the British nation and king.

Document 29

The Remonstrance of the Irish Princes in John of Fordun, *Scotichronicon*, ed. Thomas Herne, 5 vols. (Oxford, 1722), 3: 908–26. Translated by James Muldoon.

Like the English request to the papacy which resulted in *Laudabiliter*, this was a request, this time by the Irish, that the pope authorize a course of action that was underway in any event. The Irish had invited Edward Bruce, brother of Robert Bruce whose victory over the English at Bannockburn (1314) had stopped English expansion in Scotland, to rule them. The Remonstrance was an explanation of the Irish situation and a defense of their refusal to recognize Edward II of England as Lord of Ireland. The Remonstrance may be viewed as the conquest and settlement of Ireland as seen by the conquered. The inability of the English to understand and to appreciate the native culture was typical of European overseas expansion for the next several hundred years.—ed.

To the most holy Father in Christ, John, by the grace of God supreme Pontiff, his devoted children, Donald O'Neill, king of Ulster and by hereditary right true heir to the whole of Ireland, and also the under-kings and nobles and the whole Irish people, with humble recommendation of themselves and devout kisses of his blessed feet. Lest the sharp-toothed and viperous calumny of the English and their untrue representations should to any degree excite your mind against us and the defenders of our right, which God forbid, and so that there may be no ground for what is not well known and is falsely presented to kindle your displeasure, for our defense we pour into your ears with a mighty out-cry by means of this letter an entirely true account of our origin and our form of government, if government it can be called, and also of the cruel wrongs that have been wrought inhumanly on us and our forefathers by some kings of England, their evil ministers and English barons born in Ireland, wrongs that are continued still. We do this in order that you may be able to approach the subject and see in which party's loud assertion truth is found. And thus being carefully and sufficiently informed so far as the nature of the case demands, your judgment, like a naked blade, may smite or correct the fault of the party that is in the wrong. . . . And in those days, our chief apostle and patron, St. Patrick, sent to us at the inspiration of the Holy Spirit by your predecessor Celestine in the year 435, taught the truths of the Catholic faith with the fullest success to our fathers. And after the faith had been preached and received, 61 kings of the same blood, without intervention of alien blood, kings admirable in the faith of Christ and filled with works of charity, kings that in temporal things acknowledged no superior, ruled here uninterruptedly in humble obedience to the Roman Church until the year 1170. And it was they, not the English nor others of any nation, who eminently endowed the Irish Church with lands, ample liberties and many possessions, although at the present time she is, for the most part, despoiled of those lands and liberties by the English. And although for so long a time those kings with their own power had firmly defended against tyrants and kings of divers countries the inheritance that God had given them and had always kept their birthright of freedom unimpaired yet, at last, in the year of the Lord 1170, at the false and wicked representation of King Henry of England, under whom and perhaps by whom St. Thomas of Canterbury, as you know, in that very year suffered death for justice and defense of the Church, Pope Adrian, your predecessor, an Englishman not so much by birth as by feeling and character, did in fact, but unfairly, confer upon that same Henry whom for his said offense he should rather have deprived of his own kingdom this lordship of ours by a certain form of words, the course of justice entirely disregarded and the moral vision of that great pontiff blinded, alas, by his English inclinations. . . . For from the time when in consequence of that grant the English iniquitously but with some show of religion entered within the limits of our kingdom, they have striven with all their might and with every treacherous artifice in their power, to wipe our nation out entirely and to eliminate it completely. By base and deceitful craftiness they have prevailed against us so far that without any authority from a superior, they have driven us by force from the spacious places where we dwelled and from the inheritance of our fathers. They have compelled us to seek mountains, woods, barren tracts, and even caverns in the rocks to save our lives, and for a long time back to make our dwellings there like beasts. Yet even in such places as these they harass us constantly and do all they can to expel us from them and seek unduly to seize for themselves every place we occupy, falsely asserting in their blind madness that there is to be no free abode for us in Ireland but that all the land is entirely theirs by right. Whence, by reason of this and much more of the same kind, relentless hatred and incessant wars have arisen between us and them, from which have resulted mutual slaughter, continual plundering, endless rapine, detestable and too frequent deceits and perfidies. But alas, all correction and due reform fail us, for want of a head. And so for many years the native Irish clergy and people have stood in too serious and terrible danger not alone as regards what is perishable and bodily, but further still, through this want, the greatest danger, that of souls, is hanging over them, and that beyond an ordinary degree. For we hold it as an established truth that more than 50,000 human beings of each nation, in addition to those cut off by famine, distress, and prison, have fallen by the sword in consequence of that false representation and the grant resulting from it, since the time when it was made. . . . Know, most holy Father, that King Henry of England, who was authorized in the manner already stated to enter Ireland, and also the four kings who have succeeded him, have clearly gone beyond the limits of the grant made them by the pope's bull in certain specific articles, as appears plainly from the very text of the bull. For the said Henry, as is embodied in the bull, undertook to extend the bounds of the Irish Church, to preserve its rights uninjured and entire, to bring the people under the rule of law and to train them in a good way of life, to implant virtue and to root out the weeds of vice and to make a yearly payment of one penny from every house to blessed Peter the apostle. Henry himself, as well as his aforesaid successors and their wicked and crafty English ministers in no respect indeed keeping this promise, but departing altogether from the terms of the grant, have of set purpose and design accomplished in fact the opposite of all the foregoing engagements. . . . Likewise, the Irish people, whom in explicit terms they had promised to shape to good morals and to bring under laws, they so shape that their holy and dove-like simplicity has been surprisingly altered into a serpentine craftiness through daily life with them and through their bad example. They also deprive the Irish people of the written laws by which, for the most part, they were formerly governed, and of all other law, save what could not be uprooted, enacting for the extermination of our race the most wicked and unjust laws, some of which are presented here as examples of English wickedness.

In the King of England's court in Ireland these laws are rigidly enforced: any person who is not an Irishman may bring any Irishman into court on any cause of action without restriction, but every Irishman, cleric or layman, with the exception of prelates, is refused all recourse to law by the very fact of being Irish. Also, as usually happens for the most part when by perfidy and guile some Englishman kills an Irishman, however noble and inoffensive, whether cleric or lay, regular or secular, even if an Irish prelate should be killed, no punishment or correction is inflicted by the said court on such a nefarious murderer. . . . Also, every Irishwoman, whether noble or otherwise, who marries any Englishman, is entirely deprived of the third part of his lands and possessions after his death precisely because she is Irish. Likewise, wherever the English can oppress an Irishman by main force they do not allow the Irish to dispose of their property according to their own wishes or to make a last will and testament. Nay, they appropriate for themselves all the goods of such persons and deprive the Church of its right and of their own authority make serfs by violence of the blood that has been free from all antiquity. . . . Likewise, where they were bound to implant virtues and root out the weeds of vice, they have cut out by the roots the virtues already planted and themselves have brought in vices. . . . Let these few cases, notorious to everyone, out of the countless misdeeds of that nation serve as examples. . . . And though acts of this kind appear horrible and detestable to all Christians, yet to those of that oft-mentioned nation, as by too hard a daily experience we feel, they seem honorable and praiseworthy, since those that do them reap not at all the punishment of which they are deserving, but by a too flagrant antithesis the reward of praise that they do not merit is heaped upon them. For not only their laymen and secular clergy but also some of their regular clergy assert dogmatically the heresy that it is no more a sin to kill an Irishman than it is to kill a dog or any other brute. And in maintaining this heretical position, some of their monks boldly affirm that if it should happen to them, as it often does, to kill an Irishman, they would not on that account refrain from saying mass, not even for a day. . . . And falling out of this heresy into another error, all of them indifferently, secular and regular, assert with obstinacy that it is lawful for them to take away from us by force of arms whatever they can of our lands and possessions of every kind, making no conscientious scruple about it even when they are at the point of death. And all the land they hold in Ireland they hold by usurpation in this way. And of whatever condition or station he may be that should withstand this error or preach in opposion to them, for that alone he is proclaimed an enemy to the king and kingdom of England, as guilty of death and outlawed by the King's council. For, lusting eagerly for our lands, they it is that, to the no small loss of the kings and kingdom of England, by sowing perpetual dissentions between them and us, have craftily and deceitfully kept us apart from them, lest of our own free will we should hold from the King directly the lands that are rightfully our due. That this is a characteristic policy of theirs is well established, and from it spring frequent acts of bad faith and treachery. For they never cease from sowing similar dissentions not merely between persons only distantly related but even between brothers and near relations. And as in way of life and speech they are more dissimilar from us and in their actions from many other nations than can be described by us in writing or in words, there is no hope whatever of our having peace with them. For such is their arrogance and excessive lust to lord it over us and so great is our due and natural desire to throw off the unbearable yoke of their slavery and to recover our inheritance wickedly seized upon by them, that as there has not been hitherto, there can not now be or ever henceforward be established, sincere good will between them and us in this life. For we have a natural hostility to each other arising from the mutual, malignant and incessant killing of fathers, brothers, nephews, and other near relations and friends so that we can have no inclination toward reciprocal friendship in our time or in that of our sons. Likewise it can not escape your attention, since it is obvious to everyone, that the Roman curia does not receive a penny from every house in Ireland as was promised. In this way then . . . have the kings of England and their oft-mentioned subjects observed the articles of the aforementioned bull to the Irish Church and nation. . . . Let no one wonder then that we are striving to save our lives and defending as we can the rights of our law and liberty against cruel tyrants and usurpers, especially since the said king who calls himself Lord of Ireland and also the said kings his predecessors have wholly failed in this respect to do and exhibit orderly government to us. . . . Wherefore, if for this reason we are forced to attack that king and our said enemies that dwell in Ireland, we do nothing unlawful but rather our action is meritorious and we neither can nor should be held guilty of perjury or disloyalty on this account, since neither we nor our fathers have ever done homage or taken any other oath of fealty to him or his fathers. And therefore, without any conscientious misgivings, so long as life endures we will fight against them in defense of our right and will never cease to attack and assail them until through want of power they shall desist from unjustly injuring us and the justest of Judges shall take evident and fitting vengeance upon them for their tyrannous oppression and other most wicked deeds. This we believe with a firm faith will soon come to pass. . . . Therefore, on account of the aforesaid wrongs and infinite other wrongs that can not easily be comprehended by the wit of man and yet again on account of the injustice of the kings of England and their wicked ministers and the constant treachery of the English of mixed race, who, by the ordinance of the Roman curia, were bound to rule our nation with justice and moderation and have set themselves wickedly to destroy it. In order to shake off the hard and intolerable yoke of their slavery and to recover our native liberty, which for a time through them we lost, we are compelled to wage deadly war with them, preferring under stress of necessity to put ourselves like men to the trial of war in defense of our right, rather than to bear like women their atrocious outrages.

Document 30

The Statutes of Kilkenny (1366) in *Statutes and ordinances and acts of the parliament of Ireland, King John to Henry V*, ed. H. F. Berry (Dublin: His Majesty's Stationery Office, 1907), pp. 431–37, 439, 445–47, 451.

The Statutes of Kilkenny are an interesting example of the way in which the English tried to deal with the Irish. The most famous part of these statutes concerns the prohibition of the Irish language and Irish customs for those among the Irish who wished to be reckoned as loyal subjects of the king. Although some Irish historians have argued that these laws are analogous to the system of apartheid practiced in South Africa, this would seem to be inaccurate. The principle of apartheid assumes fundamental biological differences between Whites and Blacks. The Statutes of Kilkenny assumed that the differences between the English and the Irish were cultural and that an Irishman was capable of becoming Anglicized if he wished to do so. A more reasonable analogy would be to the practice used in colonial Massachusetts to acculturate the Indians, namely the establishment of Praying Towns where Indians who wished to become Christians could live in order to acquire the values and habits of Englishmen which were considered a necessary prerequisite to baptism. In both cases cultural differences were involved, not biological ones.—*ed.*

Whereas at the conquest of the land of Ireland, and for a long time after, the English of the said land used the English language, mode of riding and apparel, and were governed and ruled, and their subjects called Betaghes, by the English law, in which time God and Holy Church, and their franchises according to their conditions were maintained [and themselves lived] in subjection; but now many English of the said land forsaking the English language, fashion, mode of riding, laws and usages, live and govern themselves according to the manners, fashion, and language of the Irish enemies; and also have made divers marriages and alliances between themselves and the Irish enemies aforesaid; whereby the said land and the liege people thereof, the English language, the allegiance due to our lord the King, and the English laws there, are put in subjection and decayed, and the Irish enemies exalted and raised up, contrary to right; our lord the King considering the mischiefs aforesaid, in consequence of the grievous complaints of the commons of his said land, summoned to his Parliament held at Kilkenny, the Thursday next after Ash Wednesday, in the fortieth year of his reign, [18 Feb. 1366] before his well-beloved son Lionel Duke of Clarence, his lieutenant in the parts of Ireland, to the honour of God and of his glorious Mother, and of Holy Church, and for the good government of the said land, and quiet of the people, and for the better observance of the laws, and punishment of evil doers, there are ordained and established by our said lord the King, and his said lieutenant, and our lord the King's council there, with the assent of the archbishops, bishops, abbots, and priors (in that which appertains to them to assent to), the earls, barons, and others the commons of the said land at the said parliament there being and assembled, the ordinances and articles under written, to be held and kept perpetually upon the penalties contained therein. . . .

Also it is ordained and established, that no alliance by marriage, gossipred, fostering of children, concubinage or by amour, or in any other manner, be henceforth made between the English and Irish on the one side or on the other. And that no Englishman, or other person, being at peace, give or sell to any Irish, in time of peace or war, horses or armour, or any manner of victuals in time of war. And if any do to the contrary, and thereof be attaint, that he have judgment of life and limb, as a traitor to our lord the King.

Also, it is ordained and established, that every Englishman use the English language, and be named by an English name, leaving off entirely the manner of naming used by the Irish; and that every Englishman use the English custom, fashion, mode of riding and apparel, according to his estate; and if any English, or Irish living amongst the English, use the Irish language amongst themselves, contrary to this ordinance, and thereof be attaint, that his lands and tenements, if he have any, be seized into the hands of his immediate lord, until he come to one of the Places of our lord the King, and find sufficient surety to adopt and use the English language, and then that he have restitution of his said lands, by writ to issue out of the said Place. In case that such person have not lands or tenements, that his body be taken by some of the officers of our lord the King, and committed to the next gaol, there to remain until he, or another in his name, find sufficient surety in the manner aforesaid. And that no Englishman who has to the value of one hundred shillings of lands or tenements, or of rent by the year, ride otherwise than on a saddle in the English fashion, and he that shall do the contrary and be thereof attaint, that his horse be forfeited to our lord the King, and his body committed to prison, until he make fine according to the King's pleasure, for the contempt aforesaid. And also, that beneficed persons of Holy Church, living amongst the English, use the English language; and if they do not, that their Ordinaries have the issues of their benefices until they use the English language in the manner aforesaid. . . .

Also, whereas diversity of government and divers laws in one land cause diversity of allegiance and disputes among the people, it is agreed and established, that no English having disputes with other English, henceforth make distraint or take pledge, distress or vengeance against any other, whereby the people may be troubled, but that they sue each other at the common law, and that no English be governed in the settlement of their disputes by March or Brehon law, which by right ought not to be called law, but bad custom; but that they be governed, as right is, by the common law of the land, as the lieges of our lord the King; and if any do to the contrary, and thereof be attaint, that he be taken and imprisoned, and adjudged as a traitor. And that no difference of allegiance henceforth be made between the English born in Ireland, and the English born in England, by calling them English hobbe, or Irish dog, but that all be called by one name, the English lieges of our lord the King, and that he who shall be found doing to the contrary be punished by imprisonment for a year, and afterwards fined, at the King's will; and by this ordinance it is not the intention of our lord the King but that it may be lawful for any one who can, to take distress for services and rents due to them, and for damage feasant, as the common law requires. . . .

Also, whereas a land, which is at war, requires that every person do render himself able to defend himself, it is ordained and established, that the commons of the said land of Ireland, who are in divers marches of war, use not henceforth the games which men call hurlings, with great clubs at ball upon the ground, from which great evils and maims have arisen, to the weakening of the defence of the said land, and other games which men call coitings, but that they apply and accustom themselves to use and draw bows and throw lances, and other gentle games which appertain to arms, whereby the Irish enemies may be the better checked by the liege commons of these parts; and if any do or practice the contrary, and of this be attaint, that he be taken and imprisoned, and fined at the will of our lord the King. . . .

Also, it is ordained that no Irish of the nations of the Irish be admitted into any cathedral or collegiate church by provision, collation, or presentation of any person whatsoever, or to any benefice of Holy Church amongst the English of the land; and that if any be admitted, instituted, or inducted into such benefice, it be held void, and that the King have his presentation of the said benefice for that vacancy, to what person soever the advowson of such benefice may belong, saving their right to present or make collation to the said benefice, when it shall be vacant another time.

Also, it is agreed and established, that no house of religion, which is situate among the English, be it exempt or not, henceforth receive any Irishmen [to their] profession, but receive Englishmen, without taking into consideration that they be born in England or in Ireland, and that [in the case of] any that shall do otherwise, and thereof be attaint, the temporalities be seized into the hand of our lord the King, to remain at his will. And that no prelate of Holy Church receive any villein to any orders without the assent and testimony of his lord, made to him under his seal.

Also, whereas the Irish minstrels, coming among the English, spy out the secrets, customs and policies of the English, whereby great evils have often happened, it is agreed and forbidden that any Irish minstrels, that is to say, tympanours, pipers, story tellers, babblers, ryhmers, harpers, or any other Irish minstrels, come amongst the English; and that no English receive them or make gift to them. And that he who does so, and thereof be attaint, be taken and imprisoned, as well the Irish minstrels as the English that receive them or give them anything, and that afterwards they be fined at the King's will, and the instruments of their minstrelsy be forfeited to our lord the King. . . .

Also, it is agreed and assented, that one peace and war be throughout the entire land, so that if any Irish or English be at war in one county, the counties around them shall make war and harass them in their marches, so soon as they shall be warned by the wardens of the peace of the said county, or by the sheriff where the war arises; [and if they do not, they be held as maintainers of felons; and if those of the country where the war arises] suffer their marches to be laid waste by the enemy, and will not rise to check the malice of the enemy, after they be reasonably warned by the wardens of the peace or by the sheriff, or cry raised in the countries of the said county, that then they be held as maintainers of felons. . . .

VI

The Open-Door Policy in Medieval Asia

Introduction

When Jesuit missionaries entered China in the sixteenth century, they did so believing that they were the first visiting Europeans. They were not at first aware that Marco Polo's Cathay, which had been reached by an overland route, was the China that they had entered from the sea, and it was not until the beginning of the seventeenth century that Jesuit missionaries proved that Cathay and China were the same country.[1] Furthermore, the Jesuits did not know that the imperial capital at Peking had been the seat of an archbishop in the fourteenth century and that Franciscan missionaries had already begun making converts. Some enthusiastic Franciscans had even expected the conversion of the emperor of Cathay and, following his example, the conversion of the entire society. The evidence for this ecclesiastical penetration of China during the Middle Ages was buried in the papal archives until materials from the archives were published beginning in the late sixteenth century.[2]

At first glance, there might seem to be little or no connection between medieval and modern contact with China. In fact, however, two links survived the general collapse of direct European contact with Asia, which followed the ouster of the Mongols from China in 1368. In the first place, Marco Polo's book of travels circulated continuously, first in manuscript and then in printed editions, reminding Europeans that there was a rich empire to the east that could be reached under the right circumstances.[3] In addition, the Franciscan friars may have retained some awareness of the missionary journeys made to the East by their predecessors.[4] These traditions came together in the career of Columbus, a man who had read Marco Polo and who was befriended at the low point of his career by the Franciscan community at La Rábida.

Another important link between the medieval experience with Asia and

---

1. Penrose, *Travel and Discovery*, pp. 268–70.
2. Because the Franciscans had taken the lead in the Asian mission, many of the letters were first published by the Order's official historian, Luke Wadding, *Annales Minorum*, 8 vols. (Lyons: 1654).
3. There are at least 138 surviving manuscripts of Marco Polo's *Travels*. The first printed edition appeared in the 1480s. Penrose, *Travel and Discovery*, p. 22.
4. Samuel Eliot Morrison, *The European Discovery of America*, vol. 2, *The Southern Voyages* (New York: Oxford Univ. Press, 1974), p. 34. Franciscans were also among the first missionaries to reach India.

149

the modern was the papacy. To a large extent, papal attitudes toward non-European and non-Christian societies during the period of early modern expansion overseas had been shaped by the papacy's experience with similar societies during the Middle Ages. This experience shaped the policies developed by various popes for dealing with the problems posed to missionaries by the cultural practices of non-Christian, European societies. The most important such problems involved the marriage practices of infidels and the doctrines and liturgical practices of the Christian communities of Asia.[5] The policies developed for coping with these problems were incorporated into papal judicial decisions and studied by canon lawyers who comprised the mainstay of the papal administrative staff. When sixteenth- and seventeenth-century popes faced problems involving different cultural practices, and the possibility of making accomodations with them, the legally trained curial officials were able to reach into the files for precedents upon which to base their decisions. The refusal to make major accomodations for non-European cultures in the modern era was rooted in similar refusals in the Middle Ages.[6]

Contact with Asia was a logical outgrowth of three factors: trade, missionary interest, and the crusades. Europeans had imported silks and spices from Asia for centuries. Missionaries were always interested in converting infidels, especially those who bordered Europe. Finally, the failure of the early crusades encouraged potential crusaders in the later Middle Ages to seek allies against the Moslems from among the other nations that bordered the expanding Moslem world. The first significant attempt to initiate contact with the peoples of Asia, begun at the Council of Lyon in 1245, stemmed from the fear that the Mongols who had already destroyed Kievan Russia, and who were moving relentlessly against Poland and Hungary, would move on into Western Europe.[7] Pope Innocent IV (1243–54) commissioned two Franciscan friars, John of Plano Carpini and Lawrence of Portugal, to meet with the leader of the Mongols and to determine his intentions toward Europe (doc. 31). The friars were to seek the conversion of the Mongols as well. The discovery of Nestorian

5. The problems posed for Christian missionaries by the marriage customs of non-Christians are discussed in John T. Noonan, Jr., *Power to Dissolve* (Cambridge, Mass.: Belknap Press of the Harvard Univ. Press, 1972), pp. 347–59, and James Muldoon, "Missionaries and the Marriages of Infidels: The Case of the Mongol Mission," *The Jurist* 2/3 (Spring and Summer, 1975): 125–41.

6. The problem of adapting the Christian liturgy to the cultural styles of the various non-European cultures that the missionaries encountered was a major issue for the Catholic Church in the seventeenth and eighteenth centuries. The problem is discussed in the *New Catholic Encyclopedia*, s.v. "Chinese Rites Controversy," by F. A. Rouleau. The Jesuits did make concessions to Chinese cultural practices: see George Dunne, *Generation of Giants* (Notre Dame, Indiana: Notre Dame Univ. Press, 1962).

7. The history of the Mongols is treated in René Grousset, *The Empires of the Steppes*, trans. Naomi Walford (New Brunswick, N.J.: Rutgers Univ. Press, 1970).

Christians among members of the khan's household gave rise to the belief that the Mongol leader was sympathetic to Christianity and encouraged the hopes of those who sought the conversion of the Mongols. Plano Carpini's *History of the Mongols*, his record of the mission, was the first extensive description of the Mongols, their history, customs, and, as far as he could determine them, their goals. The journey rendered the Franciscan quite respectful of the Mongols' power.

Some years later, another Franciscan, William of Rubruck, made a similar journey to Central Asia, but he did so apparently on his own initiative. The record of his travels, covering the years 1253–55, provided the most detailed description of the Mongols and their way of life that was to appear in the Middle Ages (doc. 32). One of the most striking scenes in the book dealt with a proposed debate on religious topics that was to be held in the presence of the Mongol khan. The Franciscan was to debate with a representative of the Moslems and with a representative of some other sect, perhaps Taoism. Such debates were not uncommon in thirteenth century Europe, usually pitting Christians against Jews, as Joinville observed (ch. 1, doc. 7). The purpose was to convince nonbelievers by the power of human reason alone.

By the end of the thirteenth century, European leaders could look upon the Mongols in one of two ways. Either the Mongols were enemies with whom no agreements were possible or they were potential allies against the Moslems. As Joinville pointed out, St. Louis, had experience of both approaches to the Mongols (doc. 33). The rude reception met by the French king's representatives at the Mongol court meant that no meaningful alliance was possible between Louis and the Mongols. The search for allies in the struggle against both the Moslems and the Mongols led to the search for a Christian king, Prester John, whose kingdom was somewhere in Asia.[8] The existence of Christian communities in Asia had given rise to stories about a Christian kingdom, surrounded by the Mongols, that was facing destruction unless it received help from the Christians of the West. An alliance between Prester John and the Christian rulers of Europe might lead to the destruction of the Mongol threat to Europe, so a good deal of attention was paid to the search for this elusive king and his kingdom.

The high point of European contact with Asia came in the late

---

8. The story of Prester John intrigued Europe until the sixteenth century. The location of his kingdom varied according to the storyteller. In the late fifteenth century, Ethiopia came to be identified with his kingdom. The search for Prester John is discussed in Vsevolod Slessarev, *Prester John: The Letter and the Myth* (Minneapolis: Univ. of Minnesota Press, 1959). Interest in finding Christian communities in Asia flourished during this period: see, Francis M. Rogers, *The Quest for Eastern Christians: Travels and Rumor in the Age of Discovery* (Minneapolis: Univ. of Minnesota Press, 1962).

thirteenth and the early fourteenth centuries. Merchants, like the Polo family of Venice, and missionaries continued to travel the road to Cathay, apparently in increasing numbers. Marco Polo's book about his adventures in the East (doc. 34) and the handbook for merchants written by Francesco Balducci Pegolotti (doc. 38) suggest that more Italian merchants went to Asia than the few examples that we possess would indicate. Hope for the conversion of the infidels continued to flourish, although hopes for the speedy reconciliation of the Christians already living in the East was fading. The experiences of John of Monte Corvino with the Nestorians had led him to believe that conversion of the infidels would be accomplished only if the Nestorians did not interfere (doc. 35). The situation was probably not helped when Pope Benedict XII (1334-42) responded to the request of a group of Christians living in China for some clergy to minister to them by insisting on liturgical uniformity with Rome and by discoursing at length about papal primacy, an issue that divided Latin Christians from Eastern Christians (doc. 36). Although the participants did not realize it, the visit of these Asian Christians to Rome in 1338 marked the beginning of the end for missionary efforts in Asia. The bishop whom Benedict XII assigned to accompany them on the return trip, John of Marignolli, eventually reached Peking in 1342, only to return to the West in 1347. The collapse of the Mongol Empire and the ouster of the Mongols from China by the Ming Dynasty in 1368 meant the end of Christian missionary efforts in China because the Chinese identified Christianity with the hated Mongols, who had employed Christians in their civil service. Letters and missions continued to issue from the papal court to various eastern rulers until 1370 when the last mission, the fate of which remains unknown, was dispatched.

The reports of the missionaries and merchants provided Europeans with a wide range of information about various segments of Asian society. The picture of Asia included both fact and fancy, but in either case the wealth of Asia was emphasized. Furthermore, the inhabitants of Asia were clearly not primitive barbarians who would benefit from the civilizing influence of European domination. The great kingdom that Marco Polo described was clearly more advanced in many ways than any kingdom in Europe. It was Europe that was barbarous, not China. On through the eighteenth century, China fascinated Europeans. Some European political theorists even saw Chinese society as a model to be emulated, not one to be scorned as primitive.[9]

9. The impact upon European culture of the renewed contacts between Europe and Asia is discussed in Donald F. Lach, *Asia in the Making of Europe*, vol. 1 in 2, *The Century of Discovery* (Chicago: Univ. of Chicago Press, 1965).

Bibliography

The basic work on the papal contacts with the Mongols is Giovanni Soranzo, *Il Papato, l'Europa christiana e i Tartari* (Milan: Università cattolica del Sacro Cuore, 1930). A more recent study that brings the bibliography up to date is I. de Rachewiltz, *Papal Envoys to the Great Khans* (Stanford: Stanford Univ. Press, 1971). Other useful works include: Leonardo Olschki, *Marco Polo's Precursors* (Baltimore: The Johns Hopkins Univ. Press, 1943), and Arthur C. Moule, *Christians in China Before the Year 1550* (London: Society for Promoting Christian Knowledge, 1930). The sudden appearance of the Mongols and their strange ways gave rise to a number of myths about their origins that are discussed in Charles W. Connell, "Western Views of the Origins of the 'Tartars': An Example of Myth in the Second Half of the Thirteenth Century," *Journal of Medieval and Renaissance Studies* 3 (1973): 115–37.

The Christians of India who claimed to be a church founded by the Apostle Thomas are discussed in Leslie W. Brown, *The Indian Christians of St. Thomas. An Account of the Ancient Syrian Church of Malabar* (Cambridge, Eng.: Cambridge Univ. Press, 1956). The attempt to accomodate the practices of the Christians of the Malabar Coast to those of the Latin Church are discussed in the *New Catholic Encyclopedia*, s.v. "Malabar Rites Controversy," by V. Cronin.

It is interesting to note that at the same time as Europeans were beginning to reach out toward Asia, some Chinese travellers reached the eastern fringes of Europe: see E. Bretschneider, *Mediaeval Researches from Eastern Asiatic Sources*, 2 vols. (London: 1888; reprint ed., New York: Barnes and Noble, 1967). During the fifteenth century, a Chinese fleet explored the Indian Ocean and the lands that bordered it, including the shores of East Africa, in an effort that paralleled the early Portuguese efforts to explore the coast of West Africa. The most convenient introductions to this generally overlooked aspect of Chinese history are, Donald F. Lach and Carol Flaumenhaft, *Asia on the Eve of Europe's Expansion*, The Global History Series (Englewood Cliffs, N.J.: Prentice Hall, 1965), pp. 115–20, and Nora Buckley, "The Extraordinary Voyages of Admiral Cheng Ho," *History Today* 25 (July 1975): 462–71.

Document 31

"Journey of Friar John of Pian de Carpine to the Court of Kuyuk Khan," in *The Journey of William of Rubruck to the Eastern Parts of the World, 1253–55,* ed. William W. Rockhill, Hakluyt Society Publications, New Series, no. 4 (London: The Society, 1900), pp. 4–6, 23, 27–30.

When John of Plano Carpini undertook this first mission to the Mongols at the command of Pope Innocent IV, he was already 65 years old. He had engaged in an active career as one of the early leaders of the Franciscan Order, having served as provincial superior of the provinces of Germany and Spain. He lacked, however, any knowledge of the languages spoken in Asia. His associate, Brother Benedict, was Polish and had had some contacts with the Christian principalities that existed on the fringes of the Mongol empire. In July of 1246 the two friars reached the Mongol camp near Karakorum in Mongolia where they observed the installation of the new Great Khan. This mission had little practical effect, and the friars returned to the West bearing only a letter from the Great Khan asking that the pope and the other rulers of Europe submit to him. Upon returning from the mission, John of Plano Carpini reported to Innocent IV and wrote an account of his journey. This account received wide circulation after Vincent of Beauvais included it in his *Speculum Historiale,* a popular compendium of knowledge in the later Middle Ages.—ed.

Having settled then all these matters at Kiew, on the second day after the feast of the Purification of Our Lady (February 4, 1246), we started out from Kiew for other barbarous peoples, with the horses of the Millenarius and an escort. We came to a certain town which was under the direct rule of the Tartars and is called Canov; the prefect of the town gave us horses and an escort as far as another town in which was a certain Alan prefect who was called Micheas, a man full of all malice and iniquity, for he had sent to us to Kiew some of his body-guard, who lyingly said to us, as from the part of Corenza, that we being ambassadors were to come to him; and this he did, though it was not true, in order that he might extort presents from us. When, however, we reached him, he made himself most disagreeable, and unless we promised him presents, would in no wise agree to help us. Seeing that we would not otherwise be able to go farther, we promised to give him some presents, but when we gave him what appeared to us suitable, he refused to receive them unless we gave more;

and so we had to add to them according to his will, and something besides he subtracted from us deceitfully and maliciously.

After that we left with him on the second day of Quinquagesima (19th February), and he led us as far as the first camp of the Tartars, and on the first Friday after Ash Wednesday (23rd February), while we were stopping for the night as the sun went down, the Tartars broke in on us in arms in horrible fashion asking who we were. We answered them that we were envoys of the Lord Pope, and then, having accepted some food from us, they left at once. Starting again at morn, we had only gone a little way when their chiefs who were in the camp came to us, and inquired of us why we came to them, and what was our business. We answered them that we were the envoys of the Lord Pope, who was the lord and father of Christians; that he had sent us to the King as well as to the princes and all the Tartars, because he desired that all Christians should be friends of the Tartars and at peace with them. Moreover, as he wished that they should be mighty with God in heaven, he, the Lord Pope, advised them as well through us as by his letters, that they should become Christians and receive the faith of Our Lord Jesus Christ, for otherwise they could not be saved. He told them furthermore that he was astonished at the slaying of human beings done by the Tartars, and especially of Christians and above all of Hungarians, Moravians and Poles, who were his subjects, when they had injured them in nothing nor attempted to injure them; and as the Lord God was gravely offended at this, he cautioned them to abstain henceforth from such acts, and to repent them of those they had done. Furthermore we said that the Lord Pope requested that they should write to him what they would do and what was their intention; and that they would give answer to him to all the above points in their letters. Having heard our motives, and understood and noted them down, they said that, in view of what we had said, they would give us pack-horses as far as Corenza, and supply a guide; and at once they asked for presents, which we gave them, for we must needs do their will. . . .

It was at this place (the Golden Orda) that we were called into the Emperor's presence; after that Chingay the prothonotary had written down our names and the names of those who had sent us, and also those of the chief of the Solanges and of the others, he repeated them all, shouting with a loud voice before the Emperor and all the chiefs. When this had been done each of us had to bend the left knee four times, and they cautioned us not to touch the threshold, and having searched us carefully for knives, and not having found any, we entered the door on the east side, for no one dare enter that on the west side save the Emperor; and the same rule applies if it is the tent of a chief; but those of low rank pay little attention to such matters. And when we entered his tent, it was the first occasion since he had been made Emperor (that he had given an audience). He received likewise the ambassadors, but very few persons entered his tent. Here also such great quantities of presents were given him by the ambassadors, silks, samites, purples, baldakins, silk girdles worked in gold, splendid furs and other things, that it was a marvel to see. . . .

After these things had happened the Emperor sent his prothonotary Chingay to tell us to write down what we had to say and our business, and to give it to him; this we did, writing down all we had previously said at Bati's, as has been stated above. After an interval of several days, he had us again called, and told us, through Kadac, the procurator of the whole empire, and in the presence of the prothonotaries Bala and Chingay, and of many others of his secretaries, to say all we had to say; and this we did right willingly. Our interpreter on that occasion, as well as on the other, was Temer, a knight of Jerosalv's, now a clerk with him, and another clerk of the Emperor's. And he (i.e., Kadac) asked us on the latter occasion if there were any persons with the Lord Pope who understood the written languages of the Ruthenians or Saracens or Tartars. We replied that we did not use either the Ruthenian, Tartar, or Saracenic writing, and that though there were Saracens in the country, they were far distant from the Lord Pope. We added that it appeared to us the best plan for them to write in Tartar, and to have it translated to us, and that we would carefully write it down in our language, taking both the (original) letter and the translation to the Lord Pope. On this they left us and went back to the Emperor.

On the feast of Saint Martin (11th November) we were again summoned, and Kadac, Chingay, Bala and several others of the secretaries came to us, and the letter was translated to us word for word; and as we translated it into Latin they made us explain each phrase, wishing to ascertain if we had made a mistake in any word; and when the two letters were written they made us read them together and separately for fear we had left out anything, and they said to us: "Be sure you understand it all, for it must not be that you do not understand everything, when you have reached such very distant lands." And having told them: "We understand it all," they re-wrote the letter in Saracenic, so that it might be read to the Lord Pope if he could find any one in our part of the world able to do so.

It is the custom of the Emperor of the Tartars never to address in person a stranger, no matter how great he may be; he only listens, and then answers through the medium of someone, as I have explained. Whenever they explain any business to Kadac, or listen to an answer of the Emperor, those who are under him (i.e., his own subjects), remain on their knees until the end of the speech, no matter how great they may be. One may not, for it is not the custom, say anything more about any question after it is disposed of by the Emperor. This Emperor has a pro-curator, prothonotaries and secretaries, and also all the other officers for public as well as private affairs, except advocates, for they carry out with-out a murmur all judgments according to the Emperor's decision. The other princes of the Tartars do in like manner as regards those things which pertain to their offices.

This Emperor[1] may be forty or forty-five years or more old; he is of medium stature, very prudent and extremely shrewd, and serious and sedate in his manners; and he has never been seen to laugh lightly or show any levity, and of this we were assured by Christians who were constantly with him. We were also assured by Christians who were of his household that they firmly believed that he was about to become a Christian. As signal evidence of this he keeps Christian clerks and gives them allowances, and he has always the chapel of the Christians in front of his great tent, and (these priests) chant publicly and openly and beat (a tablet) ac-cording to the fashion of the Greeks at appointed hours, just like other Christians, and though there may be ever so great a multitude of Tartars and of other people. And the other chiefs do not have this.

Our Tartars who were to come back with us told us that the Emperor proposed sending his ambassadors with us. He wished, however, I think, that we should ask him to do so, for one of our Tartars, the elder of the two, told us to ask it; but it not seeming to us good that they should come, we replied that it was not for us to ask it, but that if the Emperor of his own will sent them, we would with God's help guide them safely. There were various reasons, however, for which it seemed to us inexpedi-ent that they should come. The first reason was that we feared they would see the dissensions and wars among us, and that it would encourage them to march against us. The second reason was that we feared they were in-tended to be spies. The third reason was that we feared lest they be put to death, as our people for the most part are arrogant and hasty: thus it was that when the servants who were with us at the request of the Cardinal Legate in Germany were going back to him in Tartar dress, they came near being stoned by the Germans on the road, and were forced to leave off that dress. And it is the custom of the Tartars never to make peace with those who have killed their envoys till they have wreaked vengeance upon them. The fourth reason was that we feared they would carry us off, as was once done with a Saracen prince, who is still a captive, unless he is dead. The fifth reason was that there was no need for their coming, for they had no other order or authority than to bring the letters of the Emperor to the Lord Pope and the other princes (of Christendom), which we (already) had, and we believed that evil might come of it.

1. Guyuk Khan (1240–48).

Therefore it pleased us not that they should come. The third day after this, which was the feast of Saint Brice (13th November), they gave us permission to leave (*licentiam*) and a letter of the Emperor signed with his seal, and then they sent us to the Emperor's mother, who gave to each of us a fox-skin gown with the fur outside and wadding inside, and also a piece of purple—of which our Tartars stole a palm's length from each, and also more than half of another piece which was given to our servant; but though it was no secret to us, we did not choose to make any ado over it.

Document 32

William of Rubruck, *The Journey of William of Rubruck to the Eastern Parts of the World*, 1253–55, ed. William W. Rockhill, Hakluyt Society Publications, new series, no. 4 (London, The Society, 1900), pp. 228–37.

Almost nothing is known about William of Rubruck except that in 1253 he set off to meet with Mongol Khan, bearing greetings from St. Louis, and that he returned in 1255. His mission was the most purely religious in character of all the thirteenth-century missions to the East. Although his description of the Mongols and their way of life was the most thoughtful description available to medieval men, the excerpt presented here reflects another aspect of his work, the naive belief that Christians could convert infidels to the faith by the sheer force of logical argument. The debate among the representatives of the religions present at the Mongol court was not untypical of thirteenth-century missionary efforts.—*ed.*

The next day (25th May) (the Chan) sent his secretaries to me, who said: "Our lord sends us to you to say that you are here Christians, Saracens and Tuins.[1] And each of you says that his doctrine is the best, and his writings—that is, books—the truest. So he wishes that you shall all meet together, and make a comparison, each one writing down his precepts, so that he himself may be able to know the truth." Then I said: "Blessed be God, who put this in the Chan's heart. But our Scriptures tell us, the servant of God should not dispute, but should show mildness to all; so I am ready, without disputation or contention, to give reason for the faith and hope of the Christians, to the best of my ability." They wrote down my words, and carried them back to him. Then it was told the Nestorians that they should look to themselves, and write down what they

---

1. A term for those who worship idols.

wished to say, and likewise to the Saracens, and in the same way to the Tuins.

The next day (26th May) he again sent secretaries, who said: "Mangu Chan[2] wishes to know why you have come to these parts." I replied to them: "He must know it by Baatu's letters." Then they said: "The letters of Baatu have been lost, and he has forgotten what Baatu wrote to him; so he would know from you." Then feeling safer I said: "It is the duty of our faith to preach the Gospel to all men. So when I heard of the fame of the Moal people, I was desirous of coming to them; and while this desire was on me, we heard that Sartach was a Christian. So I turned my footsteps toward him. And the lord king of the French sent him letters containing kindly words, and among other things he bore witness to what kind of men we were, and requested that he would allow us to remain among the men of Moal. Then he (i.e., Sartach) sent us to Baatu, and Baatu sent us to Mangu Chan; so we have begged him, and do again beg him, to permit us to remain."

They wrote all these things down, and carried it back to him on the morrow.

Then he again sent them to me, saying: "The Chan knows well that you have no mission to him, but that you have come to pray for him, like other righteous priests; but he would know if ever any ambassadors from you have come to us, or any of ours gone to you." Then I told them all about David and Friar Andrew, and they, putting it all down in writing, reported it back to him.

Then he again sent them to me, saying: "You have stayed here a long while; (the Chan) wishes you to go back to your own country, and he has inquired whether you will take an ambassador of his with you." I replied to them: "I would not dare take his envoys outside his own dominions, for there is a hostile country between us and you, and seas and mountains; and I am but a poor monk; so I would not venture to take them under my leadership." And they, having written it all down, went back.

Pentecost eve came (30th May). The Nestorians had written a whole chronicle from the creation of the world to the Passion of Christ; and passing over the Passion, they had touched on the Ascension and the resurrection of the dead and on the coming to judgement, and in it there were some censurable statements, which I pointed out to them. As for us, we simply wrote out the symbol of the mass, "*Credo in unum Deum.*" Then I asked them how they wished to proceed. They said they would discuss in the first place with the Saracens. I showed them that that was not a good plan, for the Saracens agreed with us in saying that there is one God: "So you have (in them) a help against the Tuins." They agreed with

2. Mangu or Mongka was the Khan from 1251 to 1259.

this. Then I asked them if they knew how idolatry had arisen in the world, and they were in ignorance of it. Then I told them, and they said: "Tell them these things, then let us speak, for it is a difficult matter to talk through an interpreter." I said to them: "Try how you will manage against them; I will take the part of the Tuins, and you will maintain that of the Christians. We will suppose I belong to that sect, because they say that God is not; now prove that God is." For there is a sect there which says that whatever spirit (*anima*) and whatever virtue is in anything, is the God of that thing, and that God exists not otherwise. Then the Nestorians were unable to prove anything, but only to tell what the Scriptures tell. I said: "They do not believe in the Scriptures; you tell me one thing, and they tell another." Then I advised them to let me in the first place meet them, so that, if I should be confounded, they would still have a chance to speak; if they should be confounded, I should not be able to get a hearing after that. They agreed to this.

We were assembled then on Pentecost eve at our oratory, and Mangu Chan sent three secretaries who were to be umpires, one a Christian, one a Saracen, and one a Tuin; and it was published aloud: "This is the order of Mangu, and let no one dare say that the commandment of God differs from it. And he orders that no one shall dare wrangle or insult any other, or make any noise by which this business shall be interfered with, on penalty of his head." Then all were silent. And there was a great concourse of people there; for each side had called thither the most learned of its people, and many others had also assembled.

Then the Christians put me in the middle, telling the Tuins to speak with me. Then they—and there was a great congregation of them—began to murmur against Mangu Chan, for no other Chan had ever attempted to pry into their secrets. Then they opposed to me one who had come from Cathay, and who had his interpreter; and I had the son of master William, who began by saying to me: "Friend, if you think you are going to be hushed up (*conclusus*), look for a more learned one than yourself." I remained silent. Then (the Tuin) inquired by what I wished to begin the discussion, by the subject how the world was made, or what becomes of the soul after death. I replied to him: "Friend, this should not be the beginning of our talk. All things proceed from God; He is the fountainhead of all things; so we must first speak of God, of whom you think differently from us, and Mangu Chan wishes to know who holds the better belief." The umpires decided that this was right. . . .

On Pentecost day (31st May) Mangu Chan called me before him, and also the Tuin with whom I had discussed; but before I went in, the interpreter, master William's son, said to me that we should have to go back to our country, and that I must not raise any objection, for he understood that it was a settled matter. When I came before the Chan, I had to bend the knees, and so did the Tuin beside me, with his interpreter. Then (the Chan) said to me: "Tell me the truth, whether you said the other day, when I sent my secretaries to you, that I was a Tuin." I replied: "My lord, I did not say that; I will tell you what I said, if it pleases you." Then I repeated to him what I had said, and he replied: "I thought full well that you did not say it, for you should not have said it; but your interpreter translated badly." And he held out toward me the staff on which he leaned, saying: "Fear not." And I, smiling, said in an undertone: "If I had been afraid, I should not have come here." He asked the interpreter what I had said, and he repeated it to him. After that he began confiding to me his creed: "We Moal," he said, "believe that there is only one God, by whom we live and by whom we die, and for whom we have an upright heart." Then I said: "May it be so, for without His grace this cannot be." He asked what I had said; the interpreter told him. Then he added: "But as God gives us the different fingers of the hand, so he gives to men divers ways. God gives you the Scriptures, and you Christians keep them not. You do not find (in them, for example) that one should find fault with another, do you?" "No, my lord," I said; "but I told you from the first that I did not want to wrangle with anyone." "I do not intend to say it," he said, "for you. Likewise you do not find that a man should depart from justice for money." "No, my lord," I said. "And truly I came not to these parts to obtain money; on the contrary I have refused what has been offered me." And there was a secretary present, who bore witness that I had refused an iascot and silken cloths. "I do not say it," he said, "for you. God gave you therefore the Scriptures, and you do not keep them; He gave us diviners, we do what they tell us, and we live in peace."

He drank four times, I believe, before he finished saying all this. And I was listening attentively for him to say something else of his creed, when he began talking of my return journey, saying: "You have stayed here a long while; I wish you to go back. You have said that you would not dare take my ambassadors with you; will you take my words, or my letters?" And from that time I never found the opportunity nor the time when I could show him the Catholic Faith. For no one can speak in his presence but so much as he wishes, unless he be an ambassador; for an ambassador can say whatever he chooses, and they always ask if he wishes to say something more. As for me, it was not allowed me to speak more; I had only to listen to him, and reply to his questions. So I answered him that he should make me understand his words, and have them put down in writing, for I would willingly take them as best I could. Then he asked me if I wanted gold or silver or costly clothing. I said: "We take no such things; but we have no travelling money, and without your assistance we cannot get out of your country." He said: "I will have you given all you require while in my possessions; do you want anything more?" I replied: "That suffices us." Then he asked: "How far do you wish to be taken?" I said: "Our power extends to the country of the king of Hermenia; if we were (escorted) that far, it would suffice me." He answered: "I will have you taken that far; after that look out for yourself."

Document 33

Jean, Sire de Joinville, "Chronicle of the Crusade of St. Lewis," in *Memoirs of the Crusades*, trans. Frank Marzials (London: J. M. Dent, 1908; reprint ed., New York: E. P. Dutton, 1958), pp. 253–59.

One of the great dreams of those who led the crusades was the creation of an alliance between European Christians and the Mongols. Both groups were threatened by the expansion of the Moslem world and, to the Europeans, the Mongols seemed ripe for conversion as well. If an alliance could be achieved, the Moslems would be squeezed between the two wings of the combined army in one last crusade. The mission that St. Louis sent to inquire about such an alliance returned with the information that the Mongols saw the French king's proposal as meaning the subjugation of the French to the Mongols. St. Louis soured on the idea of an alliance, but that did not prevent variations on the idea from surfacing later. The version of the Prester John story, which the Mongols related to the French ambassadors, may have been designed to convince the French that there was no possibility of finding allies in Asia with whom the Europeans could ally themselves against the Mongols armies.—*ed.*

As I have told you before, while the king was sojourning in Cyprus, envoys came from the Tartars and gave him to understand that they would help him to conquer the kingdom of Jerusalem from the Saracens. The king sent back these envoys, and sent with him, by his own envoys, a chapel which he had caused to be fashioned all in scarlet; and in order to draw the Tartars to our faith, he had caused all our faith to be imaged in the chapel: the Annunciation of the angel, the Nativity, the baptism that God was baptised withal, and all the Passion, and the Ascension, and the coming of the Holy Ghost; and with the chapel he sent also cups, books, and all things needful for the chanting of the mass, and two Preaching Brothers to sing the mass before the Tartars.

The king's envoys arrived at the port of Antioch; and from Antioch it took them full a year's journeying, riding ten leagues a day, to reach the great King of the Tartars. They found all the land subject to the Tartars, and many cities that they had destroyed, and great heaps of dead men's bones.

They inquired how the Tartars had arrived at such authority, and killed and utterly confounded so many people; and this was how, as the envoys reported it to the king: The Tartars came, being there created, from a great plain of sand where no good thing would grow. This plain began from certain rocks, very great and marvellous, which are at the world's end, towards the East; and the said rocks have never been passed by man, as the Tartars testify. And they said that within these rocks are enclosed the people of Gog and Magog, who are to come at the end of the world, when Antichrist shall come to destroy all things.

In this plain dwelt the people of the Tartars; and they were subject to Prester John, and to the Emperor of Persia, whose land came next to his, and to several other misbelieving kings, to whom they rendered tribute and service every year, for the pasturage of their beasts, seeing they had no other means of livelihood. This Prester John, and the King of Persia, and the other kings, held the Tartars in such contempt that when they brought their rents they would not receive them face-wise, but turned their backs upon them.

Among the Tartars was a wise man, who journeyed over all the plains, and spoke with the wise men of the plains, and of the different places, and showed them in what bondage they stood, and prayed them all to consider how best they might find a way of escape from the bondage in which they were held. He wrought so effectually that he gathered them all together at the end of the plain, over against the land of Prester John, and explained matters to them. And they answered that whatever he desired, that they would do. And he said that they would achieve nothing unless they had a king and lord over them. And he taught them after what manner they might obtain a king; and they agreed.

And this was the manner: out of the fifty-two tribes that there were, each tribe was to bring an arrow marked with its name; and by consent of all the people it was agreed that the fifty-two arrows so brought should be placed before a child aged five years; and the arrow that the child took first would mark the tribe from which the king would be chosen. When the child had so lifted up one of the arrows, the wise men caused all the other tribes to draw back; and it was settled that the tribe from which the king was to be chosen should select among themselves fifty-two of the wisest and best men that they had. When these were elected, each one brought an arrow marked with his name. Then was it agreed that the man whose arrow the child lifted up should be made king. And the child lifted up one of the arrows, and it was that of the wise man by whom the people had been instructed. Then were the people glad, and each rejoiced greatly.

And the wise man bade them all be silent, and said, "Lords, if you would have me to be your king, swear to me by Him who made the heavens and the earth, that you will keep my commandments." And they swore it.

The ordinances that he established had for purpose the maintenance of peace among the people; and they were to this effect: that none should steal another man's goods, nor any man strike another, on penalty of losing his fist; that no man should have company with another's wife or daughter, on penalty of losing his fist, or his life. Many other good ordinances did he establish among them for the maintenance of peace.

VICTORY OF THE TARTARS OVER PRESTER JOHN— VISION OF ONE OF THEIR PRINCES—HIS CONVERSION

After he had established order and arrayed them, the king spoke in this wise, "Lords, the most powerful enemy that we have is Prester John. And I command you to be all ready, on the morrow, to fall upon him; and if it so happens that he defeats us—which God forbid!—let each do as best he can. And if we defeat him, I order that the slaying last three days and three nights, and that none, during that space, be so rash as to lay hand on the booty, but all be bent on slaying the people; for after we have obtained the victory, I will distribute the booty, duly and loyally, so that each shall hold himself well paid." To this they all agreed.

On the morrow they fell upon their enemies, and, as God so willed, discomfited them. All those whom they found in arms, and capable of defence, they put to the sword; and those whom they found in religious garb, the priests and other religiouses, they slew not. The other people belonging to Prester John's land, who were not in that battle, made themselves subject unto the Tartars.

One of the princes of the tribes spoken of above, was lost for three months, so that no one had news of him; and when he came back he was neither athirst nor an hungered, for he thought he had remained away no more than one night at the most. The news that he brought back was this: that he had gone to the top of a tall hillock and had found thereon a great many folk, the fairest folk that he had ever seen, the best clothed and the best adorned; and at the end of the hillock he saw sitting, a king, fairer than the rest, and better clothed, and better adorned; and this king sat upon a throne of gold. At his right sat six kings, crowned, richly adorned with precious stones, and at his left six kings. Near him, at his right hand, was a queen kneeling, and she prayed and besought him to think upon her people; at his left hand knelt a man of exceeding beauty, and he had two wings resplendent as the sun. And round the king were a great foison of fair folk with wings. Then the king called the prince to him, and said, "Thou art come from the host of the Tartars." And he replied, "Sire, that is so, truly." And the king said, "Thou shalt go to thy king and tell him that thou hast seen me, who am lord of heaven and earth; and thou shalt tell him to render thanks to me for the victory I have given him over Prester John, and over his people. And thou shalt tell him also, as from me, that I give him power to bring the whole earth under his subjection." "Sire," said the prince, "how will he then believe me?" "Thou shalt tell him to believe thee by these signs: that thou shalt go and fight against the Emperor of Persia, with three hundred of thy people, and no more; and in order that your great king may believe that I have power to do all things, I shall give thee the victory over the Emperor of Persia, who will do battle against thee with three hundred thousand armed men, and more; and before thou goest to do battle against him, thou shalt ask of thy king to give thee the priests and men of religion whom he has taken in the (late) battle; and what these teach, that thou shalt firmly believe, thou and all thy people." "Sire," said the prince, "I cannot go hence, if thou dost not cause me to be shown the way."

Then the king turned towards a great multitude of knights, so well armed that it was a marvel to see them; and he called one of them, and said, "George, come hither." And the knight came and knelt before him. Then the king said to him, "Rise, and lead me this man safe and sound to his tent." And this the knight did at the dawning of a certain day.

As soon as all his people saw the prince, they made such joy of him, as did all the host likewise, that it was past the telling. He asked the great king to give him the priests, and he gave them to him; and then the prince and all his people received the priests' teaching so favourably that they were all baptised. After these things the prince took three hundred men-at-arms, and caused them to be confessed and to make ready for battle, and then went and fought against the Emperor of Persia, and defeated him, and drove him from his kingdom, so that the said emperor came flying to the kingdom of Jerusalem; and this was the same emperor who discomfited our people, and took Count Walter of Brienne prisoner, as shall be told to you hereinafter.

MANNERS OF THE TARTARS—PRIDE OF THEIR KING—ST. LEWIS REPENTS OF HAVING SENT AN ENVOY TO HIM

The people of this Christian prince were so numerous that the king's envoys told us that he had in his camp eight hundred chapels on wagons. Their manner of living is such that they eat no bread, and live on meat and milk. The best meat they have is horseflesh; and they put it to lie in brine and dry it afterwards, so that they can cut it as they would black bread. The best beverage they have, and the strongest, is mare's milk, flavoured with herbs. There was presented to the great king of the Tartars a horse laden with flour, who had come a three-months journey's distance; and he gave it to the envoys of the king.

There are among them a great many Christian folk who hold the creed of the Greeks, and there are, besides, the Christians of whom we have already spoken, and others. These Christians the Tartars send against the Saracens when they wish to make war on the Saracens; and contrariwise they use the Saracens in any war against the Christians. All manner of childless women go with them to war, and they give pay to such women as they would do to men, according to their strength and vigour. And the king's envoys told us that the men and women soldiers ate together in the quarters of the chiefs under whom they served; and that the men dared not touch the women in any sort, because of the law that their first king had given them.

The flesh of all manner of beasts dying in the camp is eaten. The women who have children see after them, and take care of them; and also prepare the food of the people who go to battle. They put the raw meat between their saddles and the lappets of their clothing, and when the blood is well pressed out, they eat it quite raw. What they cannot eat, there and then, they throw into a leather bag; and when they are hungry they open the bag and always eat the oldest bits first. . . .

But now let us go back to the matter in hand, and tell how the great King of the Tartars, after he had received the king's envoys and presents, sent to gather together, under safe conduct, several kings who had not as yet submitted to him; and when they were come he caused the king's chapel to be pitched, and spoke to them after this manner, "Lords, the King of France has sued for mercy, and submitted himself to us, and behold here is the tribute he has sent us; and if you do not submit yourselves to us we will send and fetch him for your destruction." Many there were who, through fear of the French king, placed themselves in subjection to that Tartar king.

With the king's envoys returned other envoys from the great King of the Tartars, and these brought letters to the King of France, saying, "A good thing is peace; for in the land where peace reigns those that go about on four feet eat the grass of peace; and those that go about on two feet till the earth—from which good things do proceed—in peace also. And this thing we tell thee for thy advertisement; for thou canst not have peace save thou have it with us. For Prester John rose up against us, and such and such kings"—and he named a great many—"and we have put them all to the sword. So we admonish thee to send us, year by year, of thy gold and of thy silver, and thus keep us to be thy friend; and if thou wilt not do this, we will destroy thee and thy people, as we have done to the kings already named." And you must know that it repented the king sorely that he had ever sent envoys to the great King of the Tartars.

Document 34*

Marco Polo, The Book of Ser Marco Polo, ed. Henry Yule, 2 vols. (London: Murray, 1926), 1: 13–14, 26, 362–64, 394–95.

Marco Polo's book about his travels in Asia in the late thirteenth century has not always been accepted as authentic; for a time it seemed too fantastic to be true. However, with increased knowledge of European contacts with Asia in that period, the story of the Polo family's experiences seems quite possible. Marco Polo went to China accompanied by his father and uncle, who had been there previously but returned to Europe seeking missionaries for a return journey. The Great Khan had requested that they bring one hundred wise men with them, but when the Polos left Europe in 1271, they were accompanied by only two Dominican friars, who refused to go beyond Armenia. After a journey that lasted three and a half years, the Polos reached the Khan's court in 1275. For the next twenty years, the three Venetians lived in China and served Kublai Khan. During this service, Marco obtained first-hand information about China, information that he later put into his famous book. After returning home in 1295, Marco's life was less exotic. His memoirs were compiled apparently only because having been taken prisoner in one of the periodic wars between Genoa and Venice, one of his fellow prisoners wrote down Marco's stories about the East. His final years, until his death in 1324, may have been embittered by the refusal of his fellow Venetians to believe his stories.

One of the attractions of Marco Polo's description of China was the picture he drew of a large, wealthy, and peaceful kingdom. In his time, the Mongols were secure in their possession of China, having completed its conquest in 1260 under Kublai Khan. Marco saw the Mongol dynasty at its peak. He did not live to see their defeat and expulsion from China in 1368. As a result, his description of China was not a description of typical China, something neither he nor his readers realized. While the wealth that China possessed must have attracted the interest of some of his listeners, the idea of a large and peaceful society lacking the divisive wars that marked European society in the thirteenth and fourteenth centuries must have attracted the interest of others.—ed.

When that Prince, whose name was Cublay Kaan, Lord of the Tartars all over the earth, and of all the kingdoms and provinces and territories

---

* Reprinted by permission of John Murray (Publishers) Ltd.

of that vast quarter of the world, had heard all that the Brothers had to tell him about the ways of the Latins, he was greatly pleased, and he took it into his head that he would send them on an Embassy to the Pope. So he urgently desired them to undertake this mission along with one of his Barons; and they replied that they would gladly execute all his commands as those of their Sovereign Lord. Then the Prince sent to summon to his presence one of his Barons whose name was Cogatal, and desired him to get ready, for it was proposed to send him to the Pope along with the Two Brothers. The Baron replied that he would execute the Lord's commands to the best of his ability.

After this the Prince caused letters from himself to the Pope to be indited in the Tartar tongue, and committed them to the Two Brothers and to that Baron of his own, and charged them with what he wished them to say to the Pope. Now the contents of the letter were to this purport: He begged that the Pope would send as many as a hundred persons of our Christian faith; intelligent men, acquainted with the Seven Arts, well qualified to enter into controversy, and able clearly to prove by force of argument to idolaters and other kinds of folk, that the Law of Christ was best, and that all other religions were false and naught; and that if they would prove this, he and all under him would become Christians and the Church's liegemen. Finally he charged his Envoys to bring back to him some Oil of the Lamp which burns on the Sepulchre of Our Lord at Jerusalem. . . .

And what shall I tell you? when the Two Brothers and Mark had arrived at that great city, they went to the Imperial Palace, and there they found the Sovereign attended by a great company of Barons. So they bent the knee before him, and paid their respects to him, with all possible reverence [prostrating themselves on the ground]. Then the Lord bade them stand up, and treated them with great honour, showing great pleasure at their coming, and asked many questions as to their welfare, and how they had sped. They replied that they had in verity sped well, seeing that they found the Kaan well and safe. Then they presented the credentials and letters which they had received from the Pope, which pleased him right well; and after that they produced the Oil from the Sepulchre, and at that also he was very glad, for he set great store thereby. And next, spying Mark, who was then a young gallant, he asked who was that in their company? "Sire," said his father, Messer Nicolo, " 'tis my son and your liegeman." "Welcome is he too," quoth the Emperor. And why should I make a long story? There was great rejoicing at the Court because of their arrival; and they met with attention and honour from everybody.

So there they abode at the Court with the other Barons. . . .

You must know that for three months of the year, to wit December, January, and February, the Great Kaan resides in the capital city of Cathay, which is called Cambaluc, [and which is at the north-eastern extremity of the country]. In that city stands his great Palace, and now I will tell you what it is like.

It is enclosed all round by a great wall forming a square, each side of which is a mile in length; that is to say, the whole compass thereof is four miles. This you may depend on; it is also very thick, and a good ten paces in height, whitewashed and loop-holed all round. At each angle of the wall there is a very fine and rich palace in which the war-harness of the Emperor is kept, such as bows and quivers, saddles and bridles, and bowstrings, and everything needful for an army. Also midway between every two of these Corner Palaces there is another of the like; so that taking the whole compass of the enclosure you find eight vast Palaces stored with the Great Lord's harness of war. And you must understand that each Palace is assigned to only one kind of article; thus one is stored with bows, a second with saddles, a third with bridles, and so on in succession right round. . . .

In the middle of the second enclosure is the Lord's Great Palace, and I will tell you what it is like.

You must know that it is the greatest Palace that ever was. [Towards the north it is in contact with the outer wall, whilst towards the south there is a vacant space which the Barons and the soldiers are constantly traversing. The Palace itself] hath no upper story, but is all on the ground floor, only the basement is raised some ten palms above the surrounding soil [and this elevation is retained by a wall of marble raised to the level of the pavement, two paces in width and projecting beyond the base of the Palace so as to form a kind of terrace-walk, by which people can pass round the building, and which is exposed to view, whilst on the outer edge of the wall there is a very fine pillared balustrade; and up to this the people are allowed to come]. The roof is very lofty, and the walls of the Palace are all covered with gold and silver. They are also adorned with representations of dragons [sculptured and gilt], beasts and birds, knights and idols, and sundry other subjects. And on the ceiling too you see nothing but gold and silver and painting. [On each of the four sides there is a great marble staircase leading to the top of the marble wall, and forming the approach to the Palace.]

The Hall of the Palace is so large that it could easily dine 6,000 people; and it is quite a marvel to see how many rooms there are besides. The building is altogether so vast, so rich, and so beautiful, that no man on earth could design anything superior to it. The outside of the roof also is all coloured with vermilion and yellow and green and blue and other hues, which are fixed with a varnish so fine and exquisite that they shine like crystal, and lend a resplendent lustre to the Palace as seen for a great way round. This roof is made too with such strength and solidity that it is fit to last for ever.

[On the interior side of the Palace are large buildings with halls and chambers, where the Emperor's private property is placed, such as his treasures of gold, silver, gems, pearls, and gold plate, and in which reside the ladies and concubines. There he occupies himself at his own convenience, and no one else has access.]. . . .

Now you must know that the Great Kaan hath set apart 12,000 of his men who are distinguished by the name of *Keshican*, as I have told you before; and on each of these 12,000 Barons he bestows thirteen changes of raiment, which are all different from one another: I mean that in one set the 12,000 are all of one colour; the next 12,000 of another colour, and so on; so that they are of thirteen different colours. These robes are garnished with gems and pearls and other precious things in a very rich and costly manner. And along with each of these changes of raiment, i.e. 13 times in the year, he bestows on each of those 12,000 Barons a fine golden girdle of great richness and value, and likewise a pair of boots of *Camut*, that is to say of *Borgal*, curiously wrought with silver thread; insomuch that when they are clothed in these dresses every man of them looks like a king! And there is an established order as to which dress is to be worn at each of those thirteen feasts. The Emperor himself also has his thirteen suits corresponding to those of his Barons; in colour, I mean (though his are grander, richer, and costlier), so that he is always arrayed in the same colour as his Barons, who are, as it were, his comrades. And you may see that all this costs an amount which it is scarcely possible to calculate.

Now I have told you of the thirteen changes of raiment received from the Prince by those 12,000 Barons, amounting in all to 156,000 suits of so great cost and value, to say nothing of the girdles and the boots which are also worth a great sum of money. All this the Great Lord hath ordered, that he may attach the more of grandeur and dignity to his festivals.

And now I must mention another thing that I had forgotten, but which you will be astonished to learn from this Book. You must know that on the Feast Day a great Lion is led to the Emperor's presence, and as soon as it sees him it lies down before him with every sign of the greatest veneration, as if it acknowledged him for its lord; and it remains there lying before him, and entirely unchained. Truly this must seem a strange story to those who have not seen the thing!

Document 35

Letter of John of Monte Corvino in *Cathay and the Way Thither*, eds. Henry Yule and Henri Cordier, Hakluyt Society Publications, nos. 33, 37, 38, 41. 4 vols. (London: The Society, 1913–16), 3: 45–51.

John of Monte Corvino (1247–ca. 1328) was a Franciscan friar who set out for China in 1291, arriving in 1295 only after a long detour through India. As a result, he possessed an unusually wide knowledge of the East for a European. About fifteen years after reaching China, he wrote three letters to his fellow Franciscans in Europe seeking their support for his work. In response to these letters, Pope Clement V (1305–14) appointed him first archbishop of Khanbalik, that is Peking, and sent several friars to assist him. The letters reflected the optimism about the possibility of converting the Chinese that marked much of the European interest in China. At the same time, the realities of missionary work crept through the optimistic veneer. Monte Corvino's major success at converting infidels appears to have amounted to baptizing a number of young boys whom he had purchased and formed into a Christian community. His work among the Nestorians was more successful, perhaps because he was willing to translate the Mass and other liturgical materials into the native language, an accomodation that the papacy seems to have been unwilling to make.—ed.

I, Friar John of Monte Corvino, of the order of Minor Friars, departed from Tauris, a city of the Persians, in the year of the Lord 1291, and proceeded to India. And I remained in the country of India, wherein stands the church of St. Thomas the Apostle, for thirteen months, and in that region baptized in different places about one hundred persons. The companion of my journey was Friar Nicholas of Pistoia, of the order of Preachers, who died there, and was buried in the church aforesaid.

I proceeded on my further journey and made my way to Cathay, the realm of the Emperor of the Tartars who is called the Grand Cham. To him I presented the letter of our lord the Pope, and invited him to adopt the Catholic Faith of our Lord Jesus Christ, but he had grown too old in idolatry. However he bestows many kindnesses upon the Christians, and these two years past I am abiding with him.

The Nestorians, a certain body who profess to bear the Christian name, but who deviate sadly from the Christian religion, have grown so powerful in those parts that they will not allow a Christian of another ritual to have ever so small a chapel, or to publish any doctrine different from their own.

To these regions there never came anyone of the Apostles, nor yet of the Disciples. And so the Nestorians aforesaid, either directly or through others whom they bribed, have brought on me persecutions of the sharpest. For they got up stories that I was not sent by our lord the Pope, but was a great spy and impostor; and after a while they produced false witnesses who declared that there was indeed an envoy sent with presents of immense value for the emperor, but that I had murdered him in India, and stolen what he had in charge. And these intrigues and calumnies went on for some five years. And thus it came to pass that many a time I was dragged before the judgment seat with ignominy and threats of death. At last, by God's providence, the emperor, through the confessions of a certain individual, came to know my innocence and the malice of my adversaries; and he banished them with their wives and children.

In this mission I abode alone and without any associate for eleven years; but it is now going on for two years since I was joined by Friar Arnold, a German of the province of Cologne.

I have built a church in the city of Cambaliech, in which the king has his chief residence. This I completed six years ago; and I have built a bell-tower to it, and put three bells in it. I have baptised there, as well as I can estimate, up to this time some 6,000 persons; and if those charges against me of which I have spoken had not been made, I should have baptized more than 30,000. And I am often still engaged in baptizing.

Also I have gradually bought one hundred and fifty boys, the children of pagan parents, and of ages varying from seven to eleven, who had never learned any religion. These boys I have baptized, and I have taught them Greek and Latin after our manner. Also I have written out Psalters for them, with thirty Hymnaries and two Breviaries. By help of these, eleven of the boys already know our service, and form a choir and take their weekly turn of duty as they do in convents, whether I am there or not. Many of the boys are also employed in writing out Psalters and other things suitable. His Majesty the Emperor moreover delights much to hear them chaunting. I have the bells rung at all the canonical hours, and with my congregation of babes and sucklings I perform divine service, and the chaunting we do by ear because I have no service book with the notes.

A certain king of this part of the world, by name George, belonging to the sect of Nestorian Christians, and of the illustrious family of that great king who was called Prester John of India, in the first year of my arrival here attached himself to me, and being converted by me to the truth of the Catholic faith, took the lesser orders, and when I celebrated mass he used to attend me wearing his royal robes. Certain others of the Nestorians on this account accused him of apostasy, but he brought over a great part of his people with him to the true Catholic faith, and built a church on a scale of royal magnificence in honour of our God, of the Holy Trinity, and of our lord the Pope, giving it the name of the *Roman Church*.

This King George six years ago departed to the Lord a true Christian, leaving as his heir a son scarcely out of the cradle, and who is now nine years old. And after King George's death his brothers, perfidious followers of the errors of Nestorius, perverted again all those whom he had brought over to the church, and carried them back to their original schismatical creed. And being all alone, and not able to leave his Majesty the Cham, I could not go to visit the church above-mentioned, which is twenty days' journey distant.

Yet, if I could but get some good fellow-workers to help me, I trust in God that all this might be retrieved, for I still possess the grant which was made in our favour by the late King George before mentioned. So I say again that if it had not been for the slanderous charges which I have spoken of, the harvest reaped by this time would have been great!

Indeed if I had had but two or three comrades to aid me 'tis possible that the Emperor Cham would have been baptized by this time! I ask then for such brethren to come, if any are willing to come, such I mean as will make it their great business to lead exemplary lives, and not to make broad their own phylacteries.

As for the road hither I may tell you that the way through the land of the Goths, subject to the Emperor of the Northern Tartars, is the shortest and safest; and by it the friars might come, along with the letter-carriers, in five or six months. The other route again is very long and very danger-ous, involving two sea-voyages; the first of which is about as long as that from Acre to the province of Provence, whilst the second is as long as from Acre to England. And it is possible that it might take more than two years to accomplish the journey that way. But, on the other hand, the first-mentioned route has not been open for a considerable time, on account of wars that have been going on.

It is twelve years since I have had any news of the Papal court, or of our Order, or of the state of affairs generally in the west. Two years ago in-deed there came hither a certain Lombard leech and chirurgeon, who spread abroad in these parts the most incredible blasphemies about the court of Rome and our Order and the state of things in the west, and on this account I exceedingly desire to obtain true intelligence. I pray the brethren whom this letter may reach to do their possible to bring its contents to the knowledge of our lord the Pope and the Cardinals, and the agents of the Order at the court of Rome.

I beg the Minister General of our Order to supply me with an Anti-phonarium, with the Legends of the Saints, a Gradual, and a Psalter with the musical notes, as a copy; for I have nothing but a pocket Breviary with the short Lessons, and a little missal: if I had one for a copy, the boys of whom I have spoken could transcribe others from it. Just now I am engaged in building a second church, with the view of distributing the boys in more places than one.

I have myself grown old and grey, more with toil and trouble than with years; for I am not more than fifty-eight. I have got a competent knowl-edge of the language and character which is most generally used by the Tartars. And I have already translated into that language and character the New Testament and the Psalter, and have caused them to be written out in the fairest penmanship they have; and so by writing, reading, and preaching, I bear open and public testimony to the Law of Christ. And I had been in treaty with the late King George, if he had lived, to translate the whole Latin ritual, that it might be sung throughout the whole extent of his territory; and whilst he was alive I used to celebrate mass in his church, according to the Latin ritual, reading in the before-mentioned language and character the words of both the preface and the Canon.

And the son of the king before-mentioned is called after my name, John; and I hope in God that he will walk in his father's steps.

As far as I ever saw or heard tell, I do not believe that any king or prince in the world can be compared to his majesty the Cham in respect of the extent of his dominions, the vastness of their population, or the amount of his wealth. Here I stop.

Dated at the city of Cambalec in the kingdom of Cathay, in the year of the Lord 1305, and on the 8th day of January.

Document 36

Benedict XII, Serena facie (13 June 1338), Acta Benedicti XII (1334–1342), ed. Aloysius L. Tautu, Fontes, series 3, vol. 8 (Vatican City: Pontificia commissio ad redigendum codicem iuris canonici orientalis, 1958), pp. 44–47. Translated by James Muldoon.

In 1338, a party of Christian Alans visited the West in order to obtain priests. The Alans, who had originally lived along the shores of the Black Sea, had been converted by John of Monte Corvino. At John's death they had been left without Catholic clergy, so an embassy was sent to obtain a successor. This letter, which the Alans were to present to their leaders upon their return, contained a number of points of doctrine and ecclesiastical practice that the pope considered crucial. The theme of the letter, the unity of the Christian Church under the headship of the pope who possessed the plenitudo potestatis—the fullness of power in the Church, a power derived from Christ Himself—was the driving theme of the medieval papacy. Not only was there to be unity of doctrine, but unity of liturgical practice as well. For example, Benedict XII stressed that the communion host must be made from unleavened bread while the Eastern Church, headed by the Patriarch of Constantinople, used leavened bread. Although some concessions to the liturgical practices of the various Christian groups in Asia might appear to have been useful, the medieval popes made none. Complete submission to Rome in all matters was required. The brief mention of the ban against polygamy was a reference to a common problem for missionaries working in lands where polygamy was practiced. Should a convert be allowed to retain all those of his wives who wished to remain with him, or must he leave all but his first wife who would be, according to Church law, his only true wife? Although some lawyers did raise the possibility that all the wives could be kept, the papacy rejected that opinion.

This letter illustrates the increasingly hard line that the Catholic Church was taking against compromises of any sort in the matter of making converts. Converts would be expected to adopt what was in fact a western European style of life and the Roman liturgy. This intransigent policy was rather different from the attitude of early Church, which allowed a number of concessions in order to ease the way of converts.—ed.

To the beloved men, Fodim Jovens, Chyansam Tongi, Chemboga Vensy, and Johannis Jochoy and Rubeo Pinzano, princes of the Alans, and to each and every Christian living in the eastern lands, greetings. . . .

It was with a shining countenance and a joyful spirit that we received your ambassadors, the princes, your sons, who came to our presence recently. A gracious audience being granted to them for everything which they wished to place before us, we understood those matters they placed before us with the aid of a faithful translator. They in turn fully understood our response and those matters which we explained to them.

Through both the letters presented to us by your ambassadors (a series of which we had translated) and through those things that they told us . . . we perceived the great devotion that you and the other Christian Alans of those regions bear for us and for the Roman Church, the mother and mistress of all the faithful, and for the Catholic faith, without which there is no salvation for anyone. We also perceived that you desired to be instructed and strengthened in that same faith in the same manner as the aforementioned Roman Church holds and preaches it. . . .

And so that the Catholic faith, which we and the Roman Church, together with the whole body of Christians, profess, preach, and hold firmly, might become known more clearly to you and to the other Christians of the aforementioned regions and so that you may be able to follow, profess, and hold it more firmly, we explain it more openly and more clearly as follows. . . .

We believe that there is one, true, holy, Catholic, and apostolic Church, in which baptism and true remission of all sins is given to one. . . .

That same Catholic Church also holds and teaches that there are seven sacraments of the Church. . . .

That same Catholic Church makes the sacrament of the Eucharist from unleavened bread, holding and teaching that in that sacrament bread and wine are truly transformed into the body and the blood of Jesus Christ.

Concerning matrimony, the Church holds that neither men nor women are allowed to have several spouses at the same time. The bond of matrimony being dissolved, however, through the death of the other partner, [successive second or third marriages] are said to be licit if there is no canonical impediment of any sort standing in the way.

[We believe that] the holy Roman Church holds the highest and fullest primacy and headship over the entire Catholic Church . . . together with the plenitude of power. Among other things, the pope is bound to defend the truth of the faith, so, if any question concerning the faith arises, he ought to settle the matter according to his own judgement. . . . All the Churches and their prelates are subject to him and owe him obedience and reverence. . . .

We propose with the grace of God to send to those lands certain ambassadors or our legates to console you and the other Christians of those regions and to conform you to the Roman Church's practice, and to bring back the erring to the Church.

Document 37

John de' Marignolli, "Recollections of Travel in the East," *Cathay and the Way Thither*, ed. Henry Yule and Henri Cordier, Hakluyt Society Publications, nos. 33, 37, 38, 41, 4 vols. (London: The Society, 1913–16), 3: 213–16.

John de' Marignolli (1290–1357), a Franciscan, was one of a party of clerics sent to China by Pope Benedict XII to serve the Alans. Arriving in Peking in the early summer of 1342, Marignolli resided there for three or four years. He later returned to Europe, travelling by way of India, and arrived at the papal court in 1353. He never returned to Asia, becoming a bishop in Italy and later joining the court of the Holy Roman Emperor. There is no indication that he was any more successful in making converts than his predecessors had been. Some of the interest of this excerpt lies in his discussion of the Christians of St. Thomas who dwelled in India. He was also interested in dispelIng the mystery about the source of pepper.—ed.

Towards the end of the third year after our departure from the Papal Court, quitting Armalec[1] we came to the Cyollos Kagon, i.e. to the Sand

---

1. The capital of the khans of Turkestan.

Hills thrown up by the wind. Before the days of the Tartars nobody believed that the earth was habitable beyond these, nor indeed was it believed that there was any country at all beyond. But the Tartars by God's permission, and with wonderful exertion, did cross them, and found themselves in what the philosophers call the torrid and impassable zone. Pass it however the Tartars did; and so did I, and that twice. . . . After having passed it we came to Cambalec,[2] the chief seat of the Empire of the East. Of its incredible magnitude, population, and military array, we will say nothing. But the Grand Kaam,[3] when he beheld the great horses and the Pope's presents, with and when he saw us also, rejoiced greatly, being delighted, yea exceedingly delighted with everything, and treated us with the greatest honour. And when I entered the Kaam's presence it was in full festival vestments, with a very fine cross carried before me, and candles and incense, whilst *Credo in Unum Deum* was chaunted, in that glorious palace where he dwells. And when the chaunt was ended I bestowed a full benediction, which he received with all humility.

And so we were dismissed to one of the Imperial apartments which had been most elegantly fitted up for us; and two princes were appointed to attend to all our wants. And this they did in the most liberal manner, not merely as regards meat and drink, but even down to such things as paper for lanterns, whilst all necessary servants also were detached from the Court to wait upon us. And so they tended us for nearly four years, never failing to treat us with unbounded respect. And I should add that they kept us and all our establishment clothed in costly raiment. And considering that we were thirty-two persons, what the Kaam expended for everything on our account must have amounted, as well as I can calculate, to more than four thousand marks. And we had many and glorious disputations with the Jews and other sectaries; and we made also a great harvest of souls in that empire.

The Minor Friars in Cambalec have a cathedral church immediately adjoining the palace, with a proper residence for the Archbishop, and other churches in the city besides, and they have bells too, and all the clergy have their subsistence from the Emperor's table in the most honourable manner.

And when the Emperor saw that nothing would induce me to abide there, he gave me leave to return to the Pope, carrying presents from him, with an allowance for three years' expenses, and with a request that either I or some one else should be sent speedily back with the rank of Cardinal, and with full powers, to be Bishop there; for the office of Bishop is highly venerated by all the Orientals, whether they be Christians or no. He should also be of the Minorite Order, because these are the only priests that they

2. Peking.
3. Khan.

are acquainted with; and they think that the Pope is always of that Order because Pope Girolamo[4] was so who sent them that legate whom the Tartars and Alans venerate as a saint, viz., Friar John of Monte Corvino of the Order of Minorites, of whom we have already spoken.

We abode in Cambalec about three years, and then we took our way through Manzi, with a magnificent provision for our expenses from the Emperor, besides about two hundred horses; and on our way we beheld the glory of this world in such a multitude of cities, towns, and villages, and in other ways displayed, that no tongue can give it fit expression.

And sailing on the feast of St. Stephen, we navigated the Indian Sea until Palm Sunday, and then arrived at a very noble city of India called Columbum,[5] where the whole world's pepper is produced. Now this pepper grows on a kind of vines, which are planted just like in our vineyards. These vines produce clusters which are at first like those of the wild vine of a green colour, and afterwards are almost like bunches of our grapes, and they have a red wine in them which I have squeezed out on my plate as a condiment. When they have ripened, they are left to dry upon the tree, and when shrivelled by the excessive heat the dry clusters are knocked off with a stick and caught upon linen cloths, and so the harvest is gathered.

These are things that I have seen with mine eyes and handled with my hands during the fourteen months that I stayed there. And there is no roasting of the pepper, as authors have falsely asserted, nor does it grow in forests, but in regular gardens; nor are the Saracens the proprietors but the Christians of St. Thomas. And these latter are the masters of the public steel-yard,[6] from which I derived, as a perquisite of my office as Pope's legate, every month a hundred gold *fan*, and a thousand when I left.

Document 38

Francesco Balduccio Pegolotti, "Notices of the Land Route to Cathay," in *Cathay and the Way Thither*, ed. Henry Yule and Henri Cordier, Hakluyt Society Publications, nos. 33, 37, 38, 41. 4 vols. (London: The Society, 1913–16), 3: 213–16.

We know almost nothing of Pegolotti except that he was an employee of the Bardi family, one of the great banking houses of Renaissance Italy. This brief work was probably written around 1340. The author himself seems never to have travelled the route that he described and for which he provided such useful information as the cost of provisions

4. Jerome Musci, who became Pope Nicholas IV (1288–92).
5. Modern Quilon in India.
6. Market-place.

and the lengths of the various stages of the journey. The implication of this handbook is that the trip to China was commonly made by Italian businessmen in the fourteenth century, so that Marco Polo's experiences, while perhaps more interesting than the experiences of the ordinary businessman, nevertheless were not very unusual.—ed.

In the Name of the Lord, Amen!

This book is called the Book of Descriptions of Countries and of measures employed in business, and of other things needful to be known by merchants of different parts of the world, and by all who have to do with merchandize and exchanges; showing also what relation the merchandize of one country or of one city bears to that of others; and how one kind of goods is better than another kind; and where the various wares come from, and how they may be kept as long as possible.

The book was compiled by Francis Balducci Pegolotti of Florence, who was with the Company of the Bardi of Florence, and during the time that he was in the service of the said Company, for the good and honour and prosperity of the said Company, and for his own, and for that of whosoever shall read or transcribe the said book. And this copy has been made from the book of Agnolo di Lotti of Antella, and the said book was transcribed from the original book of the said Francesco Balducci. . . .

In the first place, you must let your beard grow long and not shave. And at Tana you should furnish yourself with a dragoman. And you must not try to save money in the matter of dragomen by taking a bad one instead of a good one. For the additional wages of the good one will not cost you so much as you will save by having him. And besides the dragoman it will be well to take at least two good men servants, who are acquainted with the Cumanian tongue. And if the merchant likes to take a woman with him from Tana, he can do so; if he does not like to take one there is no obligation, only if he does take one he will be kept much more comfortably than if he does not take one. Howbeit, if he do take one, it will be well that she be acquainted with the Cumanian tongue as well as the men.

And from Tana travelling to Gittarchan you should take with you twenty-five days' provisions, that is to say, flour and salt fish, for as to meat you will find enough of it at all the places along the road. And so also at all the chief stations noted in going from one country to another in the route, according to the number of days set down above, you should furnish yourself with flour and salt fish; other things you will find in sufficiency, and especially meat.

The road you travel from Tana to Cathay is perfectly safe, whether by day or by night, according to what the merchants say who have used it. Only if the merchant, in going or coming, should die upon the road, everything belonging to him will become the perquisite of the lord of the country in which he dies, and the officers of the lord will take possession of all. And in like manner if he die in Cathay. But if his brother be with him, or an intimate friend and comrade calling himself his brother, then to such an one they will surrender the property of the deceased, and so it will be rescued.

And there is another danger: this is when the lord of the country dies, and before the new lord who is to have the lordship is proclaimed; during such intervals there have sometimes been irregularities practised on the Franks, and other foreigners. (They call Franks all the Christians of these parts from Romania westward.) And neither will the roads be safe to travel until the other lord be proclaimed who is to reign in room of him who is deceased.

Cathay is a province which contained a multitude of cities and towns. Among others there is one in particular, that is to say the capital city, to which is great resort of merchants, and in which there is a vast amount of trade; and this city is called Cambalec. And the said city hath a circuit of one hundred miles, and is all full of people and houses and of dwellers in the said city.

You may calculate that a merchant with a dragoman. and with two men servants, and with goods to the value of twenty-five thousand golden florins, should spend on his way to Cathay from sixty to eighty sommi of silver, and not more if he manage well; and for all the road back again from Cathay to Tana, including the expenses of living and the pay of servants, and all other charges, the cost will be about five sommi per head of pack animals, or something less. And you may reckon the sommo to be worth five golden florins. You may reckon also that each ox-waggon will require one ox, and will carry ten cantars Genoese weight; and the camel-waggon will require three camels, and will carry thirty cantars Genoese weight; and the horse-waggon will require one horse, and will commonly carry six and half cantars of silk, at 250 Genoese pounds to the cantar. And a bale of silk may be reckoned at between 110 and 115 Genoese pounds.

VII

Intellectuals and the Wider World

Introduction

For Christian intellectuals of the Middle Ages, the non-European world provided a field for spiritual, not military, conquest. Christ's injunction to teach all men was taken seriously by numerous missionaries. Behind the missionaries in the field, scholars tried to provide the tools that would make the conversion of the infidels easier. These tools included commentaries on the beliefs of the Moslems, a major object of missionary efforts, and discussions of the legal right of the Christians to invade and conquer infidel kingdoms.

Peter the Venerable and Thomas Aquinas provide examples of the intellectual approach to conversion of the infidel. The Order of Cluny, of which Peter was a member, was actively involved in encouraging the reconquest of Spain and in converting to Christianity those Moslems who remained in the areas retaken by the Christians.[1] To make the work of the missionaries easier by providing them with material about the history and doctrines of the Moslem faith, Peter wrote or had written several treatises about the Moslems and the founder of their religion. The picture he presented of Mohammed was a most unflattering one, and his understanding of basic Moslem doctrines was weak. His description of Mohammed as essentially a Christian heretic, not as the founder of a radically different religion, was typical medieval orthodoxy (doc. 39). To some extent, this belief must have encouraged missionaries to be optimistic about converting the Moslems because their beliefs were already similar to Christian ones, or so the missionaries thought.

Where Peter the Venerable reflected the uncritical enthusiasm of the twelfth-century crusader, Thomas Aquinas reflected the fascination of thirteenth-century intellectuals with classical Greek philosophy.[2] Rather than seeking to convert the Moslems by ridiculing the founder of their religion, Aquinas sought to provide his fellow Dominican missionaries with arguments that could be employed to bring infidels to the faith (doc. 42). Beginning with what he took to be the most sophisticated

1. Jonathan Sumption, *Pilgrimage: An Image of Mediaeval Religion* (Totowa, N.J.: Rowman and Littlefield, 1975), pp. 118–19.
2. As Gilson has pointed out, Aquinas took the position that, "Being a rational animal, man should rule his conduct according to the laws of reason." Etienne Gilson, *History of Christian Philosophy in the Middle Ages* (New York: Random House, 1955), p. 380. This being the case, the Moslems could be reached on the level of reason, which is common to all men.

notions about God that had been achieved by human reason alone, without the use of Christian revelation, the work of the ancient Greeks, and especially the work of Aristotle, Aquinas wrote a lengthy treatise on the nature of God and His qualities that, he assumed, could be used as a basis for dealing with non-Christians on a plane that was open equally to Christians and infidels. One goal of this effort was to prove that the truths of the Christian religion did not contradict natural reason. The popularity of such an approach to the work of conversion is reflected in the scene of William of Rubruck debating with the Nestorians and the Moslems at the camp of the Mongol Khan. (ch. 6 doc. 32).

The success of the early phase of the crusades and the enthusiasm of Europeans for continuing the work of conquering the infidel caused some thirteenth-century thinkers to consider the implications of continuous wars of conquest against the non-Christian world. As Pope Innocent IV, a noted canon lawyer, asked, by what right did the Christians conquer lands from the Moslems. Was it simply because they were not Christians? His answer denied Christians the right to deprive non-Christians of their lands and power. Christians did, however, have the right to reconquer lands taken from Christians in the Moslem wars of expansion several centuries earlier. On the other hand, he also argued that if infidel rulers refused to allow Christian missionaries access to their kingdoms, then Christians would be justified in using armed force to insure the safety of missionaries who wished to enter such lands (doc. 40).

Innocent IV's recognition of the natural rights of infidels and his consequent establishment of limits on Christian expansion formed one pole of the legal debate over the rights of infidels vis-à-vis Christians. Innocent IV's greatest student, the canonist known as Hostiensis, took a position opposite to that of his master. Hostiensis argued that the coming of Christ ended the right of infidels to possess property and governmental authority lawfully. Christians were the only people with the right to own these. The infidels retained possession of their lands and power, but they were essentially usurpers, and Christians were within their rights in seeking to deprive infidels of their goods and power. As a result, any war by Christians against infidels was a just war (doc. 41).

Until the late sixteenth century, the legal debate about the rights of infidels continued using the terms fashioned by Innocent IV and Hostiensis. Only then, in the Protestant Reformation with its rejection of the canon law tradition and with the appearance of creative legal minds such as Hugo Grotius, was modern international law formulated.[3] Until the

3. For a discussion of the literature on the question of Grotius's relation to his medieval predecessors, see James Muldoon, "The Contribution of the Medieval Canon Lawyers to the Formation of International Law: A Bibliographical Survey," *Traditio* 28 (1972): 483–97.

time of Grotius, those who objected to European expansion often did so in the language of Innocent IV. When the king of Poland sought to block further expansion of the Teutonic Knights into his territory, he employed the services of Paulus Vladimiri, a leading canonist, to attack the premises on which the Knights justified their expansion. Like Innocent IV before him and the sixteenth-century Spanish critics of expansion after him, Vladimiri rejected the claim that infidels possessed no rights. Infidels who posed no threat to Christians had the right to be left alone. He even pointed out that if Hostiensis' position was accepted, then any number of horrible crimes would thereby be justified (doc. 44).

Finally a word must be said about medieval proposals for universal peace, which included world conquest and the placing of all mankind under a single ruler, a European ruler.[4] Critics of the turbulent politics of medieval Europe occasionally argued that peace would only occur when men lived together under one ruler; this was, so the critics claimed, the natural state of things. The poet Dante, for example, proposed a world monarchy under the leadership of the Holy Roman Emperor (doc. 43). Like Aquinas, Dante was influenced by classical Greek thought on the nature of unity and harmony, and, like Aquinas, he believed that a logical presentation of the need for world unity would convince the leaders of European society to begin the necessary work. Like Aquinas's belief that a logical presentation of religious doctrine would win converts, Dante's hope for world unity through argument was doomed to failure.

In all of these proposals for Christian expansion, there is one thing missing, any hesitation about bringing blessings to the non-European world in the form of European Christian values. Like the defenders of expansion in the period following the voyages of Columbus, and unlike some contemporary critics, medieval critics of expansion attacked not the principle but the means used and the abuses that could result. They were convinced that non-Europeans would benefit from conversion to Christianity, if from nothing else that the Europeans had to offer.

4. R. W. and A. J. Carlyle, *A History of Mediaeval Political Theory in the West,* 6 vols. (Edinburgh and London: William Blackwood, 1903–36), 6: 111–27.

Bibliography

The Cluniac order played a significant role in both the crusades and in the church reform movement which was developing at the same time. The two movements had much in common, and each centered on the right ordering of the world, something that was also central to the life of the Cluniac monasteries. Concerning the history of the order, see Lucy M. Smith, *Cluny in the Eleventh and Twelfth Centuries* (London: P. Allen, 1930). Cluny's role in the process of church reform is discussed in Gerd Tellenbach, *Church, State and Christian Society at the Time of the Investiture Controversy*, trans. R. F. Bennet, Studies in Mediaeval History (Oxford: Basil Blackwell, 1940). The hope that the Moslems in Spain might be converted peacefully has recently been discussed by Robert I. Burns, "Christian-Islamic Confrontation in the West: the Thirteenth Century Dream of Conversion," *American Historical Review* 76 (December 1971): 1386–1434. Underlying the belief of Aquinas and Dante that the conversion of the infidel and the right ordering of the world could be approached in a logical, rational manner is the assumption that there is a natural law that all men can know if they apply themselves. It is the responsibility of the philosopher to make known this law to all men, Christian and infidel alike. A good, brief introduction to the notion of natural law is by A. Passerin d'Entreves, *Natural Law* (London: Hutchinson, 1951). As for the place of natural law in the thought of Aquinas, see D. J. O'Connor, *Aquinas and Natural Law* (London: Macmillan, 1967). The most recent study of the life and work of Aquinas is James A. Weisheipl, *Friar Thomas d'Aquino: His Life, Thought, and Work* (Garden City, N.Y.: Doubleday, 1974). Although Dante is thought of as a religious poet, his work was permeated by strong political opinions and his writings cannot be understood without considering the political milieu in which he functioned. A good introduction to Dante's thought is Thomas G. Bergin, *Dante* (Boston: Houghton Mifflin, 1965). The poet as political thinker is discussed in A. Passerin d'Entreves, *Dante as Political Thinker* (Oxford: Clarendon, 1952).

In recent years, the political opinions of the medieval canon lawyers have attracted a good deal of scholarly interest. Works on the canonists that consider the canonistic discussions of the rights of infidels include: Walter Ullmann, *Medieval Papalism*, (London: Methuen, 1949), and James Muldoon, "*Extra ecclesiam non est imperium*: The Canonists and the Legitimacy of Secular Power," *Studia Gratiana* 9(1966): 553–80.

Document 39*

Peter the Venerable, "Summa totius haeresis Saracenorum," from James Kritzeck, *Peter the Venerable and Islam* (Princeton: Princeton Univ. Press, 1964), pp. 205–6. Translated by James Muldoon.

Peter the Venerable (1092–1156), the ninth abbot of the Cluniac order, was apparently the first European Christian to study the doctrines of the Moslems. His aim was to provide for Christian missionaries in Spain a guide to the teachings of Mohammed and a brief history of the origins of Moslem teachings. The fact that the monks of Cluny were active supporters of the crusading movement and that a number of Cluniac monasteries were founded in Spain in the wake of the reconquest of the peninsula from the Moslems encouraged him in this work. Unlike many of his contemporaries, however, Peter the Venerable desired peaceful conversion of the Moslems if at all possible. He hoped that missionaries grounded in a thorough knowledge of Moslem beliefs would be able to win the infidels to Christianity and eliminate the need for armed conquest in Spain. His opinion that Mohammed was a Christian heretic, not the founder of an absolutely new religion, helped to shape the approach of European to the Moslems for over five centuries.—*ed.*

Thus were they instructed by the most wicked and impious Mohammed, a man who rejected all the sacraments of the Christian faith by means of which men are saved. Indeed, he has drawn almost one third of the human race, by what judgement of God we do not know, to the devil and to eternal death because they have listened to his foolish stories.

For this reason it seems that who he was and what he taught ought to be discussed so that those who read this book might better understand what they read, and that they might understand how detestable both his life and his doctrine are. Some think that he was that Nicholas who was one of the seven deacons and that the doctrine of the so-called Nicholaits, which is censured in the Apocalypse of John, is the law of the modern Saracens. Some talk foolishly about them and others, both incurious about what he wrote and ignorant of what deeds he accomplished, as in other situations, believe various falsehoods about them.

As the chronicle translated by Anastasius, the Librarian of the Roman Church, from Greek into Latin clearly states, in the time of Emperor Heraclius, some time after the era of the Roman Pope Gregory I, about 550 years ago he [Mohammed] emerged from the Arab nation, a man of low birth. At first he was an adherent of the ancient idolatry, like the other Arabs of that time, uneducated, with almost no learning at all. Knowledgeable in business matters and practical affairs [he emerged] from poverty and obscurity to wealth and fame. Little by little he grew in power, first by attacking those around him and especially his blood relatives, using craft, rapine, and assault. Some he killed secretly, some publicly, increasing fear of him so that he began to aspire to the kingship over his people.

And when he met with resistance on all sides and with contempt for his low-born status, he realized that he could not achieve what he desired by the power of the sword, so he attempted to become king in the guise of religion and using the name of prophet. And because he lived as a barbarian among the barbarians and as an idolator among idolators, and among those who were above all nations ignorant of and unlearned in the law, both human and divine, and knowing that they would be easy to seduce, he began to devote himself to the wicked work that he had conceived. And since he had heard that God's prophets were great men, calling himself His prophet, so that he might appear to be performing a good action, he began to lead them away from idol worship. He did not, however, lead them to the true God, but to that erroneous heresy to which he had already given birth.

When meanwhile, by the judgement of Him Who is called "terrible in His deeds over the sons of men" and Who "takes pity on some and hardens the hearts of others according to His will," Satan gave him success in his error and sent the monk Sergius who belonged to the Nestorian sect and who had been expelled from the Church across Arabia and joined the heretical monk to the pseudo-prophet. So then when Sergius joined Mohammed, he supplied what Mohammed lacked and explained to him the sacred scriptures, both the Old Testament and the New, which he interpreted in part according to his master Nestorius who denied that Our Savior was God and in part according to his own interpretation, and he imbued him with apocryphal fables so that he made him a Nestorian Christian. And so that the totality of wickedness might come together in Mohammed and so that nothing might be lacking for his damnation or that of others, Jews joined the heretic and, lest he become a true Christian, they deceitfully provided this man who was greedy for novelties not the truth of the scriptures but, in secretive whispers, their own fables in which they even now abound. So from the best scholars, Jews, and heretics, was Mohammed taught. He produced his Koran and wove it together from the fables of the Jews and from children's tales of heretics, a wicked scripture in his own barbarous fashion.

Document 40

Innocent IV, *Commentaria Doctissima in Quinque Libros Decretalium* (Turin: apud haeredes Nicolai Beuilaquae, 1581), fol. 176–77. Translated by James Muldoon.

At the Council of Lyons in 1245, Pope Innocent IV initiated European contacts with central Asia (and, eventually, with China and India), which attracted so much missionary interest in the thirteenth and fourteenth centuries. In addition to this, however, Innocent IV was also a famous canon lawyer and he was led to speculate on the relations between Christian and non-Christian societies. Some lawyers, inspired perhaps by the crusades, had argued that Christians had the absolute right to rule all non-Christians. Innocent IV denied this and instead discussed the natural right of all men to choose their own leaders without interference. He recognized the potential conflict between the right of all men to govern themselves and the responsibility of the Christian Church to preach to all men. The optimism that characterized thirteenth-century missionary activity seems to have encouraged him to believe that conversion and not conquest would occur. His discussion of the natural right of infidels to govern themselves was an important step in the development of international law. It was often quoted in the sixteenth-century debate over the rights of the inhabitants of the New World in the face of the Spanish conquest of the Americas.—ed.

There is no doubt that it is proper for the pope to encourage the faithful to defend the Holy Land and the faithful who live there and to grant them indulgences (for this purpose). . . . But is it licit to invade a land that infidels possess or which belongs to them? And we respond that in truth the earth is the Lord's and His power is over the entire world and all who live in it, for He is the creator of everything, He made everything. . . . Men can select rulers for themselves as [the Israelites] selected Saul and many others. . . . Sovereignty, possessions, and jurisdiction can exist licitly, without sin, among infidels, as well as among the faithful. Things were made for every rational creature . . . and because of this, we say it is not lawful for the pope or for the faithful to take sovereignty or jurisdiction from infidels, because they hold them without sin, but we believe rightly, however, that the pope who is the vicar of Jesus Christ has power not only over Christians but also over all infidels, for Christ had power over all men. . . . Thus to Peter and his successors he gave the keys to the kingdom of heaven. . . . Elsewhere He said, "Feed My sheep." Both infidels and the faithful belong to Christ's flock by virtue of their creation, although the infidels do not belong to the sheepfold of the Church, and so it seems from the aforementioned, that the pope has jurisdiction over all men and power over them in law but not in fact, so that through this power which the pope possesses I believe that if a gentile, who has no law except the law of nature [to guide him], does something contrary to the law of nature, the pope can lawfully punish him, as for example in Genesis 19 where we see that the inhabitants of Sodom who sinned against the law of nature were punished by God. Since, however, the judgements of God are examples for us, I do not see why the pope, who is the vicar of Christ, cannot do the same and he ought to do it as long as he has the means to do so. And so some say that if they worship idols [the pope can judge and punish them] for it is natural for man to worship the one and only God, not creatures. Also, the pope can judge the Jews if they violate the law of the Gospel in moral matters if their leaders do not punish them. . . . However, the pope can grant indulgences to those who invade the Holy Land for the purpose of recapturing it although the Saracens possess it . . . [but] they possess it illegally . . . and against those infidels who now hold the Holy Land where Christian princes once ruled, the pope can lawfully order and command that [infidel rulers] not molest unjustly the Christians who are their subjects. . . . Indeed, if they treat Christians badly the pope can deprive them of the jurisdiction and sovereignty they possess over Christians by judicial sentence. . . . Infidels should not be forced to become Christians, because all should be left to their own free will in this matter. . . . The pope can order infidels to admit preachers of the Gospel in the lands that they administer, for every rational creature is made for the worship of God. . . . If infidels prohibit preachers from preaching, they sin and so they ought to be punished. In all the aforementioned cases and in all others where it is licit for the pope to command those things, if the infidels do not obey, they ought to be compelled by the secular arm and war may be declared against them by the pope and not by anyone else.

Document 41

Hostiensis, *Lectura quinque decretalium*, 2 vols. (Paris: 1512), 2: 124–25. Translated by James Muldoon.

Henry of Segusia (ca. 1200–1271), generally known as Hostiensis because he was cardinal-bishop of Ostia, was a canon lawyer and student of Innocent IV. In spite of the fact that his writings generally reflected the teachings of Innocent IV, in the case of infidel rights

Hostiensis chose not to follow his master's teaching. Instead, he followed a line of argument that can be traced back to the end of the twelfth century. According to this view, the coming of Christ deprived all non-Christians of any legitimate claim to power and authority. Given the support of a well-known canonist, such as Hostiensis, the view that infidels had no right to oppose Christian armies because they had no legal right to the lands they occupied became a major justification for the conquest of the non-Christian world outside of Europe as late as the seventeenth century.—ed.

It seems to me that with the coming of Christ every public office and every government and all sovereignty and jurisdiction, both by law and from just cause, was taken from infidels and given over to the faithful through Him who has the highest power and cannot err. . . . And we assert that by law infidels ought to be subject to the faithful and not the reverse. . . . We concede, however, that infidels who recognize the sovereignty of the Church ought to be tolerated by the Church, because they should not be forced to accept the faith.

Document 42*

Thomas Aquinas, On the Truth of the Catholic Faith (Summa Contra Gentiles) Book I: God, trans. Anton C. Pegis (Garden City, N.Y.: Doubleday, 1955), pp. 61–63, 71–76.

St. Thomas Aquinas (1225–74) was one of the foremost philosophers of the Middle Ages and the one whose work is the most widely known in the modern world. Like many other thinkers of the thirteenth century, he was optimistic about the possibility of reconciling ancient pagan thought with Christian thought. To that end, he devoted his life to studying and writing commentaries on the works of Aristotle and to writing a great synthesis of Christian truth, the Summa Theologiae. The Summa Contra Gentiles appears to have been written to provide missionaries of the Dominican Order, of which Aquinas was a member, a handbook of teachings about God and religious truths that were accessible to all men by the use of natural reason alone. This reflects the optimism of many thirteenth-century missionaries that Christianity would win over infidels by the force of argument rather than by force of arms.—ed.

The Author's Intention in
the Present Work

[1] Among all human pursuits, the pursuit of wisdom is more perfect, more noble, more useful, and more full of joy.

It is more perfect because, in so far as a man gives himself to the pursuit of wisdom, so far does he even now have some share in true beatitude. And so a wise man has said, "Blessed is the man that shall continue in wisdom" (Ecc. 14:22).

It is more noble because through this pursuit man especially approaches to a likeness to God Who "made all things in wisdom" (Ps. 103:24). And since likeness is the cause of love, the pursuit of wisdom especially joins man to God in friendship. That is why it is said of wisdom that "she is an infinite treasure to men! which they that use become the friends of God" (Wis. 7:14).

It is more useful because through wisdom we arrive at the kingdom of immortality. For "the desire of wisdom bringeth to the everlasting kingdom" (Wis. 6:21).

It is more full of joy because "her conversation has no bitterness, nor her company any tediousness, but joy and gladness" (Wis. 7:16).

[2] And so, in the name of the divine Mercy, I have the confidence to embark upon the work of a wise man, even though this may surpass my powers, and I have set myself the task of making known, as far as my limited powers will allow, the truth that the Catholic faith professes, and of setting aside the errors that are opposed to it. To use the words of Hilary, "I am aware that I owe this to God as the chief duty of my life, that my every word and sense may speak of Him."

[3] To proceed against individual errors, however, is a difficult business, this for two reasons. In the first place, it is difficult because the sacrilegious remarks of individual men who have erred are not so well known to us so that we may use what they say as the basis of proceeding to a refutation of their errors. This is, indeed, the method that the ancient Doctors of the Church used in the refutation of the errors of the Gentiles. For they could know the positions taken by the Gentiles since they themselves had been Gentiles, or at least had lived among the Gentiles and had been instructed in their teaching. In the second place, it is difficult because some of them, such as the Mohammedans and the pagans, do not agree with us in accepting the authority of any Scripture, by which they may be convinced of their error. Thus, against the Jews we are able to argue by means of the Old Testament, while against heretics we are able to argue by means of the New Testament. But the Mohammedans and the pagans accept neither the one nor the other. We must, therefore, have recourse to the

natural reason, to which all men are forced to give their assent. However, it is true, in divine matters the natural reason has its failings.

[4] Now, while we are investigating some given truth, we shall also show what errors are set aside by it; and we shall likewise show how the truth that we come to know by demonstration is in accord with the Christian religion. . . .

That to Give Assent to the Truths of Faith Is Not Foolishness Even Though They Are Above Reason

[1] Those who place their faith in this truth, however, "for which the human reason offers no experimental evidence," do not believe foolishly, as though "following artificial fables" (2 Peter 1:16). For these "secrets of divine Wisdom" (Job 11:6) the divine Wisdom itself, which knows all things to the full, has deigned to reveal to men. It reveals its own presence, as well as the truth of its teaching and inspiration, by fitting arguments; and in order to confirm those truths that exceed natural knowledge, it gives visible manifestation to works that surpass the ability of all nature. Thus, there are the wonderful cures of illnesses, there is the raising of the dead, and the wonderful immutation in the heavenly bodies; and what is more wonderful, there is the inspiration given to human minds, so that simple and untutored persons, filled with the gift of the Holy Spirit, come to possess instantaneously the highest wisdom and the readiest eloquence. When these arguments were examined, through the efficacy of the abovementioned proof, and not the violent assault of arms or the promise of pleasures, and (what is most wonderful of all) in the midst of the tyranny of the persecutors, an innumerable throng of people, both simple and most learned, flocked to the Christian faith. In this faith there are truths preached that surpass every human intellect; the pleasures of the flesh are curbed; it is taught that the things of the world should be spurned. Now, for the minds of mortal men to assent to these things is the greatest of miracles, just as it is a manifest work of divine inspiration that, spurning visible things, men should seek only what is invisible. Now, that this has happened neither without preparation nor by chance, but as a result of the disposition of God, is clear from the fact that through many pronouncements of the ancient prophets God had foretold that He would do this. The books of these prophets are held in veneration among us Christians, since they give witness to our faith.

[2] The manner of this confirmation is touched on by St. Paul: "Which," that is, human salvation, "having begun to be declared by the Lord, was confirmed unto us by them that hear Him: God also bearing them witness

of signs, and wonders, and divers miracles, and distributions of the Holy Ghost" (Heb. 2:3–4).

[3] This wonderful conversion of the world to the Christian faith is the clearest witness of the signs given in the past; so that it is not necessary that they should be further repeated, since they appear most clearly in their effect. For it would be truly more wonderful than all signs if the world had been led by simple and humble men to believe such lofty truths, to accomplish such difficult actions, and to have such high hopes. Yet it is also a fact that, even in our own time, God does not cease to work miracles through His saints for the confirmation of the faith.

[4] On the other hand, those who founded sects committed to erroneous doctrines proceeded in a way that is opposite to this. The point is clear in the case of Mohammed. He seduced the people by promises of carnal pleasure to which the concupiscence of the flesh goads us. His teaching also contained precepts that were in conformity with his promises, and he gave free rein to carnal pleasure. In all this, as is not unexpected, he was obeyed by carnal men. As for proofs of the truth of his doctrine, he brought forward only such as could be grasped by the natural ability of anyone with a very modest wisdom. Indeed, the truths that he taught he mingled with many fables and with doctrines of the greatest falsity. He did not bring forth any signs produced in a supernatural way, which alone fittingly gives witness to divine inspiration; for a visible action that can be only divine reveals an invisibly inspired teacher of truth. On the contrary, Mohammed said that he was sent in the power of his arms—which are signs not lacking even to robbers and tyrants. What is more, no wise men, men trained in things divine and human, believed in him from the beginning. Those who believed in him were brutal men and desert wanderers, utterly ignorant of all divine teaching, through whose numbers Mohammed forced others to become his followers by the violence of his arms. Nor do divine pronouncements on the part of preceding prophets offer him any witness. On the contrary, he perverts almost all the testimonies of the Old and New Testaments by making them into fabrications of his own, as can be seen by anyone who examines his law. It was, therefore, a shrewd decision on his part to forbid his followers to read the Old and New Testaments, lest these books convict him of falsity. It is thus clear that those who place any faith in his words believe foolishly.

That the Truth of Reason Is Not Opposed to the Truth of the Christian Faith

[1] Now, although the truth of the Christian faith which we have discussed surpasses the capacity of the reason, nevertheless that truth that the human

reason is naturally endowed to know cannot be opposed to the truth of the Christian faith. For that with which the human reason is naturally endowed is clearly most true; so much so, that it is impossible for us to think of such truths as false. Nor is it permissible to believe as false that which we hold by faith, since this is confirmed in a way that is so clearly divine. Since, therefore, only the false is opposed to the true, as is clearly evident from an examination of their definitions, it is impossible that the truth of faith should be opposed to those principles that the human reason knows naturally.

[2] Furthermore, that which is introduced into the soul of the student by the teacher is contained in the knowledge of the teacher—unless his teaching is fictitious, which it is improper to say of God. Now, the knowledge of the principles that are known to us naturally has been implanted in us by God; for God is the Author of our nature. These principles, therefore, are also contained by the divine Wisdom. Hence, whatever is opposed to them is opposed to the divine Wisdom, and, therefore, cannot come from God. That which we hold by faith as divinely revealed, therefore, cannot be contrary to our natural knowledge.

[3] Again. In the presence of contrary arguments our intellect is chained, so that it cannot proceed to the knowledge of the truth. If, therefore, contrary knowledges were implanted in us by God, our intellect would be hindered from knowing truth by this very fact. Now, such an effect cannot come from God.

[4] And again. What is natural cannot change as long as nature does not. Now, it is impossible that contrary opinions should exist in the same knowing subject at the same time. No opinion or belief, therefore, is implanted in man by God which is contrary to man's natural knowledge.

[5] Therefore, the Apostle says, "The word is nigh thee, even in thy mouth and in thy heart. This is the word of faith, which we preach" (Rom. 10:8). But because it overcomes reason, there are some who think that it is opposed to it: which is impossible.

[6] The authority of St. Augustine also agrees with this. He writes as follows, "That which truth will reveal cannot in any way be opposed to the sacred books of the Old and the New Testament."

[7] From this we evidently gather the following conclusion: whatever arguments are brought forward against the doctrines of faith are conclusions incorrectly derived from the first and self-evident principles imbedded in nature. Such conclusions do not have the force of demonstration; they are arguments that are either probable or sophistical. And so, there exists the possibility to answer them.

How the Human Reason Is Related to the Truth of Faith

[1] There is also a further consideration. Sensible things, from which the human reason takes the origin of its knowledge, retain within themselves some sort of trace of a likeness to God. This is so imperfect, however, that it is absolutely inadequate to manifest the substance of God. For effects bear within themselves, in their own way, the likeness of their causes, since an agent produces its like; yet an effect does not always reach to the full likeness of its cause. Now, the human reason is related to the knowledge of the truth of faith (a truth which can be most evident only to those who see the divine substance) in such a way that it can gather certain likenesses of it, which are yet not sufficient so that the truth of faith may be comprehended as being understood demonstratively or through itself. Yet it is useful for the human reason to exercise itself in such arguments, however weak they may be, provided only that there be present no presumption to comprehend or to demonstrate. For to be able to see something of the loftiest realities, however thin and weak the sight may be, is, as our previous remarks indicate, a cause of the greatest joy.

[2] The testimony of Hilary agrees with this. Speaking of this same truth, he writes as follows in his *De Trinitate*:

> Enter these truths by believing, press forward, persevere. And though I may know that you will not arrive at an end, yet I will congratulate you in your progress. For, though he who pursues the infinite with reverence will never finally reach the end, yet he will always progress by pressing onward. But do not intrude yourself into the divine secret, do not, presuming to comprehend the sum total of intelligence, plunge yourself into the mystery of the unending nativity; rather, understand that these things are incomprehensible.

Document 43

Dante, *Monarchy and Three Political Letters*, trans. Donald Nicholl and Colin Hardie (New York: Noonday Press, 1954), pp. 9–15.

Dante Alighieri (1265–1321), the greatest poet of traditional Europe, was, above all, a political man. His great work, the *Divine Comedy*, was written while in exile from Florence, the result, in part, of his political activities. After observing the chaotic state of Italian politics with the bitter eye of an exile, Dante concluded that peace in Italy and throughout the entire world would occur only if there was a single world ruler who possessed the power to repress the local violence that was constantly erupting. Like Aquinas, Dante was strongly influenced by the philosophy of Aristotle, and, like Aquinas, he believed that men could be brought to Christianity by the process of rational argument. Dante was one of a number of European writers of the thirteenth and four-teenth centuries who proposed grandiose solutions to the problem of world peace and order. In Dante's case, the proposal was a mixture of Aristotelian ideas about the need for unity, the tradition of the Roman imperial mission, and the desire of Christians to convert all men.—ed.

Let us now return to what was said at the beginning; that there are three main problems to be solved concerning temporal monarchy, or, as it is more commonly called, the Empire. As we promised, we intend to in-vestigate them in the order signified and on the basis of the axiom that we have established.

Thus the first question is whether temporal monarchy is necessary for the well-being of the world. Now no substantial objection either from reason or authority can be urged against it, and its truth can be demon-strated by the clearest and most cogent arguments, the first of which is derived from the authority of the Philosopher in his *Politics*. There the acknowledged authority states that when several things are directed to-wards a single end it is necessary for one of them to act as director or ruler and for the others to be directed or ruled. This statement is supported not only by the glorious renown of its author but also by inductive reason. Again, if we consider an individual man we see the same principle verified: since all his faculties are directed towards happiness, his intellectual faculty is the director and ruler of all the others—otherwise he cannot attain hap-piness. If we consider a home, the purpose of which is to train its members to live well, we see that there has to be one member who directs and rules, either the "pater familias" or the person occupying his position, for, as the Philosopher says, "every home is ruled by the eldest." And his function, as Homer says, is to rule the others and lay down laws for them; hence the proverbial curse, "May you have an equal in your home." If we consider a village, whose purpose is mutual help in questions of persons and goods, it is essential for one person to be supreme over all others, whether he is appointed from outside or raised to office by the consent of the others; otherwise, not only would the community fail to provide mutual suste-nance, but in some cases the community itself would be utterly destroyed through some members' scheming to take control. Similarly if we examine a city, whose purpose is to be sufficient unto itself in everything needed for the good life, we see that there must be one governing authority—and this applies not only to just but even to degenerate forms of government. If this were not so, the purpose of civil life would be frustrated and the city, as such, would cease to exist. Lastly, every kingdom (and the end of a kingdom is the same as that of a city but with a stronger bond of peace) needs to have a king to rule over and govern it; otherwise its inhabitants will not only fail to achieve their end as citizens but the kingdom itself will crumble, as is affirmed by the infallible Word: "Every kingdom divided against itself shall be laid waste."

If this is true of all communities and individuals who have a goal towards which they are directed, then our previous supposition is also valid. For, if it is agreed that mankind as a whole has a goal (and this we have shown to be so), then it needs one person to govern or rule over it, and the title appropriate to this person is Monarch, or Emperor.

Thus it has been demonstrated that a Monarch or Emperor is necessary for the well-being of the world.

VI

Furthermore, the order of a part stands in the same relation to the order of the whole as the part does to the whole; therefore the order within a part has as its end the order of the whole, which brings it to perfection. Hence the goodness of the order amongst the parts does not surpass the goodness of the total order; in fact the reverse is true. Now in all things this twofold order is to be found: that is, the relation of the parts towards each other; and the relation of the parts to that unity which is not itself a part (in the same way that the parts of an army are related towards each other yet are all subordinated to their commander). Hence the relation of the parts to that unity is the superior of the two orders; and the other relation is simply a function of the superior order, not vice versa. Now if this pattern of relationship is found in individual groups of human beings it must apply all the more to mankind as a group or whole, in virtue of the previous syllogism concerning the superior pattern of relationship. But it has been adequately proved in the previous chapter that this pattern is in fact found in all human groups: therefore it should also be found in the whole.

Consequently all those parts below the level of a kingdom, as well as kingdoms themselves, must be subordinate to one ruler or rule, that is, to the Monarch or to Monarchy.

VII

Furthermore, mankind in one sense is a whole (that is, in relation to its component parts), but in another sense it is itself a part. It is a whole in relation to particular kingdoms and peoples, as we have previously shown; but in relation to the whole universe it is, of course, a part. Therefore just as its component parts are brought to harmony in mankind, so mankind itself has to be brought into the harmony of its appropriate whole. The component parts of mankind are brought into harmony by a single principle (as may easily be gathered from the preceding argument); and mankind itself is similarly related to the whole universe, or to its principle (that is, God, the Monarch); this harmony is achieved by one principle only, the one Prince.

It follows that Monarchy is necessary for the well-being of the world.

VIII

And everything is at its best and most perfect when in the condition intended for it by the first cause, which is God; this is self-evident—except to those who deny that the divine goodness achieves supreme perfection. It is God's intention that every created thing, in so far as its natural capacity allows, should reflect the divine likeness. This explains why it is said: "Let us make man after our image and likeness." Although the phrase "after our image" cannot be applied to anything inferior to man, "likeness" can be applied to anything whatsoever, since the whole universe is simply a sort of shadow of the divine goodness. Therefore the human race is at its best and most perfect when, so far as its capacity allows, it is most like to God. But mankind is most like to God when it enjoys the highest degree of unity, since He alone is the true ground of unity—hence it is written: "Hear, O Israel, the Lord thy God is one." But mankind is most one when the whole human race is drawn together into complete unity, which can only happen when it is subordinate to one Prince, as is selfevident.

Therefore when mankind is subject to one Prince it is most like to God and this implies conformity to the divine intention, which is the condition of perfection, as was proved at the beginning of this chapter.

IX

Again, a son's condition is most perfect when the son, as far as his nature allows, reproduces the perfection of the father. Mankind is the son of the heavens, which is perfect in all its works; but man is begotten by man and the sun (according to the second book of the *Physics*). Therefore mankind's condition is most perfect when it reproduces the perfection of the heavens, so far as human nature allows. And just as the heavens are governed and directed in every movement by a single mover, which is God (as human reasoning in philosophy amply demonstrates), so, if our argument has been correct, mankind is at its best when all its movements and intentions are governed by one Prince as its sole mover and with one law for its direction.

Hence it is obvious that the world's well-being demands a Monarch or single government known as the Empire.

This is the argument that led Boethius to sigh:

> How happy you would be, O mankind, if your minds were ruled by the love that rules the heavens.

X

And wherever there is a possibility of dispute there has to be a judgment to settle it; otherwise there would be imperfection without a remedy to heal it, which is impossible, since God and nature never fail in essentials.

It is clear that a dispute may arise between two princes, neither of whom is subject to the other, and that this may be their fault or their subjects'; therefore a judgment between them is indispensable. However, since neither can take cognizance over the other (neither being subject to the other—and equals do not rule over equals), there needs to be a third person enjoying wider jurisdiction who by right rules over both of them. This person must be either the monarch (in which case our argument is complete) or not the monarch, in which case he himself will have an equal outside his own jurisdiction, and it will again be necessary to have recourse to a third person. Either this process will go on to infinity (which is impossible) or eventually it will lead us back to a first and supreme judge whose judgment will either directly or indirectly solve all disputes: he will be the Monarch, or Emperor.

Therefore monarchy is necessary to the world. And the Philosopher appreciated this truth when he wrote: "Things resent being badly ordered; but to have different rulers is bad; therefore, one Prince."

XI

Besides, the world is best ordered when justice is at its strongest. Hence Virgil, wishing to praise the new order that seemed to be emerging in his day, sang, "Now the Virgin is again returning; and the Saturnian reign begins once more." By "Virgin" he meant Justice, which is also called Astrea; by "Saturn's rule" he referred to the finest ages, which are also described as "golden." Justice is at its strongest only under a Monarch; therefore Monarchy or Empire is essential if the world is to attain a perfect order.

Document 6

Paulus Vladimiri, "Opinio Hostiensis," in Hermannus von der Hardt, *Magnum Oecumenicum Constantiense Concilium,* 7 vols. (Frankfurt and Leipzig, 1696–1724), 3: cols. 10–25. Translated by James Muldoon.
  Paulus Vladimiri (Pawel Wlodkowicz, d. 1435) was a leading Polish canon lawyer and rector of the University of Cracow. He represented the king of Poland at the Council of Constance (1414–17) where the Poles sought to follow up their military victory over the Teutonic Knights at the battle of Tannenberg (1410) by a diplomatic victory. The goal was to deprive the Knights of their power in eastern Europe by proving that they had no right to conquer these lands simply because they were held by infidels. Like many writers of the sixteenth century who objected to European conquest overseas, he denied the claims to conquest based on the arguments advanced by Hostiensis that were designed to prove that infidels had no rights to their property and political power.—ed.

It is the opinion of Hostiensis that with the coming of Christ every public office, every government, all sovereignty and jurisdiction was transferred from the infidels to the faithful and that today there is no jurisdiction nor any other power or dominion among infidels, since, as his opinion states, they are fundamentally incapable of possessing them. It is also his opinion that Christians ought to wage war against infidels who do not recognize the Roman Empire, etc. And he states that such war against infidels who do not recognize the Roman Empire is always just and lawful as far as Christians are concerned. Although this opinion has some followers, the doctors who write on this topic generally follow Innocent IV who held the opposite opinion. . . .
  Indeed, because this opinion seems to incite people to turbulence and gives a way to people to commit murder and rapine: because if the infidels are not the lawful possessors of their goods and jurisdictions, it is lawful for anyone to take and keep them etc.— It seems that this matter, which is full of dangers, ought of necessity be cleared up by this holy council.
  Even the most famous doctor of both laws in Italy, Peter de Ancharano . . . held Hostiensis' opinion to be improbable, drawing many absurd conclusions from it, such as Christians can, without committing sin, steal, rob, ravish, occupy, and invade the possessions and territories of infidels who do not recognize the Roman Church or Empire, even if the infidels wish to live at peace with the Christians. . . .
  On Saturday, July 6, Lord Paulus Vladimiri . . . gave this presentation together with conclusions drawn from it. . . . *The Topic.* Crusaders

were admitted into Poland by the Polish nobles to assist them against the Prussians, who were infidels at that time, and other peoples who were waging war against the Christian Poles. These crusaders who were called the Brothers of the Hospital of St. Mary of Jerusalem of the House of the Germans, were established in Poland and given certain lands along the border with the infidels. From these bases, with the aid of the Poles and of other Christians, in the succeeding years, they conquered this cruel race of infidel Prussians and occupied their domain and were known as the "Lords of Prussia."

And there they built great and well-protected cities, indeed they built great armed camps. And all of their domain was secured by the strongest possible fortifications. . . . And although the Prussians had been subjugated to the aforementioned crusaders, the cruel war that the infidels had waged against the Christians now ceased—saving situations where, provoked by the insults of the Christians, they were accustomed to respond in kind—nevertheless the crusaders did not cease to wage war right up to the present against the tamed and peaceful infidels and continued to invade their lands and domains and to provoke the infidels by their outrages of this sort against them and against other people. . . . But retaining their initial justification for their efforts, as if the savage pagan society still warred against the Christians, the crusaders call for Christian help, making it virtually a rule for themselves to invade twice every year. . . .

And so, the fame of the Order grows, its riches grow as its power grows. From both sides, from Christians and from pagans, the crusaders gather wealth and grow rich. Letters have been obtained from the Roman popes and emperors so that whatever regions, lands, or domains of the infidels they capture or occupy, they might retain.

Then the spirit of God, which blows where it will, calling the most powerful pagan princes from the error of the gentiles to the knowledge of the true faith, led them to be washed in the water of holy baptism by the Polish clergy. . . .

The crusaders considered this wonderous. They took it very hard, because their justification for occupying the possessions and domains of the infidels was now lost. They invaded these regions often, with even greater ferocity, and with great regularity according to their traditional practice. They annihilated many of the neophytes, both the baptized and the unbaptized, not even sparing the clergy. The crusaders burned the new churches belonging to the converts and did innumerable other things, which good grace requires one to pass over in silence. . . .

Conclusion 1. Although infidels are not of the sheepfold of the Church, all men are, however, undoubtedly the sheep of Christ by virtue of their creation. . . .

Conclusion 3. Christian princes should not expel Jews and other infidels from their lands nor ought they despoil them without just cause. . . .

Conclusion 5. It is not lawful to take from infidels their sovereignty, possessions or jurisdiction, even if they do not recognize the Roman Empire, because they possess them without sin and from God the Creator. God created all these things, without any distinction between the faithful and the infidels, for man whom He made in His own image. . . .

Conclusion 29. Letters of the emperor, which grant to the Prussian crusaders or to any others the right to occupy infidel lands are without legal value. They only greatly deceive Christ's faithful, since the emperor cannot give what he does not possess. Nor can letters from either the Roman pontiffs or from the emperors grant this privilege to them, especially as it is against natural and divine law. . . .

Conclusion 52. It is impious and absurd to assert that infidels are incapable of possessing any jurisdiction, office, power, or sovereignty, because this wicked assertion paves the way for murder and rapine.

Conclusion

According to the author of *The Conquest of Lisbon*, a Moslem asked the victorious Christians why they had left their homes and come to Portugal:

> Do your possessions give you no pleasure at all, or have you incurred some blame at home, that you are so often on the move? Surely your frequent going and coming is proof of an innate mental instability, for he who is unable to arrest the flight of the body cannot control the mind.[1]

The embittered speaker, facing exile, pointed out a characteristic of Europeans that others have noted—the continual restlessness of Europeans.

The European might answer that the Arabs and the Mongols were similarly restless in the Middle Ages. There is a difference, however: Mongol expansion was largely restricted to the thirteenth century, as far as Europeans were concerned, and Arabic expansion, which had begun in the seventh century, had come to an end by the twelfth century when the Turks came to dominate the Moslem world. The Turks in their turn fell both to internal decay and to European pressure beginning in the seventeenth century. Europeans, and their immediate offspring, the inhabitants of the Americas, have continued to thrust outward from their original homeland in the Frankish empire.

The Moslem opinion that European expansion was rooted in some kind of psychological disorder is an interesting one but not necessarily a complete explanation of a complex and long-lasting phenomenon. What is clear is the existence of a dynamic of expansion, the roots of which are to be found in several distinct aspects of European society.

In the first place, the expansion of Europe was inextricably linked with the universalism of the Christian Church. The Church's mission encompassed the salvation of all men. Although the initial Christian contact with an infidel society might consist only of a single adventurous preacher of the Gospel, the successful missionary would be followed by more missionaries and eventually by a complete ecclesiastical organization. On the other hand, the death of a missionary at the hands of the infidels could justify an invasion by a Christian army anxious to avenge his death and to protect further missionary endeavors. In either case, the spiritual or mili-

---

1. *De expugnatione Lyxbonensi: The Conquest of Lisbon*, p. 121.

tary conquest of infidel lands would be followed by a movement of population to the new frontier. Spiritual conquest of the infidels did not necessarily mean political domination as well. The Slavic kingdoms that emerged on the borders of German expansion used their conversion to Christianity to block further German movement eastward. The result was the entrance of kingdoms such as Poland into the orbit of western-European Christian values as equal participants, not as vassal states.

Secondly, the dependence of Europeans upon goods imported from Asia and elsewhere encouraged merchants to find new routes to the sources of the goods that Europeans desired. In some cases, such as in the Baltic lands, merchants paved the way for missionaries to follow, while in other areas, such as India, the missionaries seem to have preceded the merchants. The rise and fall of the economy in various parts of Europe took place as new routes were discovered. The successful search for a water route to Asia meant a gradual shift of economic power in Europe from the shores of the Mediterranean to the shores of the Atlantic as the Portuguese began to compete with the Venetians for the spice market. The example of Portugal encouraged merchants in other Atlantic countries to seek their own routes to the Spice Islands and participate in the trade bonanza.

The third element in Europe's dynamic of expansion resulted from the long-standing fear that Europe would be overrun by the various enemies who lived along its borders. Working on the theory that the best defense is a good offense, the crusaders strove to push back the ring of enemies that gripped Europe. This work was closely connected with the final motive for medieval expansion—the desire of European nobles and peasants for additional land. Each new frontier meant the establishment of settlements that in turn attracted more colonists from the overcrowded areas of Europe.

This mixture of motives is the explanation for European Christian expansion beyond the narrow limits of western Europe. It is important to realize that this pressure did not operate continuously at the same level throughout the period and that the basic motives did not always function harmoniously. From the beginning of the crusades in the eleventh century, on through the mid-thirteenth century, Europeans generally exerted pressure against the peoples who lived on the borders of Europe.[2] From the late thirteenth century until the early fifteenth century, however, a series of crises within Europe caused a gradual withdrawal from the

2. Friedrich Heer, *The Medieval World* (London: Weidenfield and Nicolson, 1961), pp. 1–2. Heer emphasizes that although armed conflict did take place along the frontier, a great deal of peaceful intercourse also took place.
3. Ibid., pp. 6–7.

frontiers.[3] Wars within Europe, especially the Hundred Years War between France and England, absorbed military energy that might otherwise
have been devoted to wars along the frontier. Furthermore, the Black
Death in the mid-fourteenth century sharply reduced the European population and so reduced the numbers available for colonizing new lands.
Finally, the papacy, which had encouraged and helped finance the
crusades, became preoccupied with the problem of its own survival in the
face of increasing demands for reform that eventually led to the Protestant
Reformation. Individual popes scandalized Europe by their personal be-
havior, thus dissipating the papacy's greatest strength, its role as moral
leader of Christian society. Consequently, the papacy found it almost impossible to arouse Europe to a new crusade.

Furthermore, the differing interests of those who did go out to the
frontiers led to internal quarrels in the camps of the crusaders and other
adventurers. Missionaries often objected to the entrance of merchants into
the lands of new converts because they might scandalize the natives. The
work of the crusaders was often hindered by the sale of military equipment by Christian merchants to Moslem armies. The idea of the crusade
was often distasteful to peaceful missionaries who believed that infidels
should be converted by peaceful means alone. The interests of the missionaries, crusaders, merchants, and peasants, and the goals of kings and
popes, were not easy to reconcile, thus weakening the thrust of the pressure to expand beyond the boundaries of Latin Christendom.

When significant interest in expansion reappeared in the fifteenth
century, the same motives that had moved men in the thirteenth century
to press beyond the borders of Europe came into play once more. The
traditional motives did not function in quite the same fashion as they had
previously. For example, although the rhetoric of the crusades continued
to be heard, the crusading spirit was clearly declining as a motive for
action along the borders. Furthermore, the Moslems were no longer seen
as a threat to Europe, at least not by all European rulers. The French
kings came to view the Sultan of Constantinople as an ally in their series
of wars with the Hapsburgs. Even the lure of more land did not attract
the interest of nobles and peasants as it once had done.

From the late fifteenth century onward, the strongest motive for expansion was trade. The major goal was to reach the sources of spices and
silk. For two centuries following the Portuguese discovery of a water route
to Asia, explorers from other nations tried to find other routes. The
Americas were originally only a stumbling block in the way of such a
route. The search for the Spice Islands and for Cathay led Magellan to
discover the route around South America and led English sailors in the
vain attempt to find a northwest passage across North America. With the
discovery of gold and silver in the Americas, the Spanish interest in the

New World increased but largely because the precious metals could be used to purchase silk and spices.[4]

Europeans were attracted only gradually to the idea of settling the newly discovered lands. The settlements that had developed in Asia, Goa and Macao, for example, were trading centers and administrative headquarters. There was no place for large-scale settlement by European farmers there, even if any had wished to move there. When Europeans did begin to settle overseas, especially in the Americas, they did so because there was no significant trade between these regions and Europe. Trading and administrative settlements would not have survived. What these colonists did was to bring new kinds of economic activity to the Americas—i.e., cattle ranches and sugar plantations, to give but two examples—that could eventually produce goods desired by Europeans. In this way, a colonial economy was created that fitted the demands of the European economy. In addition, the colonists brought with them attitudes and institutions that had been developed to deal with the conquered populations encountered on the frontiers of Europe. The Spanish treated the Aztecs and the Incas along the lines of their treatment of the Moslems in Spain. The treatment of the Indians in Massachusetts Bay colony appears to have been based on the treatment of the Irish by the English. What distinguished European expansion from that of other societies was the willingness to adapt old institutions to meet new colonial situations. This kind of flexibility was lacking in Mongol expansion, for example.

A twelfth-century intellectual once remarked that what appeared to be the great intellectual strides made by his generation were possible only because of the efforts of previous generations on which the current generation of scholars was building.[5] This is a commonplace, yet deserves repeating because it is often forgotten. Columbus and those who sailed after him also built on the efforts of the generations of seamen who had gradually filled in the outlines of Europe on their sailing charts. Colonial administrators, merchants, and missionaries also dealt with the newly discovered worlds in terms derived from the medieval colonizing experience of their predecessors. The European expansion overseas marked the application of practices and institutions that had been developed during the medieval colonization of Europe to a wider world. The history of Europe is the history of a continuous process of expansion since the twelfth century.

4. Much of the wealth realized from the conquest of the Americas went directly to Asia, largely for the purpose of purchasing silk. The trade went from Acapulco to Manila, where Chinese goods were traded. The best study of this trade is William L. Shurz, *The Manila Galleon* (New York: Dutton, 1939).

5. Reginald Lane Poole, *Illustrations of the History of Medieval Thought and Learning*, 2nd rev. ed. (London: 1920; reprint ed., New York: Dover, 1960), p. 102.